From Mexican Days
to the Gold Rush

Memoirs of James Wilson Marshall
and Edward Gould Buffum
Who Grew Up with California

A California Goldseeker

Courtesy The Huntington Library

The Lakeside Classics

FROM MEXICAN DAYS TO THE GOLD RUSH

*Memoirs of James Wilson Marshall
and Edward Gould Buffum
Who Grew Up with California*

EDITED BY
DOYCE B. NUNIS, JR.

The Lakeside Press

R. R. DONNELLEY & SONS COMPANY

CHICAGO

Christmas, 1993

PUBLISHERS' PREFACE

SEVERAL years ago while searching through the collections at the Newberry Library in Chicago, we came across *The Life and Adventures of James W. Marshall*, the discoverer of gold in California. We were enamored with Marshall's bittersweet story not only because he died in poverty after his chance discovery set off the greatest population movement in American history, but also because of his involvement in a series of California events that eventually led to statehood.

There was a problem, however. Marshall's story was too short to be, by itself, a *Lakeside Classic*. The solution was to find an appropriate companion story. And late last year we did just that.

The second text, *Six Months in the Gold Mines*, is Edward Gould Buffum's account of his gold prospecting hardships followed by his career in California politics and journalism.

Together, Marshall and Buffum give us a vision of an amazing five year period that saw California change from a sparsely populated, quiet, agrarian Mexican province into a multi-national melting pot of thousands who, led by bold and brash, ordinary Americans, won independence from Mexico and admittance into the Union.

Marshall came to California in 1845 and participated in the Bear Flag Revolt of 1846 which drove the Mexican appointed government from California and established the California Republic. This, in turn, gave way to American occupation following the end of the Mexican War in California. In January 1848, Marshall made his remarkable discovery which changed his life and thousands of others.

Buffum came to California in March 1847 with the 7th Regiment of New York Volunteers as part of the dispersion of American forces to conduct war with Mexico. Less than a year later—on February 2, 1848—the war was over and orders were given to disband the Volunteer Regiment. Lieutenant Buffum, like nearly all the discharged soldiers, heard of the just-announced discovery and headed for the gold fields. After a summer and fall of prospecting and a winter's wait, during which time he almost died, he gave up the search and moved to San Francisco where he resumed his journalistic career with a brief fling into California politics. Both Marshall and Buffum were there to see California become the 31st state in 1850.

With both books in hand and ready to proceed, we once again chose as editor Doyce B. Nunis, Jr., PhD, retired Professor of History at the University of Southern California. Although he is no longer in the classroom, Dr. Nunis continues his fast-paced schedule of writing and editing. In 1992 and '93 he has published books dealing with California history and edited anthologies in addition to continuing his thirty-plus year editorship of the *South-*

ern California Quarterly, the journal of the Historical Society of Southern California. He has already left his mark on the *Lakeside Classic* series by serving as editor of the 1979, 1984, and 1987 selections, and was a natural choice for this year's book since he is considered by many to be today's leading historian of California. This, we believe, you will find readily apparent, after reading his Historical Introduction plus the Prologues, Epilogues, and footnotes for both stories.

For our reprinting we have used the first edition of both books. Marshall's book first appeared in 1870. A second edition came forth in 1935. Buffum's book was introduced in 1850 and has been republished several times, the most recent being a handsome edition by The Ward Ritchie Press, Los Angeles, in 1959. Several editorial liberties have been taken with each text. In the Marshall book we have omitted the first three pages of text and the Appendix of Testimonials which seem to be either unnecessary or redundant. In the Buffum book we have shortened the Author's Introduction and eliminated the last paragraph of Chapter xii and all of Chapters xiii, xiv, and xv—information we felt did not add to the book's primary context.

As usual, we have corrected text for misspellings and what we call "erratic punctuation." We have also replaced the old-fashioned "multiple thought" chapter titles with "single thought" titles.

Our slight editing in no way affects the authors'

thoughts or expressions; instead we believe we have
fulfilled the thought expressed by the first publisher
of the Buffum book who stated: "The pages of this
work . . . have been hurried through the press without revisions expected from the author."

We are most pleased to point to the sizeable
number of illustrations we were able to obtain that
directly relate to the Historical Introduction and
texts. Note please, that the time covered by the
texts is well before the availability of the camera.
As a result, many illustrations are in art form. California repositories—particularly the California State
Library and The Huntington Library—have done
an outstanding job in collecting and cataloging a
great number of likenesses of personalities as well
as scenes of the gold fields and historical events.

Nearly every year we use the Publishers' Preface
to explain the purpose of the *Lakeside Classic* series
and the Donnelley facilities responsible for its production and distribution.

The series began in 1903 with the avowed purpose of showcasing the Company's ability to produce a book using the latest machinery that would
meet or surpass the quality then found in books
made by hand. Even with the demise of the hand-
made book our series has continued with the same
objective: To produce a top quality book using mod-
ern equipment and technology.

This is the ninety-first selection in the series. Previous titles and authors are listed at the end of the

book. As in the past, Donnelley craft people handle every production step—only materials come from outside our facilities. Electronic typesetting is handled by Donnelley Database Technology Services in Willowbrook, Illinois. This is the first year that type was transmitted to our book manufacturing division in Crawfordsville, Indiana, in digital form by using a regular telephone line. In Crawfordsville, state-of-the-art equipment in the pre-press center receives the digital information and electronically imposes the type in page format and paginated sequence on film that is pre-sized to actual press forms. Illustrative material is scanned electronically and inserted onto the appropriate pages.

Printed signatures from high-speed, narrow web offset presses are gathered and Smythe sewn. After trimming and gilding, the hard cover is affixed, and the finished books pass through a final quality check before automatic cartoning, labeling and shipping.

Maps, which are produced through our GeoSystems unit in Lancaster, Pennsylvania, continue to be an integral part of this series. For the first time the maps prepared for this edition have been generated by computers using highly specialized software systems with proprietary characteristics that help cartographers achieve special effects.

All-in-all, this book, like all previous *Lakeside Classics* is proof of our ability to reach the top level of quality and to handle all phases of production, whatever the product might be.

The ability to initiate and manage change is of central importance to our company, which enjoyed an active, growth-filled year in 1993, with more acquisitions (eight) and joint ventures (six) than ever before in its 129-year history. It is important to note the global sweep of these activities. They include an acquisition in Ireland and joint ventures in the United Kingdom, France, Spain, Poland, Hong Kong, and Korea.

The year began with some solemn news, however, as we announced in January that we would close our Chicago Manufacturing Division after more than sixty-five years. Our general management team made this most difficult decision after long-time customer Sears, Roebuck and Company ceased producing its "Big Book" general-merchandise catalog, which accounted for sixty percent of our production in Chicago. Our flagship Calumet Plant—the company's oldest operating facility—and its adjacent West Plant, are phasing out operations and will be shut down by the third quarter of 1994.

The business publications we produced in the Chicago Division for Crain Communications, Inc. are being transferred to our new Pontiac Division in downstate Illinois, which we acquired in July from Ringier America, Inc. A 53,000-square-foot expansion is under way to add capacity for the seven Crain's titles as well as for other new work. Some employees from the Chicago Division are transferring to Pontiac to produce these publications.

A plant in Senatobia, Mississippi, was also part of the Ringier purchase. Together with our plant in Mendota, Illinois, which we bought in 1992 from Combined Communication Services (CCS), these three new plants form our Specialized Publishing Services unit, which now makes us a leader in the growing trade magazine business. In this connection, we have signed a five-year contract to print 24 trade magazines for Cahners Publishing, a unit of Reed Elsevier.

Our company's net sales increases for 1993 reflected good volume gains in many of our businesses. These gains more than offset the negative effects of the lost Sears catalog business and the negative translation effect of the stronger U.S. dollar on our U.K. operations. Net income was lower than the year before, entirely because of two one-time charges for required accounting changes and a separate one-time charge primarily related to the shutdown of our Chicago plant.

We sold our 69 percent share of the Lakeside Bank to a group of investors led by three of the bank's key management people. We rose to 117th on *Fortune* magazine's 1993 list of the top 500 U.S. industrial corporations ranked by sales. In August, after more than 37 years on the New York Stock Exchange, R.R. Donnelley also was listed on the Chicago Stock Exchange.

Our ability to increase sales in these challenging times reflects R.R. Donnelley's unique competitive strengths—the benefits of strong customer relationships, unmatched cash flow and financial strength to invest for profitable growth, the economies of scale and the advantages of global reach, state-of-the-art plants and equipment, and superior technology and people. But competition is fierce, and our past successes are not sufficient to carry us into the future. That is why we are aggressively pursuing our long-term vision for profitable growth by advancing global expansion through joint ventures, acquisitions, and startups; by expanding businesses through strategic partnerships; and by developing new business lines and added-value services.

During 1993, to meet the growing needs of present and new customers, we invested $450 million to expand and upgrade our operations, including acquisitions, new equipment, additions to existing manufacturing facilities and investments in new joint ventures.

Through 1994, we will spend nearly $70 million to modernize our Warsaw, Indiana, manufacturing complex, installing two new wide-web presses. At our Lynchburg, Virginia, Division we will add 93,000 square feet for a 24-pocket patent binder, a high-speed mail line and an automated printroll material-handling system.

Another $40 million is going into our other Virginia plant, in Harrisonburg, which is constructing a 250,000-square-foot addition, giving us needed capacity to better serve the growing college and trade book segments. The Harrisonburg expansion includes five new web-offset presses as well as additional binding capacity.

Startups in 1993 included a new, 30,000-square-foot book printing plant set immediately adjacent to Penguin USA's distribution center in Newbern, Tennessee. This unique partnership guarantees Penguin press-time priority for all Penguin USA trade paperback work, and gives us a ten-year agreement to provide that service.

We further enhanced our service to trade book publishers by acquiring Haddon Craftsmen, Inc., a 100-year-old book manufacturer with 1,200 employees and four facilities in Pennsylvania. Haddon, whose high-quality printing is well-respected throughout the book industry, is now a wholly owned subsidiary.

We also acquired Tech Web, Inc. of Wheeling, Illinois, a specialty and direct-mailing printer that produces promotional stuffers, coupons, brochures, stamp sheets and magazine inserts. Tech Web complements our 1992 purchase of American Inline Graphics in Seymour, Indiana. Together, these two plants form our new Specialty Products Business.

In other expansions, R.R. Donnelley (Singapore) Pte. Ltd. added 60,000 square feet of warehouse and assembly space. Laboratorio Lito Color, acquired in early 1992, doubled its size and tripled its production capacity in San Juan del Río, Mexico, installing that country's first 32-page, web-offset press. In addition to producing catalogs, promotional materials and magazines for a growing number of Latin America customers, Lito Color uses part of its new space to replicate computer disks.

Our Crawfordsville Documentation Services Division celebrated its 10th anniversary in 1993. It is hard to believe we've been in this business for only one decade, since our Documentation Services Group accounted for sales of more than $400 million in 1992, and the total for 1993 will be higher.

The group continues to expand its advanced manufacturing network worldwide for customers. To keep up with global demand, we started up new facilities in Cumbernauld, Scotland, and Preston, Washington. We acquired the manufacturing assets of Central Point Software and Western Computer Press in Beaverton and Tigard, Oregon, respectively, and also purchased SoftCopy Inc., a computer diskette replication and fulfillment organization in Orem, Utah. SoftCopy gives us additional turnkey capacity in the Utah Valley, a fast-growing area for high-technology product development. In addition, we acquired a majority interest in TestDrive Corporation, a leader in the emerging "try-then-buy" electronic distribution market. TestDrive's CD-ROM catalog allows software prospects to test fully functional programs for a limited number of times before buying them.

We bought European Language Translations Ltd.

(ELT) of Dublin, Ireland. Today, ELT and INK International, which we purchased in 1992, form R.R. Donnelley Language Solutions, a worldwide network for software localization, translation and multilingual document production services. We also formed R.R. Donnelley France, S.A., with IBM France to operate IBM's Publication Center in Orléans. Donnelley Korea Co., Ltd., another joint venture, provides diskette replication and software packaging services near Seoul, Korea.

Benefiting from European influence, our computer documentation operations in Crawfordsville, Indiana; Hudson, Massachusetts; and Provo, Utah became the first U.S. commercial printing sites certified with ISO 9002, the international quality standard that tests how well companies meet specifications for standardized procedures and quality management. As we went to press, our facilities in Fremont, California, and Portland, Oregon, expected certification by the end of the year. Most of our documentation facilities in Europe have been ISO-certified, including Cumbernauld, Scotland; Dublin, Ireland; Apeldoorn, The Netherlands; and Thorp Arch, England.

Elsewhere abroad, in Hong Kong we formed a joint venture with financial printer Leefung-Asco to better serve our Far East clients. Domestically, we opened a full-service financial printing office in Atlanta through an alliance with The Stein Printing Co. 1993 was an excellent year for our Financial

Printing Services Group thanks to a high level of activity in securities issues and an increase in mergers and acquisitions throughout industry.

Our more traditional businesses also expanded through joint ventures. DPA Printing Company is the name of our joint venture with the Polish-American Printing Association, Ltd. DPA is in the process of leasing a plant in Krakow, Poland, where we will print magazines and newspaper inserts beginning in July 1994. In March, R.R. Donnelley and Novograph, S.A., formed Donoprint, S.A., in Tres Cantos, Spain. Donoprint markets the printing and binding services of Rotedic, Novograph's parent company, and of HelioColor, a printing operation near Madrid, which we co-own with French publisher Hachette. Donnelley Hearst Holdings is our new joint venture with Hearst Corp., which purchased Tower Publishing Services of Market Harborough, England, to home-deliver magazines in the United Kingdom, where most publications are purchased at newsstands. We have even printed the Prague telephone directory, produced at our Gateshead, England, facility.

During the third quarter, we started to print weekly newspaper coupon inserts (known as FSIs) for News America FSI. A new five-year contract makes us a major provider for News America which distributes more than 50 million copies a week to 390 Sunday newspapers across America.

Setting our sights on tabloid newspaper printing,

we signed a well-publicized, 15-year contract to produce the *National Enquirer* and *Star* beginning in 1996. Our plants in Casa Grande, Arizona; Gallatin, Tennessee; Lancaster, Pennsylvania; Newton, North Carolina; Reno, Nevada; and Warsaw, Indiana, will produce 10.5 million copies a week.

Maintaining our lead in technology, in May, our Danville, Kentucky, plant marked the long-awaited debut of Heidelberg Harris' M-3000 "gapless" press—the world's largest (253 feet long) and fastest (five million pages per hour) web-offset press. This fall we installed North America's first fully digital, four-color, web-fed printing press, the Xeikon DCP-1, at our Chicago Financial Printing Division. The Xeikon accepts digital files from a multimode computer network within R.R. Donnelley and many customer facilities. The fully digital press requires no film, plates or make-ready. We plan to purchase several more digital color presses in 1994. Taking another step toward filmless printing, we formed an alliance with Creo Products to launch computer-to-plate recorders. The systems, which record plates directly from digital files, have been installed in our Crawfordsville, Indiana, and Portland, Oregon, divisions.

In other new developments, our GeoSystems unit is providing in-city routing software for hand-held electronic devices such as the Newton™ Message-Pad™ in Apple Computer's new line of Personal Communications Assistants. Also, GeoSystems is using its new, proprietary U.S. Mapping Database to prepare a customized atlas for Reader's Digest. GeoSystems also completed an extensive digital mapping project for *Picture Atlas of the World,* the National Geographic Society's first CD-ROM-based electronic atlas.

Separately, GeoSystems and Cincinnati Bell are jointly researching electronic yellow pages for possible business-to-business applications. The prototype allows users to locate desired services by name, address and telephone number as well as by business category and geographic proximity. Our conventional business in this area remains strong. We recently signed a 10-year contract renewal to print most of the telephone directories published by Ameritech, which provides service in Illinois, Indiana, Michigan, Ohio and Wisconsin.

Enhancing our services to direct marketers, our Metromail subsidiary acquired the database assets of Computerized Marketing Technology, a leading provider of behavioral data marketing services.

Last spring, on a scale unique in our history, the company launched a series of major corporate advertisements in business and trade magazines. Under the headline "Transforming Information Into Opportunities," the campaign, which will continue in 1994, positions Donnelley as a global leader in information management with diverse capabilities and added-value services for use by a wide variety of customers and prospects.

Over the past year, we bid farewell to some long-time friends and colleagues. Company President Carl Doty retired October 1, concluding a remarkable career. Carl worked during an era of great technological evolution in the printing industry. During his 33 years of service, Carl saw the company evolve into the world's largest commercial printer, doubling in size and expanding its business to three continents.

Dr. Albert V. Crewe retired from our Board of Directors after 15 years of service. A distinguished professor of physics, Dr. Crewe's knowledge of scientific matters has been highly regarded during a period of rapid technological development and change in our company's business. He will continue to advise the company as a consultant.

Our company enters its 130th year of business in a solid position for continued growth and prosperity. Attributes such as quality, service, innovation and leadership are personified by our dedicated employees, who are working harder and more effectively in these challenging times. To them, with great appreciation, we dedicate this book.

THE PUBLISHERS

Christmas, 1993

CONTENTS

BOOK 1

THE LIFE AND ADVENTURES
OF JAMES W. MARSHALL
by George Frederic Parsons

BOOK 2
SIX MONTHS IN THE GOLD MINES
by E. Gould Buffum

ILLUSTRATIONS

THE LIFE AND ADVENTURES
OF JAMES W. MARSHALL

SIX MONTHS IN THE GOLD MINES

HISTORICAL INTRODUCTION

ALTHOUGH sailed by or briefly landed upon by early European explorers, the settlement of California, as Spain's last imperial colony, did not occur until 1769, only seven years before the American Revolution. The Spanish system of colonization called first for arrival of troops and missionaries and then by settlers. Accordingly, forts were established near what is today's San Diego, Monterey, Santa Barbara, and San Francisco. At the same time, a contingent of Franciscan friars began building what would become a series of twenty-one missions—separated by one day's travel by horse—along what was called El Camino Real (The King's Highway). Groups of Spanish settlers, who had been living in Mexico, made their appearance in 1776.

For the years immediately following, the province of California languished in the backwash of the Spanish Empire. Because of the difficulties in administering an area of over 2,500 miles in length, it was formally split—in 1804—into *Alta* or Upper and *Baja* or Lower California. Government was benevolent, problems were minor, but the colony was not prosperous. When Spain agreed to Mexican independence in 1821, there were about 3,250 *gente de razon*[1] (Spanish citizens who had immigrated from

[1] Hubert H. Bancroft, *History of California* (7 vols., San Francisco, 1884–90), II: 362, 380, 392–93.

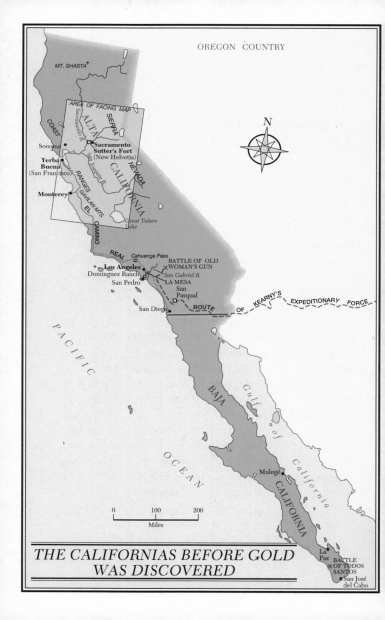

THE CALIFORNIAS BEFORE GOLD
WAS DISCOVERED

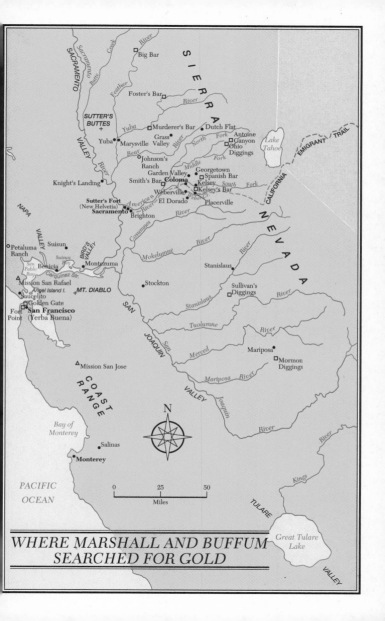

WHERE MARSHALL AND BUFFUM
SEARCHED FOR GOLD

Mexico) and only thirteen foreigners residing in all of Alta California. The province itself played no role in the Mexican struggle against Spanish rule. Many of the Franciscan missionaries, the majority of whom were Spanish-born, refused to sign an oath of allegiance to Mexico, and a few returned to their Spanish homeland. Gradually, as age took its toll, Mexican-born padres increased their presence,[2] but for the population at large it mattered little whether they were living under Spanish or Mexican rule—*that is at the outset of Alta California's Mexican period.*

The situation would gradually change between 1821, when Mexico won its independence, and 1836, when the Mexican appointed governor was ousted. The first among a number of inter-related events concerned the Mexican government's abandonment of the restrictive Spanish trade rulings which prohibited foreign traders from calling at California ports. Mexico decreed a policy of free trade based on appropriate custom duties being levied on such commerce. Second, the Mexican statutes of 1824 and 1828 provided for liberal land grants to anyone who could meet one of the following: Mexican citizenship, marriage to a Mexican citizen, or settling twenty-five miles from the ocean.[3]

[2] Maynard J. Geiger, O.F.M., *Franciscan Missionaries in Hispanic California, 1769–1848: A Biographical Dictionary* (San Marino, CA, 1969), provides individual data.

[3] W. W. Robinson, *Land in California* (Berkeley and Los Angeles, 1949), pp. 65–66.

In 1822 the Peru-based firm of McCulloch and Hartnell initiated the hide and tallow trade which very quickly became the dominant enterprise in the economic life of Alta California.[4] It also set the stage for the start of a volatile relationship between the Mexican government and a growing number of sons of the original *gente de razon* who named themselves *Californios.*

The arrival of more and more foreign ships, the bulk of which were American, resulted in a nucleus of a foreign-born, all-male population which was created through the defection of ship officers and ordinary seamen. Since shipboard life at that time was both harsh and severe, an attractive alternative was to jump ship, hide out in the back country, and after the ship left port, live among the easygoing *Californios.* Furthermore, since there was a shortage of eligible bachelors in proportion to the number of female residents, there was an infiltration of Americans—as well as a few other nationalities—into the *Californio* families.

Another factor of change became evident in 1826 when Jedediah Smith led his small band of American fur trappers overland from the Green River to Los Angeles, and returned a second time in 1827. The result was a Smith-mapped overland route— the first to define an eastern-through-the-mountains

[4]Sherman F. Dallas, "The Hide and Tallow Trade in Alta California, 1822–1846" (Unpublished Doctoral Dissertation, Indiana University, 1953), p. 77 *et seq.*

entrance to Mexican California.[5] American fur traders became the harbingers of civilian emigration as
witnessed by the Bidwell-Bartleson party's epic
1841 trek which brought thirty-four Americans,
including a woman with babe in arms to California,
a saga unto itself.[6] Only a few weeks later, the
Workman-Rowland party, twenty-three strong made
the trek over the Old Spanish Trail from Santa
Fe to Los Angeles. This route had been reopen-
ed in 1829 for the first annual trade caravan.[7]

Coupled with the ever-growing number of foreigners in Alta California came the desire and opportunity for the *Californio* youths to learn to read
and write. Typical of that trend was a school that
was organized near Monterey by an English hide
and tallow merchant. The school, which lasted only
a few years, offered tutelage to those youths who
wished it, as well as to many sons of foreign-born
business colleagues. In addition, a sizeable number
of the vessels calling at the California ports had

[5]Dale L. Morgan, *Jedediah Smith and the Opening of the
West* (Indianapolis, 1953), pp. 193–219, 236–55, 343–48;
Doyce B. Nunis, Jr., "The Fur Men: Key to Westward Ex-
pansion," *The Historian*, 23 (February, 1961): 188–90.

[6]Doyce B. Nunis, Jr., *The Bidwell-Bartleson Party 1841
California Emigrant Adventure* (Santa Cruz, CA, 1992), details the history of this first overland party of settlers.

[7]Eleanore Lawrence, "Mexican Trade Between Santa Fe
and Los Angeles, 1830–1848," *California Historical Society
Quarterly*, 10 (March, 1931): 27–39; Leroy R. Hafen and
Ann W. Hafen, *Old Spanish Trail, Santa Fe to Los Angeles*
(Glendale, CA, 1954), details the history of this trail.

books on board which quickly found their way to the hands of eager *Californios* hungry for knowledge.[8]

The last ten years of Mexican rule (1837–46) were plagued by both political unrest and troubling economic concerns on the part of the *Californios*. There was rising resentment against the policy of benign neglect by the government in Mexico City, which had fallen under the predominant influence of Antonio López de Santa Anna, who was elected president on April 1, 1833, and who would exercise enormous power during the next twenty years. By the end of 1835 he had established a highly centralized government that did not go uncontested. More than several Mexican states resisted what they deemed to be an invasion of their rights for home rule.[9] A notable example was Texas, which had been opened for colonization to Americans in 1821. Unrest, however, seethed in 1830 after the Mexican Congress prohibited slavery and further settlement by Americans. The result was a growing Texan circumvention of the prohibitions along with a deepening desire for freedom. Such was the motivation for the Texas Revolution in 1835–36 that culminated in independence and the founding of the Republic of Texas.[10]

[8] Doyce B. Nunis, Jr., *Books in Their Set Chests* ([San Francisco], 1954), *passim*.

[9] Hubert H. Bancroft, *History of Mexico* (5 vols., San Francisco, 1889), V: 131–45.

[10] William C. Binkley, *The Texas Revolution* (Baton Rouge, 1952), offers a detailed account.

Parallel with the events which transpired in Texas were similar activities occurring in Alta California. There was also increasing governmental antagonism toward the power and wealth of the Catholic Church. In August 1833, the Mexican Congress decreed that the mission effort was at an end. The missions' lands and herds were to be distributed among the Indian tribes, the members of whom had been converted to Christianity and kept at peace while toiling for the mission fathers.[11]

At the same time, the Mexican Government approved a plan to recruit and send Mexican-born citizens into the province. Known as the Híjar-Padrés party, this 250 person assemblage reached Alta California in 1834. They were coolly received. The new settlers were intent on occupying secularized land, but since that issue had not yet been resolved, Provincial Governor José Figueroa placed most of the new arrivals on the more sparsely settled northern frontier which was also home to the remaining hostile Indian tribes. As one would expect, friction quickly developed between colonists, authorities, and *Californios*. A charge of conspiracy to overthrow the government led to the deportation of the colonists' leaders.[12] In addition, the secularization

[11]The complexity of secularization is presented in Gerald J. Geary, *The Secularization of the California Missions* (Washington, D.C., 1934).

[12]The history of this scheme is brought forth in C. Alan Hutchinson, *Frontier Settlement in Mexican California* (New Haven, 1969).

process which Figueroa was implementing in a wise, humane, and orderly manner came to a sudden halt with his death in September 1835. The administrators who took over did as they pleased, unrestrained by any government direction. In the end it was the Indians, supposedly the rightful beneficiaries of secularization, who suffered most. They were ignored, forgotten, and pushed aside.[13]

Following Figueroa's death, a growing influence of foreigners began to be felt in the political sphere. They, along with a maturing group of educated *Californios*, would form a coalition that would become the political power base in Alta California. At the same time, the province was becoming infuriated with the Mexican Government's policy of sending convicts into their fast improving environs.[14]

While the government in Mexico City was confronting the ever-growing Texas crisis, little attention was given to replacing the well-liked Governor Figueroa. Five men held the office during a sixteen month period, and the last one was expelled and sent packing by irate *Californios* who then called two native sons to political prominence—Juan Bautista Alvarado, who assumed the governorship on December 7, 1836, and José Castro to serve as *jefe militar* (chief of the military).[15]

[13]This is the judgment of Andrew F. Rolle, *California, A History* (3rd ed., Arlington Heights, IL, 1978), pp. 142–43.

[14]Bancroft, *California*, I: 605–06; II: 169; III: 43, 47, 49, 459, 463–64.

[15]*Ibid.*, III: 445–75, 594.

Alvarado and the governing deputies soon issued a proclamation which declared Alta California "a free and sovereign state" until such time that Santa Anna and the Mexican Government conferred on the province full autonomy over internal affairs as provided for in Mexico's constitution of 1824.[16] Additionally, there was the extremely upsetting matter of exorbitant custom duties levied by the Mexican Government on imports. By 1836 nearly every item purchased carried a tax which increased the price by 80 to 100 percent.[17]

While these events were unfolding in Alta California, Mexico was being torn by widespread political dissension and turmoil that included a yearlong French occupation of Vera Cruz soon followed by an internal struggle for the presidency which was finally resolved in October 1841 when Santa Anna assumed dictatorial presence. This brash move centralized power at the national level and eventually brought about the appointment of General Manuel Micheltorena as California's new governor.[18]

In late August and early September 1842, Micheltorena, in a great show of strength with 200 regular army troops and 300 hastily recruited convicts, arrived in San Diego and marched north to Los Angeles and then to the capital in Monterey. Days before

[16] *Ibid.*, pp. 470–71n.
[17] Hubert H. Bancroft, *California Pastoral* (San Francisco, 1888), pp. 459–92.
[18] Bancroft, *Mexico*, V: 186–288.

the group arrived in Monterey, a courier brought the horrific news that *the United States navy had occupied Monterey!* It was an ominous beginning for his governorship.[19]

Such, indeed, was the case. In what turned out to be a humorous sidebar, Commodore Thomas ap Catesby Jones, commander of the Pacific squadron, acting on faulty intelligence that the United States had declared war against Mexico and compounded by the rumor that Mexico had ceded California to Great Britain, sailed into Monterey Bay, seized the provincial capital, and raised "Old Glory." Two days later, after verifying the fact that a state of war did not exist, Jones apologized to the officials in residence, returned the Mexican flag to its rightful place, and sailed away.[20]

Micheltorena proved to be a wretched governor. His rule was further decimated by the dreadful conduct of his troops, who had quickly become an undisciplined, hard-drinking, lawless band—easily given to robbery and violence. Their disgraceful and unbridled conduct only further alienated the *Californios* while feeding the fires of resentment already burning in the hearts of the remaining abused populace. Micheltorena was quick to realize that he could not count on any local citizenry support in the event of an effort to overthrow him. And so to compensate for the inadequacy of his own troops to

[19]Bancroft, *California*, IV: 286–97.
[20]*Ibid.*, pp. 289–329.

defend his rule, he set out to woo the foreign element by offering munificent land grants—certainly an attractive appeal to the ever increasing number of arriving settlers.

One of his first contacts was John A. Sutter, a German-born, Swiss émigré, who arrived in California in 1839 and settled near the confluence of the American and Sacramento Rivers in 1841 on a land grant given him by Governor Alvarado. There he built his famed establishment, christened Sutter's Fort. It was destined to become a legendary name, one familiar to all overland immigrants since it was literally the Ellis Island for early California.

In response to Micheltorena's request for aid, Sutter raised an armed contingent—a "Mounted Rifle Company [of] about 100 Men of all Nations," as well as 100 trained Indians, both infantry and cavalry. Sutter's force hastily joined Micheltorena's command near present-day Salinas, where upon Captain Sutter was promptly promoted to colonel.[21]

The revolting *Californios* in the northern part of the province, led by Alvarado and Castro, were far outnumbered by Micheltorena's force. This being the case, they wisely decided to avoid conflict and moved south to join larger groups of revolutionaries led by the capable Pío Pico. Once joined, the contending forces met in the Cahuenga Pass and for two days dueled with their limited artillery. During

[21] *Ibid.*, pp. 455–83; Douglas S. Watson, ed., *The Diary of Johann August Sutter* (San Francisco, 1932), pp. 18, 21–23.

this interlude several Americans supporting the
Pico-Alvarado-Castro side persuaded Sutter and
other mercenaries to abandon Micheltorena in the
field. When the governor learned of this serious defection, he meekly surrendered. The triumphant
Californios marched him and his remaining troops
to San Pedro where they were summarily loaded on
to a ship that returned them to Mexico. Again, the
Californios chose one of their own leaders, Pío Pico
of Los Angeles, to be the new governor.[22] Signifi-
cantly, with the departure of Micheltorena and his
troops, there was not a single Mexican-appointed
governmental official in Alta California by 1845.

At this time in the United States, events were
converging on a momentous decision in the nation's
history—war with Mexico. The background to this
conflict was set forth in the 1844 presidential election when the dark-horse nominee, James K. Polk,
campaigned on a platform that later would be
called "Manifest Destiny." He promised the nation,
if elected, the annexation of the Republic of Texas,
the acquisition of the Oregon Territory and *the
Mexican territory of California*, plus a tariff reduc-
tion, an independent treasury, and not to run again
for the presidency. Like few presidents, before or
after, he kept his promises.[23]

[22]Bancroft, *California*, IV: 484–517.
[23]For elaboration, see the splendid biography authored by
Charles G. Sellers, Jr., *James K. Polk, Constitution—1843–
1846* (Princeton, NJ, 1966).

There were, of course, high risks associated with these goals. Annexation of Texas would almost surely bring about war with Mexico or perhaps the seizure of Texas by Great Britain, who had long been dallying with the new republic.[24] The situation in the west was exacerbated by the overbearing tactics of José Castro in Alta California because of his proclamations expelling all foreigners and stopping further immigration. Polk saw in this the fine hand of Great Britain and suspected that the British were already at work formulating plans to seize California in order to strengthen its claim to the Oregon Country.[25]

On March 4, 1845, Polk was inaugurated. In his address he reaffirmed his campaign platform regarding Texas and the Oregon Country which in essence were direct challenges to Mexico and Great Britain. Two days later Mexico severed diplomatic relations with the United States, and two months later began to strengthen its military forces to resist the United States. The final straw concerned the location of the southern boundary of Texas. Should

[24]Conclusions reached in Ephraim D. Adams, *British Interests and Activities in Texas 1838–1846* (Baltimore, 1910), have been partially discredited by Frederick Merk, *Slavery and the Annexation of Texas* (New York, 1972), who maintains that Britain's involvement in the possible annexation of Texas was invented by the pro-slavery element to push for speedier annexation by the United States.

[25]Gene M. Brack, *Mexico Views Manifest Destiny, 1821–1846* (Albuquerque, 1975), p. 142; K. Jack Bauer, *The Mexican War, 1846–1848* (New York, 1974), p. 11.

it be the Nueces River as staunchly argued by
the Mexicans or the Rio Grande as passionately
claimed by the Texans.[26]

Fortunately for the United States, the Oregon
question was solved rather amicably, but not before
the Polk government blustered and thundered.

From America's point of view, the timing of the
tirade was letter perfect. British politics were in
something of a muddle, which confused the diplomatic efforts. Britain soon relinquished its claim to
the Columbia River boundary, and we relented
from our challenge of "54-40 or fight." The result
came in the form of a British proposal to extend the
49th parallel as the border between the United
States and far western Canada. It was quickly ratified by the Senate on June 6, 1846.[27]

The situation with Mexico, however, was quickly
deteriorating. After a diplomatic failure followed
by a deployment of troops on both sides of the
Rio Grande, the Mexican commander soon notified
General Zachary Taylor that as far as he was concerned hostilities had commenced. And so they did
that very day, April 24, 1846, when a force of 1,600
Mexican cavalry troops crossed the Rio Grande and
humbled a reconnoitering detachment of American

[26] James D. Richardson, ed., *A Compilation of the Messages
and Papers of the Presidents* (20 vols., New York, 1897) V:
2230–31.
[27] Frederick Merk, *The Oregon Question: Essays in Anglo-
American Diplomacy and Politics* (Cambridge, MA, 1967),
pp. 255–336, 410–17.

dragoons. Taylor immediately informed Washington and the war was on.[28]

Ignorant of what was transpiring between the United States and Mexico, Alta California was not totally unaware that something of an extraordinary nature was casting an ominous shadow across the province's future. A hint of what was to come was signaled by the unexpected appearance of Captain John C. Frémont, the noted western explorer, who arrived at Sutter's Fort in early December 1845 with a detachment of fifteen men. While waiting for spring-like weather, he visited Monterey and was queried by local officials as to the reason a United States army contingent should be present in Mexican California. His reply that he was on an exploratory journey was accepted and he was allowed to set up an encampment away from the settlements.[29]

In the early weeks of 1846, the remainder of his command appeared. Once united they decamped to the highest peak in the Gavilan Mountains, built a crude fortification, and had the gall to hoist an American flag while in Mexican territory. Naturally, this did not rest well with the civil prefect in Monterey who proclaimed Frémont and his troops to be a band of robbers and summoned volunteers to

[28] Allan Nevins, ed., *Polk: The Diary of a President, 1845–1849* (New York, 1952), pp. 81–86, 89; Richardson, ed., *Messages and Papers of the Presidents,* V: 2292.

[29] Neal Harlow, *California Conquered: War and Peace on the Pacific, 1846–1850* (Berkeley and Los Angeles, 1982), pp. 61–64.

defend the province. Seeing that the situation was tenuous at best, Frémont broke camp and headed north for Oregon.[30] And now a touch of mystery!

About a month after Frémont's departure, a note containing what is believed to be the official United States policy regarding California was carried to Monterey by Lieutenant Archibald H. Gillespie, who was serving in the role of a secret agent. When hearing of Frémont's presence and hasty departure, the young officer set out immediately to join Frémont, which he did about a month later. Although the contents of the material carried by Gillespie have never been revealed, the meeting did produce a change of mind. Frémont did an about-face and began his return to the Sacramento River valley. By the end of May 1846, he and his command were encamped at Sutter's Buttes.[31]

Although seemingly a minor incident by today's standards, another event of major importance began to unfold. It began with two American émigrés—John Marsh and Charles M. Weber—who suggested to other American settlers that they begin imitating their Texas counterparts. The *Californios* at this time were openly debating whether to place all of California under the protection of France, Great

[30] *Ibid.*, pp. 64–73.

[31] *Ibid.*, pp. 74–85; Werner H. Marti, *Messenger of Destiny: The California Adventures, 1846–1847 of Archibald H. Gillespie, U. S. Marine Corps* (San Francisco, 1950), p. 8 *et seq.*; John C. Frémont, *Memoirs of My Life* (Chicago and New York, 1887), p. 489.

Britain or the United States. There was little allegiance to Mexico. By the summer of 1846, unaware that war with Mexico was a reality, a small group of American immigrants, no doubt emboldened by the presence of Frémont, commenced a revolt and unfurled a hastily lettered and drawn Bear Flag as a symbol of liberty and independence. This extraordinary movement, subsequently named the Bear Flag Revolt, led to the abortive establishment of the so-called California Republic which lasted only a month—June 10 to July 9, 1846. This short-lived episode was successfully completed due to much needed support from Frémont's force. It was quickly followed by a formal occupation of California's capital and takeover of the provincial government by naval forces under the command of Commodore John D. Sloat. The entire operation surely achieved what the relatively small band of Bear Flaggers had intended: to make certain that California would become part of the United States of America.[32]

Like the Bear Flag Revolt, the Mexican War in California was short-lived! It formally began when Commodore Sloat had "Old Glory" raised at Monterey on July 7, 1846. It ended with the signing of the Treaty of Cahuenga on January 13, 1847. At the beginning, the war was exclusively conducted by U.S. naval forces; sailors and marines, who were

---

[32] Harlow, *California Conquered*, pp. 85–114, provides the essentials of Frémont's involvement and the Bear Flaggers' efforts.

joined by a locally recruited California Battalion
of American settlers, placed under the command
of Frémont. However, there was little opposition,
other than vocal, to American occupation. This
would change abruptly when Archibald Gillespie,
recently promoted to captain, was given military
command of the Los Angeles area. In only a few
weeks he alienated the local *Californios* with his ban
on *fandangos* (dances), popular events, and assemblies. His autocratic actions sparked a revolt and
led to Los Angeles being placed under siege, which
led to the surrender of the Americans within.[33]
That humiliating defeat spurred a reconquest effort
which resulted in three separate military confrontations: the Battle of the Old Woman's Gun, which
ended in a stalemate; the surprise defeat of General
Stephen W. Kearny's travel-weary dragoons who
were arriving after a long trek from Santa Fe; and
the decisive encounter where American forces routed the dissidents at La Mesa, east of Los Angeles.
Shortly thereafter, the Mormon Battalion, recruited
by Brigham Young, and the Seventh Regiment of
New York Volunteers brought added American military strength to insure the victory. Happily, all
hostilities ended almost at once. California was
completely pacified and secured.

A little more than a year later—February 2,
1848—the war with Mexico formally ended with the
signing of the Treaty of Guadalupe Hidalgo. One of

[33] Marti, *Messenger of Destiny*, pp. 73–86.

the great ironies in history is that the treaty was signed nine days *after* gold was discovered in California by James Wilson Marshall. Had the discovery been made while California was under Spanish or Mexican rule, surely the fate of the future Golden State would have been quite different, not to mention that of the United States, as well. Within the first five years of the discovery, $209 million in gold was extracted from the hills, streams, and flatlands! Even twenty years later, the mines still produced $15 million, and by the turn of the century, total gold production amounted to $1.3 billion.[34]

As to be expected, the first to respond to the discovery were the Californians. They learned of the find by word of mouth, then by confirmed reports in the two San Francisco newspapers. Oregonians were the first outsiders to learn of the discovery, but parties were small since it was August and harvest time was fast approaching. With the spring thaw the numbers increased.

Not so in the Hawaiian Islands when the discovery was reported in the Honolulu *Polynesian* on June 24. Susceptible adventurers were quickly on their way, and by year's end twenty-two shiploads had left for San Francisco.[35]

[34] Rodman M. Paul, *California Gold: The Beginnings of Mining in the West* (Cambridge, MA, 1947), pp. 345–48.
[35] The dissemination of news around the world of the gold discovery and its resulting emigration is based on the Nunis article titled, "The 'Strangers' Amongst Them," *Westways Magazine*, 59 (May, 1967): pp. 24–27.

Chileans, too, were quick to respond. A veritable stampede ensued after the Chilean brigantine *J. R. S.* brought the news to Valparaiso. Before May 1849, over 5,000 had taken ship for the gold fields, well in advance of the oncoming hordes of eastern and midwestern Americans who were slowly making their way overland.

By October, Mexico was astir with excitement, and due to their proximity, Sonorans were among the early arrivals. In the first eight months some 4,600 to 6,000 Mexicans journeyed northward. And, like the Chileans, many brought their wives and children.

At the end of 1848, California's population (excluding Indians) had grown from 14,000 to 20,000. Twelve months later it had jumped to more than 100,000. Americans accounted for most of the 1849 increase, arriving by the hundreds on ships and by the thousands via the Overland Trail. The vast majority of Americans arrived a year or more after the discovery. Their tardy appearance was not only because of the slow dissemination of news, but also the widespread skepticism that prevailed due to the extent of the gold strike. That attitude changed abruptly when couriers from California presented a tea caddy containing 230 ounces of pure gold to President Polk, who boldly declared in his annual message to Congress:

"It was known that mines of the precious metals existed to a considerable extent in California at the time of acquisition. Recent discoveries render it probable that these mines are more extensive and valuable than was anticipated. The accounts of the abundance of gold in that territory are of such extraordinary character as would scarcely command belief were it not corroborated by the authentic reports of public service officers who have visited the mineral district and derived the facts which they detail from personal observation."[36]

Europeans did not escape the infectious gold fever. Although they, too, were late in receiving the news, the discovery was immediately accepted in Europe as true because of Polk's affirmation to Congress. By thousands they booked passage to the mines—the greatest exodus coming from Great Britain and Ireland, then Germany and lastly France. Furthermore, British speculators had committed £1,200,000 to finance gold seeking companies.[37]

Unhappy Ireland, reeling from the effects of the potato famine, sent thousands from her green shores. Many Irish mining camps sprang up, and by 1852 half the population of San Francisco was Irish.

Chaotic conditions which reigned in the German states following the 1848 Revolution, compounded by successive crop failures, influenced many a German to seek the golden fleece in California. Mining camps at Stoutenburg, Mosquito Gulch, and Dutch

[36]Richardson, ed., *Messages and Papers of the Presidents*, V: 2486; Donald D. Jackson, *Gold Dust* (New York, 1980), pp. 61–62.

[37]Nunis, "The 'Strangers' Amongst Them," pp. 25–27, focuses on European, Australian, and Chinese emigrant gold seekers.

Flat were peopled by German miners who were easily assimilated and made welcome in California by the Americans.

The French, too, were excited by stories of the gold find. Many Frenchmen were involved in the backwash of the severe depression that resulted from the abortive Revolution of 1848, and looked to striking it rich as a quick remedy. Emigrant companies could be found all over France. Subscription and joint stock ventures as well as private and public sponsorship financed many mining enterprises. Even a lottery was established, and prizes included pre-paid passages to California, however, many gullible and penniless Frenchmen found themselves stranded on arrival at the Golden Gate. In 1850, the French government organized and sponsored *La Compagnie des Gardes Mobiles* to transport former soldiers to the mines. The initial detachment of 131 men arrived in San Francisco and with military precision marched to their camp area. Once there, they continued to maintain a military organization and discipline. The presence of such a group fanned the rising fury of anti-foreignism and the *Gardes Mobiles* were even suspected as being part of an overt conspiracy by France to seize California.

Other European emigration was extremely small. Few responded when the news hit Norway and Sweden and the same could be said for Russians and Poles. The Spaniards and Italians provided no more than a sprinkling of gold seekers.

Trans-Pacific emigration was more memorable. Although small in number, the Australian contingent left an unmistakable imprint on San Francisco's history. Begun as a colony for convicts after the American Revolution, many Botany Bay internees elected to seek wealth and freedom in California, but few sought their riches from the mines. Instead, most reverted to their old habits. A section of San Francisco became known as "Sydney Town" and the ex-convicts were dubbed "Sydney Ducks"—a lawless element that ravaged an already lawless community for two frightening years.

There was also the Chinese, who came as contract laborers to ease the manpower shortage in the early days of the gold rush. In 1850 the first federal census to be taken in California included 660 Chinese. They were inexperienced and worked mostly the poorer claims. To finance their passage they signed contracts which bound them to repay costs at high interest rates. Poor and illiterate, they were tolerated at first, but anti-Chinese sentiment was not long in exploding. By early 1852 there was organized popular agitation even though up to that point Chinese emigration was extremely light, but by the end of that year, *20,000 Chinese had arrived*. This sudden influx had an electrifying effect in California, and would provide a dilemma for the rest of the century. Its final solution was Congressional adoption of the exclusion policy, the seeds for which were sown in gold rush California.

Within but a scant two years, California became America's first true "melting pot," mingling a wide array of other nationalities with native-born Americans. Almost immediately it became an emotionally charged encounter since the Americans as well as the foreign-born interlopers had led such insular lives. From a 1993 perspective it is difficult to fully comprehend this extraordinary melding of so many diverse cultures and languages of men who were literally jammed together within the limited area of the gold field country and also within a compressed time period.

The situation was exacerbated by the Americans' view that California and its gold belonged to the United States, meaning its citizens. What right, the American miners asked constantly, did foreign prospectors have to American gold? Why should foreigners benefit from what was patently American wealth? There was no good answer, and the result was widespread friction that soon got out of hand.

The compounding factor was that California at the outset of the gold rush had no civil government. It was ruled by the United States army, the essential political power invested in a governor who was a military officer. Unfortunately, the military government proved unequal to the task of establishing, let alone enforcing, law and order. It simply did not have the manpower. With the termination of the Mexican War, the regiment of New York Volunteers was immediately discharged, and at the same time, regular army strength was woefully insufficient to care for the influx of over 100,000 argonauts and immigrants that flocked to the gold country in 1848 and '49. Army desertions and a huge drop in reenlistments thinned the ranks even more, and Congress did nothing to provide appropriations needed to increase and strengthen the military in California. It was simply an untenable situation for everyone concerned.

To fill the authority-void, each mining camp, in effect, became a mini-civil government, with its own laws and officials, enacted and elected in regular, popular assemblies. When it came to meting out justice for infringement of any local mining camp law, the miners served as both judge and jury. Justice was swift and emotion outweighed reason in handing down verdicts. Punishments were cruel and harsh: public whippings were commonplace; mutilations were not uncommon; hangings were frequent; banishment from camp proved to be the most humane sentence. Might made right; majority rule trampled minority rights.

It was in this vortex that the ethnic-racial mix, spawned by the gold rush, fashioned a climate of gross bigotry. Little wonder there was a dark side to the gold rush, one that bred intolerance which led to the rise of *anti-foreignism*—later called nativism—and known today as *nationalism*. California was the first in the nation to develop such a situation, and then confront such an explosive issue.

On the bright side, this enormous influx of foreigners greatly enriched the history of the state.
Even though a sizeable number of these emigrants
returned to their homes, perhaps wiser than richer, many remained to provide the basis for an expanded cosmopolitan population that has distinctly
marked California ever since. No other state in the
Union can point to an overnight "melting pot" environment comparable to that created by the gold
rush. In that respect, California was well over a century ahead of the rest of the nation, which today
increasingly shares this multi-cultural and multi-
ethnic experience.

The gold discovery also propelled California to
early statehood and in so doing helped to set the
stage for the tragedy of the Civil War. As Americans
grew in number during the first year and a half of
the gold rush, the new arrivals became increasingly
uneasy over the fact that there was no civilian government. Indeed, for the first time in their lives
they found themselves being governed by the United States army. This situation began in July 1846,
when military rule was established, first under naval
officers directed by Commodore Sloat, then under
the army beginning with General Kearny. This
whole scenario was repugnant to the long-standing
tradition of home rule or self-government. As a result, agitation began to increase to replace military
rule with civilian authority as American citizens became the major political element. In early 1849 the

quest began with San Francisco and Sacramento being the flash points of the movement.[38]

On June 3, 1849, after several steely confrontations, the last military governor, Colonel Bennet Riley, without Congressional or official authorization, created a quasi-civilian government, divided California into districts, and called for the election of delegates to decide what course of action should be initiated. The election, held on August 1, resulted in the selection of forty-eight delegates.

After formally convening, the delegates moved immediately to the task of framing a state constitution. The first order of business concerned the setting of the eastern boundary and then a momentous decision was made: slavery was to be prohibited in California! The delegates then turned their attention to structuring the government and formulating its basic laws. On October 13, their work completed, they signed the finished document and adjourned. The day before, Governor Riley issued a "Proclamation to the People" which in effect sanctioned the newly drafted constitution.[39]

November 13 was set as the date for submitting the document to the people, as well as the election of state officials and two congressmen to serve in the House of Representatives in Washington. (At

[38]See Theodore Grivas, *Military Governments in California 1846–1850* (Glendale, CA 1963), *passim*.

[39]J. Ross Browne, *Report of the Debates in Convention of California, on the State Constitution ... 1849* (Washington, DC, 1850), Appendix, p. xlvi.

this time, United States Senators were chosen by the state legislatures.) The result was a landslide of approval—12,061 in favor and 811 opposed. Peter H. Burnett was elected governor. California, *ipso facto*, had become a state—at least in its own eyes. *Officially, it was not.*

On January 1, 1850, Congressmen-elect Edward Gilbert and George W. Wright, accompanied by Senators-designate John C. Frémont and William M. Gwin, left for the nation's capital to seek California's admission into the Union. Upon their arrival, President Zachary Taylor immediately informed Congress and transmitted California's constitution for approval.[40] A long, drawn-out debate was caused by California's proposal to move from conquered territory under military rule, to formal application for statehood without going through the territorial process. Such a brash action had focused national attention on the perplexing question concerning the expansion of slavery into the area newly acquired from Mexico.

Finally, the Compromise of 1850 was accepted in a series of five laws passed between September 9 and 20. Immediately, California was admitted as the 31st state and as a free state. Further, the disputed Texas-New Mexico boundary was settled and the Utah and New Mexico territories were established.

[40]William H. Ellison, *A Self-Governing Dominion: California, 1849–1860* (Berkeley and Los Angeles, 1950), pp. 53, 79, 84.

The question of slavery in the territories was left for the inhabitants to decide by "popular sovereignty." Soon after, on September 18 and 20, new laws called for placing fugitive slave cases under federal jurisdiction and abolishing domestic slave trade in the District of Columbia.[41] The nation congratulated itself on finally putting to rest once and for all the divisive issue of slavery and expansion. That wishful thinking would hold in place until 1860 when it was shattered by secession and the advent of the Civil War.

There is no denying that acquisition through the Mexican Cession combined with the discovery of gold in California and the non-conforming move to statehood, brought forth profound constitutional, moral, and political questions, temporarily assuaged by the Compromise of 1850, that were not fundamentally solved. The final solution had to await the judgment rendered at Appomattox.

In the two books which follow, four important themes emerge that provide unique dimensions to the history of California: first, the twilight years of Mexican rule are succinctly detailed; second, the events of the Mexican War in California are aptly chronicled; third, the discovery of gold and the early days of the gold rush are graphically recounted; fourth, the struggles for self-government are ably described. These momentous events were witnessed

[41] *Ibid.*, pp. 84–101. Richard B. Morris, ed., *Encyclopedia of American History* (Rev. ed., New York, 1976), pp. 250–54.

and recorded by James W. Marshall, a pre-gold rush émigré and the man who made the initial gold discovery at Coloma, and E. Gould Buffum, an experienced journalist who was the first reporter to visit the mining district and later became an active participant in California's transition from military rule to statehood. Their first-hand accounts are well worth reading, for they are uniquely informative. They are genuine California classics.

DOYCE B. NUNIS, JR.

June, 1993

1

The
Life and Adventures
of
James W. Marshall

by
George Frederic Parsons

James Wilson Marshall
Courtesy California State Library, Sacramento

Editor's Prologue

ONLY A FEW men are destined for fame, the rest for obscurity. James Wilson Marshall's *only* claim to fame is that he was the discoverer of gold in California. That chance act brought about the gold rush, an epic story in itself, and earned him a place in the annals of the Golden State's history, along with a magnificent monument to his memory and a well done biography.[1] Yet he was of humble origin and endowed with limited talent. He would rest today in complete obscurity if it were not for the extraordinary find he made on that cold, damp morning of January 24, 1848. In that single act he literally altered the history of California and the United States.

He was born in the family's two-story stone and frame farmhouse on Round Mountain near Marshall's Corner in Hopewell Township, Hunterdon County, New Jersey, October 8, 1810, the son of Philip and Sarah (Wilson) Marshall. His great-grandfather had immigrated to colonial America

[1] Marshall's monument was erected at the site of his discovery in 1890. All biographical data has been drawn from Theresa Gay, *James W. Marshall, The Discoverer of Gold: A Biography* (Georgetown, CA, 1968), which is considered the definitive work.

about a decade or so before the American Revolution, settling in Hopewell Township. Of German origin, he came from Alsace and changed his name from Conrad Merdel to Conrad Marshall. On the latter's death in 1813, he left his property to his two grandsons, Philip (James' father) and John, since his only son was deceased. It was James' fate to be born into a family that never had to face the prospect of poverty or privation.

While he was very young, the family relocated to nearby Lambertville, New Jersey, on the Delaware River, where his father labored as a coach and wagonmaker. It was here the young boy received his education in a privately conducted school. He proved to be studious and, as a youthful fancy, began to think about becoming a teacher. When not in school, James worked alongside his father, later becoming his apprentice and then a business partner.

But tragedy and hard times overtook the family when business proved none too prosperous. His father found employment with the Baltimore and Ohio Railroad, but in late September 1834, he fell victim to typhus while helping to build the nation's first railroad and died deeply in debt. Since all the family property had to be sold to satisfy the creditors, James received no inheritance. Already restless, he decided, like so many other young men of his day, to head West. It was to be a journey of far reaching consequences.

I

Hired by Sutter

JAMES WILSON MARSHALL was born in Hopewell Township, Hunterdon County, New Jersey, on October 8, 1810.[1] His father was a coach and wagon builder, and he was taught the same trade. His early life presents no special interest; and he had arrived at man's estate—being just twenty one—when he began to turn his eyes westward, and to experience the yearning which makes the pioneer. In a short time his mind was made up, and with such leave-taking as poor men usually make when they start out into the world and turn their backs, perhaps finally, upon the place of their birth, he set forth and journeyed until he came to Crawfordsville, Indiana. Here he worked as a carpenter for some months, but the leaven of restlessness was at work within him, and he set out again shortly, this time reaching Warsaw, Illinois. After a brief stay here, he once more packed his few possessions and wandered off to the Platte Purchase, near Fort Leavenworth, in Missouri. Here, for the first time since leaving home, he appears to have had some idea of settling permanently, for he located a homestead,

[1] The original edition used the incorrect year 1812 for Marshall's birth.

worked steadily at farming and trading, and was in a modest way to prosper.[2] He was, however, attacked with fever and ague so much that after struggling against the disease for six years, he was compelled to prepare for another exodus, or make up his mind to die where he was, for the doctor said he could not expect more than a two years' lease of life.

Just at this time people were beginning to talk a good deal about a strange, new country far away in the west, called California. It was said to be a desirable place to emigrate to. The valleys were broad and fertile; the rivers were numerous; timber was plenty; and a large variety of game abounded. And there was a charm about the name and what the uncertain legends told regarding the new region that whetted the curiosity of the border men. Marshall heard of California. If he stayed in the low bottom lands he must die. He could only be killed by the Indians if he went. He decided to go. A party was being made up in the neighborhood, and gathering together his stock he joined it, and set out. They

[2]When Missouri was admitted to the Union via the Compromise of 1820, the state's northwest boundary was fashioned to preserve the Sauk and Fox Indians' reservation. In 1836 the federal government purchased the land from the Indians for $7,500 and a quantity of merchandise. Congress then sanctioned the annexation of the Platte Purchase, as it was named, to Missouri on March 28, 1837, thus extending the state's boundary to the Missouri River. James T. Adams, ed., *Dictionary of American History* (Rev. ed., 5 vols., New York, 1942), IV: 286; [W. W. Gatewood], *History of Platte County, Missouri* (St. Louis, 1885), pp. 550–55.

started about the first of May, 1844, with a train of a
hundred wagons, but owing to the heavy rains,
which had flooded the bottom lands of the Missouri
River and its tributaries that spring, they were delayed considerably. At length, they arrived at Fort
Hall, and here a consultation was held, and it was
decided that the safest route to enter California
would be by way of Oregon. All did not agree to
this, however, and the difference of opinion finally
led to a disruption of the party. Some went one
way, some another. Marshall joined a band of about
forty souls, and the company started (on horseback
and packing their provisions) about the spring of
1845. There was then, and had been for some time,
much trouble with the Indians, but this party was
not molested in any way. This fact is worthy of remark, for the reason that it was the first case of perfect immunity from attack that had been recorded
up to that time.[3]

The journey was unaccompanied therefore by
any special excitement, and after wintering in Oregon they reached California safely via Shasta in the
month of June, and coming down the Sacramento
Valley camped at Cache Creek, about forty miles
from the present site of the City of Sacramento.
Here they separated. Some trailed on to San Francisco (then known as Yerba Buena); some wandered

[3]This is not true. So long as parties traveled in tandem for
protection, their numbers provided a sufficient deterrent to
Indian attack. Only single small parties invited disaster.

off up the valley; some proceeded to Sacramento, where Sutter's Fort was established, and looked on with envy by the Mexicans, awe by the Indians, and admiration by the foreigners (as all Americans and Europeans then were). Marshall was among those who proceeded to the fort, and here, in July, 1845, he engaged to work for Sutter.

It may be well to pause here and give some idea of the California to which Marshall was first introduced in 1845. There were then very few settlers at all, and even less in the northern portion of the State. The missions were still the principal centers of business and population, but otherwise the whole country was inert, stagnant, undeveloped, barren, and almost desolate. The long held power of the Mission Fathers had been broken, and the good work they had done had been lost by the rapacity, ignorance, and obstinacy of Mexican officials and legislators. The patient labors of a hundred years had been overthrown in a twelvemonth, and the Christianized Indians had turned back to barbarism. At the many missions, where the old Fathers had used a mild despotism, and where, for generations, their every word had been law, they were cast down and despised. New rulers, secular by denomination, too often coarse and brutal by nature, tyrannical and cruel by disposition, occupied the places of authority, and ground the faces of the poor. Brigandage and lawlessness had become established in some parts of the State, and progress there was

John A. Sutter
Courtesy The Huntington Library

Sutter's Fort
Courtesy California State Library, Sacramento

9

none, save here and there where some enterprising American or other foreigner had procured a grant of land, and was cultivating a portion of it, or else raising stock.

Sutter had built the fort on the Sacramento River and was engaged in raising grain and stock, and doing a small trading business. He also made blankets, having secured the services of a number of Indians who had been taught to spin by the Mission Fathers of San Jose, and one of the first tasks in which Marshall was engaged was the construction of a number of spinning wheels for these blanket weavers. The life at the fort was a rude one, destitute of comfort and ill supplied even with necessities. The men soon wore out what clothing they had brought with them over the mountains, and thenceforward were compelled to trust to their rifles for their garments. Antelope were plentiful at that time, and from the skins of these animals most of the clothing was made. Sutter employed a band of hunters and trappers, mostly Indians, and these supplied the fort with meat, taking their pay generally in ammunition. Everything was conducted in the most primitive style. Tea, sugar, coffee, etc., were basic items completely unknown. There was flour, of a kind, but it was poorly prepared. The fort had the honor of introducing the first improvement in grinding wheat. The custom of the country was sufficiently barbarous. The grain was placed on a flat stone, and pounded with another stone, the operators being generally women. Sutter, with the assistance of his men, constructed a rude mill, which was worked by a mule, who walked round and round, causing the upper stone to revolve. The flour thus produced was coarse, but the men thought themselves lucky when it contained no lumps larger than a nutmeg. There were no candles, and consequently all hands retired as soon as it was dark, save when some enterprising individual hunted up a pitch pine knot, and thus secured an hour or so of smoky illumination.

For several months Marshall pursued the even tenor of this dull life, being occupied in stocking plows, making spinning wheels, mending wagons, and doing such general carpenter work as was required. Being a handy man, a good mechanic, and withal a shrewd natural engineer, he was extremely useful to Sutter, and they, together with a dozen more—white men and Indians—lived quietly and soberly until the fall of 1845, when an event occurred which threatened disastrous consequences to the little colony.

In order to explain what followed, it will be necessary to go back in our history some years. In 1844 the native Californians[4] raised up in revolt against Micheltorena, the Mexican Governor of California, the alleged cause of their disaffection being that he had brought over a large group of desperadoes from Mexico. Sutter, holding the office of alcalde under

[4]As pointed out in the Historical Introduction, the native Californians were also known as *Californios*.

Governor Manuel Micheltorena
Courtesy The Huntington Library

the governor, deemed it was his duty to assist him, and accordingly raised a force of white settlers and Indians. He selected as the leader of the Indians, Rufino,[5] chief of the Mokelumne tribe, a brave and shrewd man, and gave him command of two hundred Indians. One of the feats of Rufino is worthy of narration, not only as indicating the character of the man, but as illustrative of the wild life of that period. Sutter commanded a force of some sixty or seventy men, and with Indian accomplices, marched upon the Mission San Jose, where the enemy was supposed to be intrenched in large number. Having no artillery with them, it was necessary to take the mission by storm if possible, and Rufino at once undertook the task. Charging at the head of his men right up to the walls, he there caused several horses to be placed side by side, and their riders standing erect on the saddles, formed a pyramid up which the chief climbed, followed by the rest of the band, and gained the interior, though only to find that the enemy had fled. After several skirmishes, the natives retreated to the lower part of Upper California and here a final battle was fought, resulting in the defeat of Micheltorena, his capitulation, and subsequent retreat from the State. Up to this time American settlers had been fighting on both sides, but here they were now brought face to face for the first time.

[5]In the original edition Marshall mistakenly refers to this Indian chief as Raphero. All mentions of Raphero have been corrected to read Rufino.

Wisely considering that there was no necessity for them to slaughter each other, they held a conference and decided to withdraw their forces, leaving the native Californians and the Mexicans to fight it out among themselves. The native Californians were commanded by Pío Pico and Señor José Castro, and were about ninety strong. They were intrenched in a ravine, from which it would have been extremely difficult to dislodge them, and previous to the withdrawal of the American contingent, Rufino asked permission to attack Castro's force, expressing his confidence in the issue. The request was not granted, but being afterwards asked what his plan of attack would have been, he coolly replied that he intended to strip his Indians, leaving them only their muskets and bows and arrows, and then charge the enemy, reserving his fire until he was close upon them. His men, after discharging their muskets, were to have thrown them away, and taken to their bows and arrows, with which they could fire volley after volley before their antagonists would have had time to reload. He expected to be killed himself in the charge, but he believed that it would have been successful.

We now resume the thread of our story, having left the colonists at the fort peaceably engaged in agriculture, hunting, and trading. In the spring of 1846 Sutter received intelligence to the effect that the Spaniards at the Mission San Jose were inciting the Indians to attack him and burn his wheat. They

Governor Pío Pico
Courtesy The Huntington Library

General José Castro
Courtesy California State Library, Sacramento

had always regarded him with jealousy as a foreign intruder upon their soil, and at length their dislike was about to take shape in open hostilities. He soon learned that Rufino had been induced to take command of the Indians who were charged with the work of destruction, and knowing the energy, cunning, and bravery of the Mokelumne chief, he felt that a prompt and decisive response was necessary. Some time before this Rufino had killed a brother-in-law of his own. In that unsettled period, when the laws were either wholly disregarded or loosely administered, this homicide would, under ordinary circumstances, have probably entailed no punishment upon the offender; but Sutter saw in it the opportunity he needed, and being armed with the requisite authority, as a Mexican Alcalde, he caused Rufino to be arrested on a charge of murder, and brought prisoner to the fort. Undoubtedly he was doomed from the moment he set foot within those walls. His influence with his tribe, his desperate courage, and his sagacity, rendered him an enemy too formidable to be suffered to escape. A trial was granted him, and his defense was characteristically shrewd. He held a commission as lieutenant from the Mexican government, and claimed that under this instrument he was authorized to kill horse thieves, and that as the relative slain by him was an offender against the laws in this respect, he should be held blameless. The defense was plausible, but, unfortunately for himself, he was unable to prove that the slain man was a horse thief; and after a reasonable time had been given him to collect evidence on this point, he was found guilty of murder, and sentenced to be shot. Marshall and his comrades were called to execute the sentence, but they refused, and Sutter was compelled to rely upon his Indian trappers. Rufino met his fate with stoical coolness. When he was led to the place of execution, and the firing party were drawn up in front of him, it was found that a horse was standing in the line of fire, at his rear. A man was sent to remove the animal, and while the party was waiting, Rufino turned his head and asked the cause of the delay. "Why do you not shoot me?" he cried; "Are you afraid?" In another minute the signal was given, and six balls riddled the breast of the unfortunate chief, who fell forward and died without a murmur or a sigh. So impressed were Marshall and the others with his bravery that they gave him a military funeral, firing volleys over his grave in token of their respect for his undying courage.

Sutter now found it necessary to make preparations for resisting the attack of the Indians, and concluding that it would be better to carry the war into the enemy's country than to wait for their onset, he assembled all the settlers in the neighborhood, and with a force numbering twenty-five Americans and about fifteen Indians, set forth to intercept them. Having been informed that the Mokelumne Indians were camped amid a thicket on the further side of the Mokelumne River, the invading party constructed a light raft, on which they placed their arms and ammunition, and entering the water, prepared to push it across the stream. The river, however, had just been raised by a snow freshet, and on reaching the middle many of the men were carried off their feet. Those who could not swim became alarmed, and attempted to climb on the raft, in doing which it was upset, and the greater part of the arms and ammunition lost. In spite of this disaster, however, the party proceeded, and on reaching the further shore soon found the hiding place of the Indians. The latter were strongly intrenched in the midst of a mass of weeds, grass, and brush, so dense that the attacking party was compelled to cut their way through it with their knives. Marshall and one of the Indian hunters were the first to work their way to the front, where they found that the Indians had ensconced themselves behind two huge tree trunks, lying horizontally, between which they had left a narrow gap through which they could shoot their arrows. As the two men were reconnoitering, an arrow whizzed by Marshall's head and struck his companion, plowing up his scalp and lodging in the wound, without, however, penetrating the skull. The wounded man retreated, and Marshall drew out the arrow, which it appeared was poisoned. The remedies applied would have startled a surgeon, but they proved effectual. The hunter made a poultice of herbs, which Marshall supplemented with a well masticated quid of tobacco, and, strange to say, the wound healed rapidly in spite of the poison. The fight was kept up in a desultory way for several hours, but as Sutter's party had lost most of their firearms, they dared not venture upon a close attack; and so, after one had been wounded on either side, the settlers returned to the fort, while the Indians made the best of their way back to the mission. This expedition was certainly not marked by any very exciting events, nor was opportunity afforded for any grand exploits; but it had the intended effect, in preventing the Indians from carrying out their projected raid, which was finally abandoned by them.

The settlers were not molested by the Indians after this, and a short interval of quiet ensued, which we will take the advantage of to relate a little incident that may possess some interest for the good people who now inhabit the flourishing City of Sacramento. At the time we write of, Sacramento was still "in the womb of the future," and its site was a swamp of a decidedly repellent aspect. Sutter's Fort had been built well back from the river, to avoid the freshets which from time to time caused it to overflow its banks, and converted the adjacent low lying country into a shallow inland sea. When the river was confined within its banks, a ferry was necessary, and Sutter had stationed an Indian ferryman in a small hut situated on the bank, just about at the junction of Front and I streets. One day in the winter of 1846, a freshet came down, and the river flooded the country round about. Sutter waited for his ferryman to come in, but as he did not appear, it began to be feared that the freshet had carried away his boat, and left him a prisoner; so a rescue was planned. Marshall and two other men found a canoe, and soon after having patched it temporarily, started off in search of the Indian. They had hard work to get along, for the weeds and brush impeded them, but by dint of paddling, hauling, and poling, they at length reached their destination, to find the old ferryman with his squaw and family huddled together on the roof of their frail *tule* hut, which was just above the level of the water.[6] The only point of interest in the story is that Marshall and his comrade then paddled their canoe right over the site of the City of Sacramento, and that the old Indian's *tule* hut occupied the present location of the Central Pacific Railroad Depot.

[6]A "*tule*" hut was common among the Indian tribes living near rivers where the brush-like reed grew in abundance. It was used not only for building huts, but also for clothing, providing Indian women with *tule* skirts.

II

Confrontation and Revolt

THE SUMMER of 1846 came and brought serious trouble with it. Intelligence had been received that a large party of emigrants—more than four hundred—were coming across the mountains, and this news had reached the ears of the native Californians, who became alarmed at the prospect of an influx of those terribly energetic and pushy "Americanos." In truth, they had become very uneasy for some time. Accustomed to a lazy, dreamy life, in which no thought of improving the country or developing its resources found a place, they regarded the advent of these hardy, industrious, pushing foreigners with a jealousy and a fear akin to that which the Indian experiences at the approach of civilization. Already they had attempted to rid themselves of their unwelcome visitors, and though the American settlers were few in number, it had been found impossible to dislodge or to circumvent them. And if the small band already in the country had secured so firm a hold, what must be expected when four or five hundred men—the vanguard, perhaps, of an immense army of emigrants—poured down the western slopes of the Sierras, and turned their stock loose on the best lands of the great valleys?

The prospect was decidedly unpleasant, and so seriously did it alarm the Mexicans that a decision was made to gather a strong force, meet the dreaded emigrants on the eastern side of the Sierras, and turn them back, by force if necessary. And failing that, by driving off their cattle and starving them out.[1] This course having been decided upon, General José Castro sent a lieutenant with twelve men to the Mission San Rafael, to collect all the government horses at pasture there, and drive them down to San Jose, where they were to be used in mounting the troops. If the lieutenant had succeeded in his mission, it is probable that the settlement of California would have been delayed somewhat, though the issue would have been the same eventually. But he was not destined to succeed, and the cause of his failure was, naturally enough, a woman.

Nearing the Sacramento River at Knight's Landing, the officer met Mrs. Knight, and finding that she was a New Mexican woman, he entrusted her with the secret of the expedition. She listened, drew him out, and having obtained all the information he could give her, went, like a true wife, and told her husband all she had heard. Knight was indignant when informed of the plot against his countrymen,

[1] Castro's intent was not only to block further emigration but also was aimed at ridding California of all foreigners, especially Americans. To that end, he issued a number of proclamations on his own, contrary to the wishes of Governor Pío Pico. Bancroft, *California*, V: 79–80 *note*; Watson, ed., *Sutter's Diary*, p. 34.

and, manlike, would have blurted out his opinion before the officer, and thereby, perhaps, frustrated his own desires. But his wife had more sagacity, and her advice was that he should assist the lieutenant and his men to cross the river, give them fair words, and as soon as they were out of sight, saddle his best horse, raise his friends, and pursuing the Mexicans, take the horses from them before they had time to cross the San Joaquin. This advice was followed.[2]

Of note, Colonel Frémont was camped at Sutter's Buttes, the strange looking mountainous formation which attracts the eye of the traveler on the plain north of Marysville. To him Knight repaired, and told his story. Frémont listened attentively, and then informed his visitor that he could render him no assistance, being a United States officer, and therefore bound to maintain friendly relations with a power at peace with his government. However, he suggested the propriety of gathering together all the settlers, they being under no such restrictions.

[2]William Knight, a native of Maryland, was educated as a physician, but threw his "profession to the winds." He settled in New Mexico, became a Mexican citizen, and married. He came overland to California in 1841 and returned to New Mexico the next year to fetch his family. They settled on the Sacramento River in 1843 at a place named for him, Knight's Landing. With the gold strike, he operated a ferry service at a place also named for him, Knight's Ferry, on the Stanislaus River where he died on November 8, 1849. Douglas E. Kyle, ed., *Historic Spots in California* (4th ed., Stanford, CA, 1990), p. 535; *An Illustrated Atlas and History of Yolo County* ... ([San Francisco], 1879), p. 31.

Knight hurried away, and in a very short time had raised twelve men. They at once started in pursuit of the Mexicans, overtook them at the Cosumnes, captured the bulk of the horses, leaving the lieutenant and his men two animals each, and by him sent word to José Castro that they were "on the war-path." Thus did the Bear Flag War begin, and so primitive, but comprehensive, was the declaration of hostilities on the part of the settlers.

And now it became necessary to make up, by celerity of movement and decision of action, for paucity of numbers. The men who had undertaken this war knew well who they had to deal with, but were confident in their own resources, and never hesitated, or shrunk from the odds opposed to them. Two days after the capture of the horses, Merritt, who had been entrusted with the command, raised about fifteen men, started for Sonoma, and arriving there before the news of the revolt had been received, captured General Vallejo, Colonel Prudon, Colonel Reis, and Captain Vallejo.[3] On their way they were

[3]Merritt and his band of men headed for Sonoma by a circuitous route in order to avoid detection. At the same time, the party's ranks grew to thirty-three men. On June 14, General Mariano Vallejo was captured without a shot as were his brother, Captain Salvador Vallejo, and Lieutenant (not Colonel) Victor Prudon, all three of whom signed the statement of surrender. Fred B. Rogers, *William Brown Ide, Bear Flagger* (San Francisco, 1962), pp. 31–33; Bancroft, *California*, V: 113–14, *notes*. (There was no Colonel Reis involved in the surrender, but there was a Jacob P. Leese, former Alcalde of Sonoma.)

Colonel John C. Frémont
Courtesy The Huntington Library

General Mariano Vallejo
Courtesy California State Library, Sacramento

joined by ten settlers from Napa Valley, and the whole band then proceeded to Sutter's Fort, and demanded its surrender. It must be borne in mind that General Sutter was at this time an official under the Mexican government, and though it was not expected for a moment that he would take sides against his countrymen, it was deemed necessary to secure the fort and transfer its allegiance. He, at once, complied with the demand of the settlers, and they having entered the fort, proceeded to haul down the Mexican colors and raise the Bear Flag.[4]

We may as well state here how this flag came to be adopted. There was at that time a large number of grizzlies in the state, and few of the settlers had escaped a tussle with them. When, therefore, the question was raised as to the kind of flag to be adopted, the old hunters naturally thought of their four-footed enemy, and remembering his pluck and ferocity, thought no better emblem could be chosen. The way the flag was made is worthy of narration. There was no bunting to be had, and nobody was artist enough to paint a bear. So they procured a piece of sheeting, and having prepared a quantity of powdered charcoal and grease, one of the party daubed a rude image of a grizzly on the white flag with his fingers. The likeness was not an artistic

[4]There was no plan to capture Sutter's Fort since he had quickly declared for the American cause. Though he was not completely trusted, he permitted the Sonoma prisoners to be confined in the fort until their release in August. *Ibid.*, V: 122–24.

success, indeed, some of the party, who had an eye
for beauty of form, expressed doubts as to whether
the animal represented did not more closely resem-
ble a pig than a bear. However, the flag was good
enough for one to fight under, and while it floated,
the enemy seldom found time to discuss the accuracy of its design.

Shortly after this, Frémont moved down with his
exploring party to the north side of the American
River, and camped nearly opposite Sutter's Fort. He
had by this time determined to join the settlers, and
with this resolve, he prepared to resign his commission. To have sent a messenger on to Washington,
and to have awaited his return, would have been
clearly impossible, and Frémont had no intention
of adopting any such circuitous method. Having
drawn up his resignation, he charged two of his
men with the duty of conveying it to Washington,
and discharged his mind of further anxiety in the
premises. The messengers set out as though bent
upon reaching the Capital as quickly as possible,
and after making one day's journey, turned back
and rejoined their friends, who were of course very
much surprised to see them again. Frémont, previous to resigning his commission, had sounded his
men, and ascertained that they were all willing to
aid him in the conquest of California, and without
further delay the two parties joined their forces,
Sutter, Marshall, and the rest, having cast in their
lot with their countrymen also. Colonel Frémont's

The Original Bear Flag
Courtesy California State Library, Sacramento

course at this juncture is generally understood to
have been something more than the result of a mo-
mentary inspiration. His presence in the neighborhood of the outbreak at the critical moment was
perhaps accidental, but there is every reason to believe that he had received instructions to stay in
California, and combat foreign influences as much
as possible—which meant that he was to pave the
way for the eventual absorption of the country by
the United States.

The junction of forces had been scarcely completed when intelligence was received to the effect
that General Castro, with two hundred and fifty
men, was on the move to attack Sonoma, where a
small garrison had been left by the settlers. Upon
receipt of this news, the entire band of Bear Flag
warriors marched from the fort to relieve the threatened town. A description of this army would be
anything but easy. Probably since Falstaff's ragged
regiment was immortalized, no such extraordinary
gathering ever took place.[5] There was scarcely a
country or nationality under the sun unrepresent-
ed, and the costumes were as various as the races
from which the wearers sprung. There were Americans, French, English, Swiss, Austrians, Germans,
Prussians, Russians, Chileans, Greeks, Poles and
Pawnees riding along side by side and talking a

[5]The allusion here is to the polyglot regiment raised by
John Falstaff, which he described in a witty and long speech,
in Shakespeare's "King Henry IV," Part I, Scene 11.

polyglot lingual hash never exceeded in diversity since the confusion of tongues at the Tower of Babel. Some wore the relics of their homespun garments; some relied upon the antelope and the bear for their wardrobe; some were lightly habited in buckskin leggings and a coat of war paint; and their weapons were equally various. There was the grim old hunter with his long and heavy rifle; the farmer with his double-barreled shotgun; the Indian with his bow and arrows, and others with horse pistols, revolvers, sabres, ship cutlasses, bowie knives, and "pepperboxes."[6] Marshall, riding near the head of the column, glanced back at the motley array and was so struck with the quaintness of the picture, and the number of nations represented, that he exclaimed: "Well! If they whip this crowd, they can beat all the world; for Castro will whip all nations, languages and tongues." But though the Bear Flag army was a queer one to look at, it comprised as effective a body of fighting men as could have been collected. Every member of the force was inured to hardship and privation, self-reliant, fertile in resources, versed in Indian fighting, accustomed to handle firearms, and full of energy and daring.

The party proceeded towards Sonoma, and on the way picked up a piece of news which quickened

[6] A pepperbox was an early type of revolver "having five or six barrels revolving upon a central axis." Ramon Adams, *Western Words: A Dictionary of the American West* (Rev. ed., Norman, OK, 1968), p. 224.

their desire to meet the enemy. They learned that a
few days previously four American men, traveling
peaceably through the country, had been attacked
by a number of Mexicans on the ranch of General
Vallejo's wife's mother. The owner of the ranch had
done all she could to protect them, but in vain, and
the barbarous captors had taken them away, and
murdered three out of the four, mutilating their
bodies horribly. It may well be imagined that this
news did not slacken the advance of the relief party. They hurried forward, and reached Sonoma in
time to save the garrison.

In the meantime Todd, the only survivor of the
four captured Americans, had been taken by his
captors to the Petaluma Ranch, and while the Mexicans were there, a party of thirteen settlers, who
were out hunting horses, suddenly came upon
them. The enemy had eighty men, well-armed and
mounted, but the brave thirteen did not dream of
surrender. Finding themselves surrounded, in a dry
ravine, they sat down in the grass, rested their rifles
on their knees, and quietly awaited the assault. The
Mexicans charged furiously. The settlers' rifles rang
out, and four saddles were emptied in a moment,
while several men were severely wounded. This was
more than Major Joaquín, the commander, had bar-
gained for, and he drew off his forces forthwith.[7]
While this was going on, a woman in the ranch
house cut Todd's bonds, and told him to join his

[7]The commander's full name is Joaquín de la Torre.

friends. He did so, and the whole party effected their retreat in safety.

The force at Sonoma, having relieved that place, now set out, with Frémont at their head, in search of Joaquín and his band, supposing that Castro had crossed the bay with two hundred and fifty men to support him. Hearing that the Mexicans had entrenched themselves at San Rafael, they marched upon that place, and charged briskly upon it, the first three men to reach the walls were Frémont, Kit Carson, and Marshall, in the order named.[8] Here, however, their valor was thrown away, for Joaquín, hearing of their approach, had evacuated his position and was beginning to backtrack, hoping to find Sonoma unprotected. The Bear Flag army lay three days at San Rafael, watching Castro, who was seen on the opposite side of the bay with a considerable force. He, however, suspected something, and would not cross. He did, however, send three men over in a boat to reconnoitre. They were seized and shot as spies immediately on landing—whether justifiably or not is unclear, though it is probable that their deaths were inflicted more in

[8] Actually, the Bear Flaggers feared that Castro would cross the bay and try to recapture Sonoma. Because of this threat, Frémont joined forces for the first time with the Bear Flaggers, their combined party numbering about ninety men. Christopher (Kit) Carson was with Frémont as his scout, serving under a government service contract. Rogers, *Ide*, pp. 53–54, and *Bear Flag Lieutenant: The Life Story of Henry L. Ford*, (San Francisco, 1951), p. 18.

revenge for the murder of the three Americans than for any other reason.

At the end of the three days, word was brought that Joaquín was threatening Sonoma, and the settlers at once set out in pursuit of him. Strangely enough, they passed within one mile of his camp, at night, without discovering it, and he immediately started south again, and succeeded in reaching Sausalito about three hours ahead of his pursuers. Here he seized a launch that was lying there, put his saddles on board, turned his horses loose, and embarking with his men, was far out in the bay when the settlers reached Sausalito. Having no boat, or means of pursuit, they were compelled to abandon the chase; but being in urgent need of ammunition, they determined to apply to Captain Montgomery, commander of the United States sloop of war *Portsmouth*, then lying in the bay.[9]

[9] Commander John B. Montgomery (1794–1873), captain of the U.S.S. *Portsmouth*, anchored at Monterey, April 22. Eventually, it sailed for San Francisco, reaching its anchorage at Sausalito on June 3, 1846. Fred B. Rogers, *Montgomery and the Portsmouth* (San Francisco, 1958), pp. 21–24.

III

Fighting Under the Bear Flag

HAVING determined to apply to the commander of the *Portsmouth* for aid, a delegation, of which Marshall was a member, agreed to go aboard to state the case on behalf of the settlers. Captain Montgomery heard them patiently, and then said:

"Gentlemen, I am astonished at your audacity. Are you not aware that you are rebels? That you are in arms against the government of this country, and that I am an officer of the United States Navy, a power with which Mexico is at peace? I cannot entertain your proposition for a moment, and though, if you were to succeed in your endeavors, the case would be altered, it is utterly impossible that I should assist you in any way *at present.*"

The delegation, upon receiving this rejection, looked at one another in a crestfallen and melancholy way, and restraining with some difficulty an angry inclination to give the churlish captain a piece of their minds, they turned to leave the vessel, while the commander hurried below. They were about to descend the side when one of the lieutenants approached and called them to him. "You must have known," he said gravely, "that Captain Montgomery could not give you any ammunition. It would be as much as his commission was worth. Besides, a good deal of our ammunition is slightly damaged by wet, and we are going to land a quantity tomorrow for the purpose of drying it."

There was a lurking twinkle in the lieutenant's eye as he said this, but no smile appeared upon his face, and while his auditors exchanged meaning glances, for they had begun to scent a new development, he proceeded: "I have been looking around this morning for a favorable place to dry the powder, and I have chosen that spot," pointing directly to a little level plateau near the water's edge. By this time a broad grin was beginning to steal over the faces of the delegation, but repressing their mirthful tendencies, they took leave of the officer, expressing their regrets that the rules of the service were so inexorable, but assuring him that they bore Captain Montgomery no ill will, comprehending that he was but fulfilling his duty. So the interview came to an end, and though the application had been unsuccessful, strange to say the settlers were not in the least disappointed, but on the contrary appeared quite sanguine and joyous.[1]

On the morrow a boat put off from the *Portsmouth*, and a load of powder and lead was carefully landed, and placed in a most methodical manner on

[1]The conversation detailed here is pure hyperbole. Montgomery maintained an absolute stance of neutrality toward the Bear Flaggers. He did send supplies to Frémont, but none were offered to the settlers. *Ibid.*, pp. 34–48, which quotes *verbatim* many of the commander's letters.

Captain John B. Montgomery
Courtesy California State Library, Sacramento

the little plateau before mentioned. But suddenly, while the seamen were busily engaged in this work, a band of armed men burst upon them, secured their arms, and then coolly seized the ammunition and carried it off as fast as possible. Of course, the people on board the *Portsmouth* had no idea of what was going on, but when the robbers had secured the last ounce of lead and pound of powder, they politely escorted the sailors and their officer to the boat, and sent them back to the ship, unharmed. It was not to be expected that a United States man-of-war could put up with so flagrant an outrage as this attack upon her men and confiscation of her stores, and it soon became evident that Captain Montgomery was bent on vengeance. Soon after the boat returned, an unusual bustle was manifest on board the ship. A boatswain's pipe whistled loudly, the frowning ports were dropped, the guns facing the shore were run out, and using a warp maneuver, the ship started to swing her broadside around towards the spot where the audacious Bear Flag warriors still stood. Presently the grim teeth of the sloop faced the plateau, and in a moment more a sharp order was heard, followed by flashes, puffs of white smoke, and roars, one, two, three, four in number. Upon this the settlers thought it best to leave, more especially as the shots, though evidently directed at the summits of the adjoining hills, might have rolled down the declivities, and hurt somebody. This was the last heard of the ammunition.

We presume that Captain Montgomery made a report of it as "expended," and the government was none the wiser, although perhaps that boatload of powder and lead had a good deal to do with the cession of California to the United States.[2]

After this exploit, the settlers sent a party to Fort Point to spike some old guns left there by the Spaniards, and then came back to Sonoma, where they effected a more complete organization, electing officers, etc. Having done this they set out for Sutter's Fort, expecting to meet Joaquín on the way. The whole plan of their campaign was to keep the Mexican forces in the lower part of the state until the emigrants, then on their way, had had time to cross the mountains and get well into California. On arriving at the fort, Colonel Frémont received a dispatch from Commodore John S. Sloat, who had just taken Monterey, ordering him to repair to that place without delay. As one of the most interesting points connected with the later history of California, it may be worth a short digression to relate how the commodore came to take Monterey.

At this time, war was imminent between the United States and Mexico, and the former government had already determined upon the seizure of California in the event of actual hostilities. It was, however, difficult to communicate with the naval commanders on the west coast, and so they received conditional orders. Therefore, Commodore Sloat,

[2]There is no evidence to support this tale.

Commodore John D. Sloat

Monterey, California, c. 1846
Courtesy California State Library, Sacramento

47

commanding the United States frigate *Savannah*, was instructed to capture Monterey if hostilities began, but he knew as well as the government that he would be compelled to keep a very sharp lookout, lest he should be forestalled by some other power. He was lying at Mazatlán, in company with another American vessel, and the *Collingwood*, British line of battleship, under the command of Admiral Seymour, was there, also. Sloat found reason to suspect that Seymour's instructions were, also, to seize Monterey, for England at that time was regarding California with a hungry eye, and it was reported that she had made an arrangement with Mexico to hold the Golden Gate in the event of a war. It may have been merely such a transfer of property as fraudulent bankrupts sometimes make, to save it from their creditors. It may have been a *bona fide* agreement for a sale in fee. However, this is certain, that the admiral was constantly in communication with the Mexican capital, and was evidently on good terms with the government. The Commodore had no dispatches, but he had the *Collingwood* beside him, and he watched every move on board of her. On a certain day a courier arrived from the City of Mexico with dispatches for the admiral, and as soon as he perused them, it became evident something important had transpired. The boatswain's whistle piped shrilly on the decks of the lofty line of battleship; the windlass creaked as the men walked her up to her anchors with fife and drum; the topmen flew aloft and cast off the gaskets; the boats were hoisted in; the ports closed; and everything betokened a speedy departure. As soon as the commodore saw these preparations, he gave orders to heave short, and his consort followed suit. Scarcely had the huge hulk of the *Collingwood* glided out of the harbor, under a cloud of canvas, than she was followed by the American vessels. Once outside, they quickly parted company, and there ensued an anxious and exciting passage, so far as the commodore was concerned. In the first place, he was not obeying his instructions, which were to wait until hostilities had been declared. In the second place, he had received no orders as to the course he should follow if he found that England had been beforehand with him, nor would any orders have enabled him to compete with a line of battleship. What should he do if he discovered the British flag flying over Monterey, protected by the heavy guns of the *Collingwood?* Perhaps he had not himself decided, but he was perfectly clear upon one point, and that was that he was going to take Monterey, if he could.[3]

[3]This is an accurate account of the American fear of British acquisition of California and the role played by Admiral Sir George F. Seymour commanding H.M.S. *Collingwood.* Harlow, *California Conquered*, pp. 54, 132–35; Ephriam D. Adams, "British Interest in the Annexation of California," *American Historical Review*, 14 (July 1909), pp. 744–63; Sheldon G. Jackson, "The British and the California Dream: Rumors, Myths, and Legends," *Southern California Quarterly*, 55 (Fall 1975), pp. 251–70.

The passage came to an end at last, and as the vessels entered the Bay of Monterey, every eye and every glass were directed to the fort and the custom house—where, to their unspeakable delight and relief, the Mexican flag floated lazily in the summer breeze.[4] To anchor, man the boats, pull ashore, demand the surrender of the place, receive the submission of the Mexican authorities, and hoist the Stars and Stripes was the work of a very short time, since no attempt at resistance was made. This having been accomplished, the commander returned to his ship and waited for developments. Two days passed, and brought no change, but on the third the lookout descried the *Collingwood* making for the harbor. When the commodore was informed that the British man-of-war was in sight, he mused. He cast an affectionate look at the old flag floating from the fort on shore, and another at the one above his head. He paced the quarterdeck, back and forth, frowned, whistled softly, bit his lip. Eventually, his brow cleared, and calling his first officer, he gave orders to prepare for action. In a short time the guns were loaded and double-shotted, the yards slung, the hammock nettings triced up, the sailmakers aloft, the topmen in their places, the surgeon and his mates preparing for anatomical practice in the cockpit, and every one at their posts. Only the

---

[4]The Mexican flag had not flown over Monterey for some months. Harlow, *California Conquered*, p. 124; Bancroft, *California*, V: 231.

ports were kept closed, and the guns were thus concealed. These formidable preparations had scarcely
been completed when the stately *Collingwood* made
her appearance, and sailed smoothly into the harbor, anchoring not far from the *Savannah*. The
commodore sent a boat to congratulate the admiral
on his arrival. The admiral returned the visit in person. As he stepped into the gangway of the *Savannah*, his practiced eye took in the situation at a
glance, but he made no remark on the peculiar condition of the frigate, and turning quietly to the
commodore, after shaking hands, asked him "How
long has that flag been flying there, commodore?"—
pointing to the starry ensign waving over the Monterey fort. "Three days," was the reply. "Then I am
just three days too late!" rejoined the Admiral.[5]

It is curious to note upon what apparent acci-
dents the fate of great enterprises often depends.
Had the *Collingwood* arrived before the *Savannah*
California might have been an English province,
and the wealth of New Albion would have balanced
that of Australia. And had Admiral Seymour been
as enterprising or as ready to take risks, as was the
old commodore, the chances are that he would have
blown the *Savannah* out of the water, even there,
and retaken the place; for he unquestionably had

[5]The remark attributed to Admiral Seymour is fanciful. It
was never his intent to "race" the U.S. to obtain California.
That myth has since been discredited. Walter Colton, *Deck
and Port; Or Incidents of a Cruise on the United States Frigate
Congress* (New York, 1852), p. 393.

the power to do it. But the destiny of California was fixed, and it was not a British destiny.

After the usual conversation had passed between the two commanders, the admiral turned to the commodore and said "Commodore, I know you are a plain man, and therefore I will ask you plainly, now that this affair is settled, whether you received any dispatches when you were at Mazatlán?"

"I did not, Admiral," was the reply.

"Well," observed Seymour, "of course you know your own government best, and as the case has turned out, you have probably done the best thing you could have done. But considering that you were ignorant of the declaration of war between Mexico and the United States, you have done what no officer in *our* service would have ventured upon." Here he paused, and glancing for a moment from the warlike preparations around to the face of the commodore, he continued:

"Commodore, isn't this a curious time to exercise your guns?"

"I could not determine," replied the commodore, "whether I might be compelled to exercise them to some purpose—to defend that flag," nodding towards the fort.

The admiral grinned. "Now tell me," he said, "supposing you had come here and found the English flag there, and the *Collingwood* prepared to keep it there, what would you have done?"

The commodore reflected a moment, and after

hesitating an instant, broke out: "Well, Admiral, I'd have given you a broadside anyhow, I believe; and then I'd have expected you to sink me, and my government would have had to settle the matter."

That was how Commodore Sloat succeeded, and Admiral Seymour failed, in capturing Monterey, and thereby (virtually) securing California for the United States.

It was on the 7th day of July, 1846, that Commodore Sloat hoisted the American flag at Monterey. A short time later, the United States frigate *Congress*, Commodore Stockton commander, arrived, and at once took command of the naval forces.[6] On learning the condition of affairs in the interior, the progress of the Bear Flag War, and the movements of the enemy, Stockton determined to achieve the independence of California, and so deeply interested was he in the matter, that he swore he would expend half his private fortune (which was very large) rather than fail of success.

Preparations were at once made for enlisting the services of the naval force. A mixed body of sailors and marines, together with the California Battalion, were embarked on board the United States vessel *Cyane*, which had accompanied the *Savannah* from Mazatlán, and she started for San Diego. During the

[6]Commodore Robert F. Stockton (1795–1866) reached Monterey on his ship, the U.S.S. *Congress*, on July 15. He succeeded Sloat, age sixty-eight and ailing, who had requested retirement earlier, on July 29. Harlow, *California Conquered*, p. 137.

*Raising the American Flag and Taking Possession
of California by Commodore John D. Sloat,
at Monterey, July 7, 1846*

Courtesy National Archives

passage an attempt was made to impart instruction in the mysteries of military drill to the warriors of the Bear Flag, but was soon abandoned as hopeless because such a diverse group would not alter their own notions of fighting, which was somewhat akin to guerrilla warfare and proved effective in action.

After landing at San Diego, Don Andrés Pico, brother of the governor, Pío Pico, a fine, manly, warmhearted and honorable gentleman, was met with, and would have been sacrificed to the reckless fury of the settlers except for the mediation of Captain Fitch, an old resident of San Diego, who saved his life by pledging himself for his honor and uprightness.[7]

He was subsequently permitted to leave for Los Angeles with the news of the capture of San Diego. Several native Californians joined the American forces here, and through their assistance some sixty horses were procured, with which a portion of the band was mounted. Frémont then started for Los

---

[7]This incident recounted here did not take place. The *Cyane* first seized a Mexican brig, the *Juanita*, at anchor in the harbor, which had on board 40,000 percussion caps. After that excitement, "a small party left the *Cyane* and went ashore to test the opposition and to raise the American flag. They met no opposition." K. Jack Bauer, *Surfboats and Horse Marines: U.S. Naval Operations in the Mexican War, 1846-48* (Annapolis, 1969), p. 166. Henry D. Fitch (1799-1849), an American and retired sea captain, was a longtime resident of San Diego who had married a local girl. As for Andrés Pico, he was actually in Los Angeles at this time. Bancroft, *California*, III: 139-40, IV: 776.

Angeles, leaving forty men, among whom was Marshall, to garrison San Diego. After spending a month here, during which time Stockton had taken Los Angeles, they were ordered to that town, which had been in charge of Captain Gillespie. General Castro and Pío Pico had been routed, and had fled to Mexico with a few of their men.

Soon after arriving at Los Angeles, Marshall noticed that there was much discontent among the native Californians who had joined the American forces. Gillespie had established martial law, and had issued several very severe orders for the discipline of the place, which orders had much exasperated the Californians. A number of the sailors and marines had taken to drinking, and several of them had sold their muskets for liquor. There was a notable lack of watchfulness on the part of the Americans, and a cloud of discontent, that might at any moment break out into open revolt, was gathering. Marshall, with the keen observation of a frontiersman, accustomed to watch for signs and to draw conclusions from small indications, noted these things and determined to keep a strict lookout. One day he was strolling through the town, when he was attracted by the conversation of two Mexicans in a low groggery. Pretending ignorance of their language, he lulled their suspicions, and heard them talking about a certain six-pound brass cannon which they said was buried in a widow's garden near the town. He at once informed Gillespie of what he

Commodore Robert F. Stockton
Courtesy California State Library, Sacramento

had heard, but the latter laughed at the story, being confident that Stockton had collected all the cannon in the neighborhood and secured it. Still, Marshall was convinced that trouble was brewing, and he was confirmed in his suspicions on the following day, when, as he walked through the Indian quarter, he came upon a knot of men who were drinking and pledging toasts to "Castro, Revolution, and California." At this time, Marshall was employed as chief carpenter, and had just received orders to fit up the officers' quarters (which were situated in the government building) with some new furniture. Feeling certain that an attack was contemplated by the Californians, he now determined to take the responsibility of applying the lumber he had received for the furniture to a different purpose, and accordingly spent the next day in repairing and strengthening the gates of the building. He completed his work on Monday night, and on Wednesday, about midnight, his wisdom and foresight were vindicated, for at that time the Californians rose in revolt, and made an attack upon the government house. But for the good work done by him on the gates, there might have been a general massacre of the Americans, but the strong portals withstood the attack of the besiegers, the besieged had time to rally, and the assaulting party was finally forced to retreat, with a loss of some eight killed.

This, however, was but the commencement of the attack. The Californians, finding it impossible to take the quarters by storm, retired, and having gathered a force of some five hundred men, prepared to lay siege to the Americans. The location of the government house was peculiarly unfortunate. Immediately in front of it rose a hill, the summit of which commanded every portion of the courtyard and buildings, and it was at once seen that if the besiegers could mount a gun on the hill they would have the Americans at their mercy. While they were deliberating as to the best course to pursue, a shout was heard from the enemy, and looking out it was seen that they were approaching the hill, carrying with them *a six-pound brass cannon*. At this sight Marshall turned to Gillespie, and observed grimly: "There, Gillespie, there's the cannon that you wouldn't believe in!" The officer bit his lip, but made no reply. The danger, however, was pressing, and some expedient had to be devised without delay. Marshall was equal to the emergency, and at once declared that their only chance was to get a gun on the crest of the hill before the Mexicans could reach it. Gillespie thought this was good enough advice, but unfortunately they had no serviceable artillery. It was true that two or three old cannons lay in the courtyard, but they were all spiked and useless. Now, Marshall had, two or three days before, asked Gillespie for nitric acid to unspike one of these guns, and had been refused. He now advised the officer to procure some acid, but without waiting for it he took a hammer and cold chisel, and in five minutes had cleared the touch hole of a four-pounder. In the meantime, some of the men were employed in improvising cartridges for the gun, and this having been rapidly effected, a sally was made from the citadel, and a run for the top of the hill commenced. The Californians had not been idle while these preparations were occurring, but they had further to go, thus both sides' chances were about even. Neither party could see the other, as they were ascending the hill from opposite directions, and as the Americans neared the crest, the excitement became intense. If the enemy secured the position, they would themselves reach the top just in time to receive a deadly discharge from the six-pounder, and they could not tell where their opponents were. Still, they strained every nerve up the steep slope, dragging the gun with them, and at length, as they surmounted the crest, a cheer burst from them, as they saw the Californians still a considerable distance off, they having made the ascent in a more leisurely manner, being unaware that they were engaged in a match against time. It was the work of but a very few minutes to plant their gun and point it, and before the Californians had time to realize the situation, a rattling discharge came tearing in among them, bringing them to a sudden halt, which changed to a hasty retreat when they saw how they had been outmaneuvered.[8]

[8] After the initial attack on September 23, no further hostilities took place.

After this, the Californians made no more demonstrations that day; but as there was no telling when they would attack again, it was necessary to keep the position on the hill, and for this purpose a guard was placed over the gun and sentries posted about the sides and brow of the eminence. Marshall was one of these sentinels; and fearing that the Mexicans might mark the position of the tent which had been erected on the hill for the shelter of the guard, and charge upon it in the night, he suggested that it be quietly shifted after dark, to a position some distance from the gun, so as to deceive the enemy. This was done, and the watch being set, night fell, and silence reigned. Now, Marshall's frontier life had endowed him with a keenness of vision and of hearing such as none but savages and backwoodsmen possess. He could see almost as well in the dark as in the day, and a pitchy blackness that would have been hopeless obscurity to the eyes of a dweller in cities, was to him only a dim sort of twilight. On this occasion the night was very dark, and as he kept guard with his trusty rifle in his arm, ready for instant use, he continually peered through the gloom, and listened with all his ears. Presently, it seemed to him that a bush growing on the edge of the hill, had become larger. Now it may not be known to everyone that constant looking at a bush or a tree at night might produce an optical illusion such as increased size. Marshall had often experienced this, and, therefore, his first impulse was to attribute the change he had noticed to such a cause. But upon returning to the same place again, he observed that where there had been but *one* bush before, there now appeared to be *two*; and he knew bushes did not multiply in that way. His suspicions were now thoroughly aroused, and posting himself where he could watch the spot without danger of being shot, he remained there until he was relieved. No attack was made that night, and when he told the story of the bushes growing, he was laughed at. Yet, he had too much confidence in his own power of observation to be ridiculed out of his belief, and so he quietly requested that Captain Hensley accompany him to where the bushes had been seen.[9] The captain complied, thinking to have a good joke at his expense, but on arriving at the place, Marshall's suspicions were confirmed, for there, just behind the summit of the hill, were the unmistakable evidences of the recent presence of a body of men forty or fifty in number. Doubtlessly they had contemplated an attack that night, but the removal of the tent, and the watchfulness of the sentinels foiled them, and they concluded to await the dawn.

The following day the Californians appeared in force before the citadel, and demanded the surrender of the garrison, and that they should give up

[9]Marshall was a member of Company A in the California Battalion. The officer in charge of the cannon redoubt was Lieutenant (not Captain) Samuel J. Hensley. Marti, *Messenger of Destiny*, p. 78.

their arms. To this Gillespie replied that the arms did not belong to the United States, but to the men themselves, and that they were resolved to surrender them only with their lives. The besiegers held a consultation upon the receipt of this answer, being evidently disinclined to take the men's arms upon such conditions. Finally, after some time spent in negotiation, Captain Gillespie, seeing that it would be impossible to hold the place against the odds brought against him, capitulated, the terms being that he should march out with music and colors flying, and should carry his artillery out with him, and embark on the ship *Vandalia*, a merchant vessel then lying at San Pedro. The music, of course, was left to the imagination, but the little garrison marched out with colors flying, carrying their artillery. On the way down to the beach an attempt was made by some of the natives to incite an attack upon them, but the sight of the four guns, which were loaded with grape, and each attended by a grim-looking fellow carrying a burning match, exerted a wholesome influence upon the treacherous crowd, and they concluded that it was as well to let the Americans go. On reaching the *Vandalia* they embarked, having first spiked their guns, for fear the enemy might employ them. They remained here three or four days, until the United States frigate *Savannah* came into port, and the commander, Captain Mervine, at once organized an expedition to retake the Pueblo de Los Angeles.

IV

California Secured

U PON STARTING from San Pedro, Captain Mervine
had about three hundred and ten men, composed of sailors, marines, and volunteers, but no
cavalry or artillery. During the first day's march,
mounted Californians hovered continually about
this force, being careful, however, to keep well out
of range. Their object was undoubtedly to ascertain
the strength of the attacking party, and to cut off
any stragglers who might have fallen to the rear. No
attempt to hinder their progress was made this
day, and that night they stopped at Dominguez
Ranch, about fifteen miles from San Pedro. Next
morning, shortly after the march had been resumed,
a body of mounted Californians appeared at their
front, and it became evident that they had a piece
of artillery with them. Captain Mervine, upon des-
crying the enemy, formed his men into a square, the
volunteers fighting in skirmishing order, and prepared to advance upon the gun, which by this time
had been placed in position.[1] In another moment the

[1]The Californios were under command of José Antonio
Carrillo and had with them a four-pound cannon mounted
on two wagon wheels, which had been buried in a garden
when the Americans marched into Los Angeles. Bauer, *Surfboats and Horse Marines*, p. 178.

Californians fired their first shot, which was aimed too high and did little damage. The naval officers were disgusted with the conduct of the volunteers, who had thrown themselves flat upon the ground when they saw that the gun was about to be fired. Some insinuations were made about lack of courage, to which the hardy mountaineers carefully answered that they were there to fight, but not to be killed if they could avoid it, and that they saw no bravery or sense in standing up to be shot at by a fieldpiece; besides this, being skirmishers, they were not required to follow regular army discipline. They subsequently proved their gallantry and the wisdom of their tactics. The enemy having fired, the sailors charged upon the gun, hoping to capture it before it could be reloaded, but the Californians had fastened the riatas to their horses, and at once dashed off in a gallop, carrying the fieldpiece with them at a rate that their assailants could not compete with. Then, being at a safe distance, they stopped, unlimbered, loaded, and fired again, and this maneuver was repeated several more times, the sailors charging as soon as the gun was discharged, the Californians darting off with it, stopping, loading and firing, and then moving on again. The first two or three shots did no damage, being too high, but one of them caused a ludicrous incident. Some of the sailors were armed with long boarding pikes, to repel charges from the Californians lancers, and these weapons they carried perpendicularly for the most part, or sloped them slightly over the shoulder. One of the first shots, whistling above their heads, cut in two the pike of an Irish sailor, who, feeling the shock, and looking upward, exclaimed with great earnestness—"Be jabers, I'm dismasted!" But the fight now began to assume an aspect that rendered joking out of place. At length, the enemy had got the range, and a shot came plunging in among the brave fellows in the square,[2] cutting a man's leg off. His comrades crowded around, forgetting discipline in their anxiety to render him some assistance, but he waved them off, and as he sank back faint with loss of blood, murmured: "Go and take the gun, and leave me!" This casualty inspired the men with redoubled energy, and they dashed forward with a cheer. But the odds against them were too great. Again the riatas came into play; again the wild horsemen sank their spurs into the sides of their panting steeds, and again the gun was whisked away, only to take up a new position a few hundred yards further on. The mode of advance adopted by Captain Mervine was, to say the least,

[2]The square formation was introduced by the British, based on the same concept first used by the Roman armies in their successful conquests. The soldiers are formed in a square, two ranks each. The front rank, on command, would kneel to fire. The second rank then would be readied to fire while the first rank reloaded their guns. This type of formation provided for a more rapid and orderly sustained fire-power, and at the same time, with bayonets fixed, afforded a high degree of protection from either cavalry or infantry charges—a kind of human fort ringed with steel.

injudicious. The square would have been well enough in repelling cavalry, but the idea of facing artillery with such a formation was as novel as it proved mistaken. Each shot told now, and in a short time eight men were killed, for the round shot with which the gun was loaded left no wound capable of healing.[3] Still the sailors would not give up, but urgently desired their commander to let them charge like the volunteers—in open order. For some unexplained reason this request was denied, and after vainly chasing the gun, which fled before them like an *ignis fatuus* for three miles, they were compelled to abandon the undertaking and retreat to San Pedro.[4] This was the first decided repulse the American forces had sustained; and though, of course, it placed a depressing effect upon the men, they were determined to wipe it out as soon as possible, and were, indeed, confident that if allowed their own way they could have captured the gun.

Shortly after this a call for assistance at San Diego was received, and Captain Mervine sent twenty sailors and fifteen volunteers, among whom was Marshall, to support the garrison, this detail being in command of the third officer of the *Savannah*, Lieutenant George Minor. Having reached and en-

[3] Only four of the ten men wounded died. They were buried on an island in San Pedro harbor which subsequently was called Deadman's Island (today Terminal Island). *Ibid.*, p. 179. Later this encounter was named the "Battle of the Old Woman's Gun."

[4] The Latin phrase as used here means like a silly gadfly.

tered the town they began to fortify it with some
old guns from a dismantled Spanish fort, and having set themselves in posture of defense, awaited
the anticipated attack. The Californians, however,
were not disposed to advance upon the place, and
contented themselves with hovering about it while
taking potshots at any of the garrison who showed
themselves.[5] There was a hill which commanded
the garrison, and it was a favorite amusement for
them to creep to the crest of this eminence, from
the further side, and blaze away at any incautious
American who might be sitting or standing out of
doors. Our volunteers retaliated with spirit, and as
they were generally on the watch for the enemy's
sharpshooters, the crack of the latter's rifles was
pretty sure to be answered by a bullet sent in the
direction of the flash of the Californian's weapon.
Lieutenant Minor and his party held San Diego
nearly six months, during which few eventful incidents occurred, the most notable being one which
reflected no credit upon the subordinate officers

[5] Ezekial Merritt, accompanied by a dozen men, had reoc-
cupied San Diego on October 9. The Californios had effectively restricted the garrison to their barracks at the west
end of the town which was protected from assault by a
marsh. To bolster its defenses, the garrison had salvaged six
brass nine-pounder cannons from the old fort on Presidio
Hill, which was nearby. Sending out a call for help, Captain
Mervine dispatched Lieutenant George Minor and fifty-two
men on October 13 by sea on the *Magnolia* to reinforce the
San Diego garrison. *Ibid.*, p. 180; Harlow, *California Conquered*, pp. 171-72.

attached to the garrison, while it indicates the independent spirit in which the volunteers acted.

After they had been in garrison for some time and were beginning to tire of the monotony, some of the officers managed to secure a quantity of whisky, and indulged in a heavy "spree." While under the influence of *aguardiente*[6] one of them, in going the rounds, fired upon a sentinel who challenged him, and this act caused the volunteers to take decisive action. They had viewed the bad conduct of their officers with previous disapproval, but so long as they confined themselves to getting drunk, perhaps they would have put up with it. They were, however, by no means disposed to take the risk of being shot by their own friends, and so they now assembled and held a consultation, the result of which was that Marshall was deputed to call upon the commander and engage him in consultation, while the rest went to the officers' quarters, and captured and destroyed the mischievous liquor. Marshall performed his part well, and in a short time had the satisfaction of hearing a signal that had been agreed upon, and which indicated the success of the raiders. The satisfaction expressed in his face at this moment attracted the attention of Lieutenant Minor, with whom he was conversing, and he exclaimed: "Marshall, there is something the matter. You had a special object in coming to see me, and you have just received a signal of some kind. What does all this

[6]*Aguardiente* is California brandy.

mean?" Upon this, Marshall disclosed the facts, greatly to the lieutenant's chagrin and indignation. "Good Heavens!" he exclaimed, "it must never be known that my men were compelled to keep my officers from getting drunk by destroying the liquor. You must promise, all of you, to keep this quiet, and I will issue an order for the destruction of the whisky myself." This was done, and we presume it was generally supposed that the order was intended to restrain the *men* and not the officers. However, the facts were as we have stated, and the whisky was gone before Lieutenant Minor issued his order.

At the expiration of about six months, the *Congress* and *Cyane* arrived at San Diego, and Commodore Stockton prepared to make another movement upon Los Angeles. The attack was to be a concerted one, the arrangement being that Frémont, who at this time was in the Sacramento Valley, should move upon the place from the north, while Stockton attacked it from the south; and Frémont, having raised some four hundred men, had already started on the expedition. In the meantime, while Stockton was arranging his forces, General Kearny entered the territory from New Mexico leading a force of dragoons, and upon meeting Andrés Pico near San Pasqual, a fight ensued. Kearny had intended to take the enemy by surprise, but his preparations were so bad as to render this impossible. His dragoons jogged along, their sabres jingling so as to be heard three or four miles on a still, frosty night, and having been recently exposed to a pouring rain, their carbines would not go off when they got into action. Their commander had been joined by some of the volunteers, but not being impressed with their outward appearance, he made the disastrous mistake of supposing that they were of no use to him, and sent them to guard the baggage, which incensed them terribly. However, when the Californian cavalry came up, and the charge began, the dragoons were not present. They fought bravely, no doubt, but what with inefficient weapons, and ignorance of the mode of fighting adopted by their antagonists, they stood but little chance of gaining the day, and so murderous was the fire of the Californians that in less than five minutes Kearny had lost nineteen men out of the ninety composing his regiment.[7] The dragoons were beaten, and when it had been demonstrated that they could no longer hold their own, the despised volunteers stepped forward, and with their long rifles and deadly aim,

[7]General Stephen W. Kearny (1794-1848) was given command of the Army of the West in 1846. Marching from Fort Leavenworth, he easily subdued New Mexico. Leaving Santa Fe with 300 dragoons for California, he was met by Kit Carson carrying dispatches east to notify the authorities that California had been conquered, but unaware of the rebellion of the Californios after his departure. Kearny ordered 200 to return to Santa Fe and pushed on with only 100 in his command, guided by Carson. When he encountered the Californios, he was gravely outnumbered and outfought by the swift Californios. *Ibid.*, pp. 174-92; Dwight L. Clarke, *Stephen Watts Kearny, Soldier of the West* (Norman, OK, 1961), pp. 195-232.

General Stephen Watts Kearny
Courtesy California State Library, Sacramento

turned the tide of the contest, and saved their countrymen from a shameful defeat. Kearny never again
alluded to the volunteers as "riff-raff"—the term he
had used to describe his feelings when he was first
brought in contact with them.

A month was spent by Stockton at San Diego in
organizing his forces, and he then moved upon Los
Angeles, with the intention of attacking Flores, who
had taken command of the Californian forces after
the flight of Castro and Pío Pico. On the 8th of January, 1847, the contending forces met at the San
Gabriel River, eight miles south of Los Angeles.
The Americans numbered six hundred men along
with six pieces of artillery. The army under Flores
amounted to about four hundred and fifty men,
with four guns. The road crossed the river at a right
angle, and lay up a steep bank, and over a small
plateau, upon which the Californians had planted
their guns. Between the river and the plateau was a
long stretch of bottomland some six hundred yards
wide, and on the left was a copse of trees, in which
the enemy had ambushed a cavalry force, expecting
to capture the guns with a dash as they crossed the
river bottom. The American force was divided, the
guns being in front, and a considerable body bringing up the rear. The position of the Californian artillery was such that it would have been extremely
difficult and dangerous to cross the plain below the
plateau under their fire, but Stockton seriously proposed to charge across the intervening space, and

attempt to storm the battery on the crest of the hill. Fortunately, he was persuaded to leave the opening of the battle to the artillery, and before long number two gun, on which Marshall was serving, had dismounted, by well directed shots, two of the enemy's pieces. At this moment, the cavalry, concealed in the woods, emerged, and made a dash for the mischievous gun. But the men were too quick, and after wheeling their piece around, were about to fire, when Marshall exclaimed: "Give them a stand of grape!" No sooner said than done. Down came the lancers like a whirlwind. The cannoneers waited until they could see their eyes distinctly, and then applied the match. There was a roar, a burst of flame and smoke, and when it cleared away the horsemen were seen in hopeless confusion scattered and torn, while riderless animals dashed madly over the plain, and the ground was strewn with the dead and the dying. At this juncture, when the Californian officers, who fought bravely, to do them simple justice, were endeavoring to rally their men, the rear guard of the Americans opened a cross fire upon them, which completed their demoralization and drove them in headlong flight from the field. Several of the men at number two gun, however, fell in this attack, and one was killed very close to Marshall. This virtually ended the fight. The Californians could not rally, and the Americans charged up the slope and carried the plateau.

That night they camped on the San Gabriel, and

next morning started to cross the Mesa. On the Plains of the Mesa they again encountered the enemy, under Flores, and here a desperate fight took place, the American forces being most of the time massed in a square. After two hours, hard fighting hostilities were suspended by the appearance of a delegation from Los Angeles, offering to surrender the place. On the following day, Stockton marched into the town with his forces, and General Flores retreated to Sonora. Andrés Pico moved northward with the majority of his troops, to meet Frémont, who was advancing as quickly as he could towards Los Angeles. The two commanders met, and after negotiation, agreed upon the terms of the treaty by which the independence of California was secure.

So ended the Bear Flag War.[8] We have not attempted to describe it in detail, or to trace out the operations and movements of all who were concerned in it, our object being to follow the career of Marshall, mainly, and only to give such a sketch of the history of the period as will enable our readers to comprehend the nature and significance of the events in which he was an actor.

In March, 1847, he received his discharge from

[8]It should be noted that the Bear Flag Revolt (or War) was a short-lived affair. Commenced on June 10, 1846, it ended July 9 when the Californians accepted the fact that California had been occupied by the United States armed forces. Now, the struggle for California was part of the Mexican War. A number of the Bear Flaggers became members of the California Battalion fighting under the American flag.

the volunteer force, but in consequence of a misunderstanding between Frémont and Stockton on the one side, and Kearny on the other, as to which of them was entitled to the supreme command in California, the men were never paid for their services.[9] The history of this quarrel has been already written, and it is, therefore, not important for us to enter into any details concerning it; but it surely was a hardship upon the men who had contributed so largely through their exertions and gallantry to wrest the state from the hands of the Californians, that they should be deprived of the remuneration to which they were undoubtedly entitled. But for their shrewdness, intimate acquaintance with the habits and mode of warfare of their antagonists, and hardy habits, the conquest of California would doubtless have proved much more difficult. Had the forces landed from the United States men-of-war been left alone to meet the enemy, or had they been

[9]The crux of the problem was that Stockton had appointed Frémont military governor of California. Frémont refused to surrender that title (and power), not knowing that General Kearny had direct orders from Washington that conveyed such power to him. Eventually, Kearny charged Frémont with mutiny. A court-martial found him guilty and the sentence was dismissal from service. President Polk approved the court's verdict, but remitted the penalty. A proud Frémont, however, resigned his commission on February 19, 1848. *Ibid.*, pp. 347–72; Allan Nevins, *Frémont, Pathmarker of the West* (Rev. ed., New York, 1955), pp. 305–42; Andrew Rolle, *John Charles Frémont: Character as Destiny* (Norman, OK, 1991), pp. 90–106; Kenneth M. Johnson, *The Frémont Court Martial* (Los Angeles, 1968), *passim.*

only supported by Kearny's dragoons, the issue of some of the most important struggles might have been very different. It may be said that in this campaign there were no contests sufficiently serious to be dignified by the name of battles, but it must be borne in mind that population was exceedingly scanty in this state at that time, and it may safely be asserted that the proportion of fighting men to the whole community was larger than in most cases. However trivial the engagements narrated may appear, there was nothing insignificant about the issue of the campaign, and the history of the Bear Flag War will always be interesting; while the hardy settlers who inaugurated it, not only in defense of themselves but in behalf of their countrymen who were coming across the mountains, must ever be regarded with the respect and admiration due to the pioneers who hewed down the barriers that stood in the way of civilization, careless, perhaps, of the results of their energy, but nonetheless entitled to credit for their services to humanity.

V

Marshall's Chance Discovery

WE HAVE now reached a period when, the independence of the state being assured, immigration began to flow in freely. Up until this time the class of emigrants that had settled in California had consisted principally of that restless vanguard of advancing civilization which always hovers on the frontiers, and whose mission seems to be to keep moving from place to place, from territory to territory, never staying anywhere long enough to reap the full fruit of their energy and toil, until the great settler, Death, appears, and ends their uneasy career by a final remove into another world. Some few had secured large tracts of land under Spanish grants, and had affiliated with the native Californians, by marriage or otherwise, but the majority were as ready as ever to "pull up stakes" again, and journey on to some newer country, if such could have been found. The California of that time—1847—was altogether unlike the California of a year after, or any subsequent period. The influence of the old padres had been broken, and the clash of arms had rudely interrupted the sleepy placidity of their lives. The American, whose restless energy and unquenchable ambition rendered him an object of perplexity and terror to those staid old souls, had, it is true, conquered the country, but he was scarcely yet prepared to possess it. There seemed, indeed, to be a lull in the stirring life of the previous years. The people were waiting, unconsciously to themselves, for something which was to change the aspect of affairs, and was to draw the eyes of the whole world upon this little-known region. About this time, a quiet, steady man, was traveling from San Diego to New Helvetia (as Sutter's Fort was then called) pondering upon the unlucky chance which had deprived him of all recompense for the time spent in fighting the battles of his country, and wondering whether the few horses and cattle he had left behind him at the fort, were still in the land of the living. Before the breaking out of the Bear Flag War, Marshall had purchased two leagues of land, situated on the north side of Butte Creek (now known as Butte County) from Samuel J. Hensley, who owned a Spanish grant of six leagues in that district.[1] On his arrival at the fort, he at once visited this ranch, and found that the majority of his stock had strayed or been stolen during his absence. This

[1]Samuel J. Hensley (1817–66), played a prominent role in the Bear Flag Revolt and later served in the California Battalion. He was naturalized in 1844 and was granted the Rancho Aguas Nieves. Since Marshall did not wish to become a Mexican citizen, he had to buy land from someone who had received a rancho grant. Bancroft, *California*, III: 781; Robert G. Cowan, *Ranchos of California* (Fresno 1956), p. 13, Entry No. 11; p. 45, Entry No. 233; Gay, *Marshall*, pp. 83–85.

was a heavy blow to him, for his means were small, and it certainly was not calculated to inspire a man with very fervid patriotism to discover, after spending a year in the service of his country, first, that he was not to be paid for time and risk; and second, that his business had gone to ruin in consequence of his absence on this unprofitable expedition. However, he was not inclined to despond, or to waste more time in fruitless regrets; so, having cast about in his mind for the likeliest enterprise, he decided to go into the lumbering business, and forthwith returned to the fort and asked Sutter to furnish him with an Indian interpreter, purposing to explore the foothills for a suitable location for a sawmill, and foreseeing the necessity of being able to converse with the mountain tribes of Indians.[2] Sutter was at first reluctant to comply with this request, having need of Marshall's services, but after the latter had agreed to perform certain mechanical work for him, he consented, though it afterward turned out that the Indian who accompanied him knew no

[2] Actually, Sutter had initiated the idea of a sawmill in the spring of 1846 when he sent John Bidwell (1819–1900), and Dr. Robert Semple (1806–54) to explore the Feather River for a suitable site. John Bidwell, "California 1841–48; An Immigrant's Reflections Of A Trip Across the Plains ...," dictated to S. S. Boynton, 1877, p. 227, Ms., Bancroft Library; John Bidwell, "Reminiscences of the Conquest," *Overland Monthly* XVI, Series II (December 1890): 565; letter to Captain W. F. Swasey, March 10, 1881, in C. C. Royce, *John Bidwell–Pioneer, Statesman, Philanthropist; A Biographical Sketch* (Chico, CA, 1906), unpaged.

more of the country than he did himself. Marshall set out on his quest, and followed up the banks of the American River for several days, examining the country all around, but not finding what he considered to be a suitable site for his mill. The area through which he passed became more diversified as he traveled upwards. Steep cañons and considerable ranges of hills broke up the landscape, and while contributing nothing to the ease of travel, added much to the picturesqueness of the route. Presently, he branched off on the South Fork of the American River, and at length reached a place which he found was called Culloomah by the Indians, and which was afterwards known as Coloma.[3] The river here flowed through the center of a long, narrow valley, hemmed in on both sides by steep, and in some parts, almost precipitous hills. On the south side the declivity was gentlest, and here a tolerably level stretch of land invited the erection of the town which sprung up there after the discovery of gold, while the slopes beyond afforded opportunities for cultivation in later years. The river makes several bends in its course through this valley, and on the south side a point of land formed by one of these curves in the stream presented the explorer with a favorable mill site. The water power was abundant,

[3]Coloma received its name from a nearby Southern Maidu Indian village. The name first appears in the *New Helvetia Diary* on March 17, 1848, as Culloma. Gudde, *California Place Names*, p. 70.

and the surrounding hills furnished timber in apparently inexhaustible quantities. Previous to this, it had been supposed that the difficulty of bringing lumber from any point in the foothills was insurmountable, and Sutter's hunters had so impressed him with this idea that he considered Marshall's expedition little better than a waste of time. A careful examination of the locality, however, satisfied our hero that there would be no difficulty in transporting the products of the mill to the lower country, and having marked out a favorable site, he returned to the fort, and acquainted Sutter with the successful result of the journey. At the same time, he stated that he was in search of a partner with capital to assist him in building and running the mill, and Sutter at once offered to join him in the undertaking. This was about the 1st of June, 1847, and after many delays, caused principally by the attempts of others to interfere in the business, a partnership agreement was entered into between the two on or about the 19th of August. The terms of this agreement were to the effect that Sutter should furnish the capital to build a mill on a site selected by Marshall, who was to be the active partner and to run the mill, receiving certain compensation for so doing. A verbal agreement was also entered into between the parties, to the effect that if, at the close of the war with Mexico (then pending), California should belong to Mexico, Sutter, as a citizen of that Republic, should possess the mill location, Marshall holding his rights to mill privileges, and to cut timber, etc. Conversely, if the country was ceded to the United States, Marshall, as an American citizen, should own the property. The formal articles of partnership were drawn by General John Bidwell, who was then acting as clerk in Sutter's store, and were witnessed by him and Samuel Kyburg, Sutter's business manager. Shortly after these arrangements had been made, Marshall hired a man named Peter L. Wimmer, with his family, and six or seven mill hands, and with several wagons containing material, provisions, tools, etc., started for Coloma. Work on the mill was at once commenced, and prosecuted with energy and rapidity.

We now approach the most important event, not only in the life of Marshall, but in the history of California, and as many erroneous statements have been made and published from time to time concerning the manner of the first discovery, and as attempts have been made to foist a bogus discoverer upon the public, we deem it proper to enter into details with such minuteness as the historical value of the event appears to demand and to warrant.

The names of the men who were then working at the mill, and who, if living, can substantiate the accuracy of this narrative, are as follows: Peter L. Wimmer, William Scott, James Barger, Alexander Stephens, James Brown, William Johnson and Henry Bigler. Wimmer was in charge of some eight or ten Indians, whose business it was to throw out the larger sized rocks excavated while constructing the millrace in the daytime, and at night, by raising the gate of the forebay, in order for the water to carry away the lighter stones, gravel, and sand. This was the work that was going on at the mill on the 24th of January, 1848.[4]

On the morning of that memorable day Marshall went out as usual to superintend the men, and after closing the forebay gate, and thus shutting off the water, walked down the tailrace to see what sand and gravel had been removed during the night. This had been customary with him for some time, for he had previously entertained the idea that there might be minerals in the mountains, and had expressed it to Sutter, who only laughed at him. On this occasion, having strolled to the lower end of the race, he stood for a moment examining the mass of debris that had been washed down, and at this juncture, his eye caught the glitter of something that lay, lodged in a crevice, on a riffle of soft granite some six inches under the water. His first act was to stoop and pick up the substance. It was heavy, of a peculiar color, and unlike anything he had seen in the stream. For a few minutes he stood with it in his hand, reflecting, and endeavoring to recall all that he had heard or read concerning the various minerals. After a close examination, he became satisfied that what he held in his hand must be one of three

[4]The incorrect date January 19th is given in the original edition.

substances—mica, sulphurets of copper, or *gold*. The weight assured him that it was not mica. Could it be sulphurets of copper? He remembered that that mineral is brittle, and that gold is malleable, and as these thoughts passed through his mind, he turned about, placed the specimen upon a flat stone, and proceeded to test it by striking it with another. The substance did not crack or flake off; it simply bent under the blows. This, then, was gold, and in this particular manner was gold first discovered in California.

If we were writing a sensation tale, instead of a sober history, we might proceed to relate how Marshall sank pale and breathless upon a neighboring rock, and how, as he eyed the glittering metal in his hand, a vision rose before him of the mighty results of his discovery. But in fact nothing of the kind occurred. The discoverer was not one of the spasmodic and excitable kind, but a plain, shrewd, practical fellow, who realized the importance of the discovery and proceeded with his work as usual, after showing the nugget to his men and indulging in a few conjectures concerning the probable extent of the gold fields. As a matter of course, he watched closely, from time to time, for further developments, and in the course of a few days had collected several ounces of the precious metal. Although he was satisfied that it *was* gold, there were some who were skeptical, and as he had no means of testing it chemically, he determined to take some down to his partner at the fort, and have the question finally decided. Some four days after the discovery, it became necessary for him to go below, for Sutter had failed to send a supply of provisions to the mill, and the men had to be placed on short rations. So, mounting his horse and taking some three ounces of gold dust with him, he started off. Always having an eye to business, he availed himself of this opportunity to examine the river for a site for a lumber yard, whence the timber cut at the mill could be floated down; and while exploring for this purpose he discovered gold in a ravine in the foothills, and also at the place afterwards known as Mormon Island.[5] That night he slept under an oak tree, some eight or ten miles east of the fort, where he arrived about nine o'clock the next morning. Dismounting from his horse, he entered Sutter's private office, and proceeded to inquire into the cause of the delay in sending up the provisions. This matter having been explained, and the teams being in a fair way to load, he asked for a few minutes private conversation with Colonel Sutter, and the two entered a little

[5]The strike at Mormon Island was a very rich one. It was not an island but rather a sand bar separated by a ditch, located on the South Fork of the American River. The site is now covered by Folsom Lake. This was the second gold discovery made on March 2, 1848. In April it became known as the Lower Mines or Mormon Diggings. Edwin G. Gudde, *California Gold Camps* ed. by Elizabeth K. Gudde (Berkeley and Los Angeles, 1975), pp. 225, 234; Edwin G. Gudde, ed., *Bigler's Chronicle of the West* (Berkeley and Los Angeles, 1962), pp. 100–11.

room at the back of the store, reserved as a private office. Then Marshall showed the gold to him. He looked at it in astonishment, and, still doubting, asked what it was. His visitor replied that it was gold. "Impossible!" was the incredulous response of Sutter. Upon this Marshall asked for some nitric acid, to test it, and a *vaquero* was dispatched to the gunsmith's for that purpose. Now Sutter inquired whether there was another way in which it could be tested. He was told that its character might be ascertained by weighing it, and accordingly some silver coin and a pair of small scales or balances having been obtained, Marshall proceeded to weigh the dust, first in the air, and then in two bowls of water. The experiment resulted as he had foreseen. The dust went down; the coin rose lightly up. Sutter gazed, and his doubts faded, and a subsequent test with the nitric acid, which by this time had arrived, settled the question finally. Then the excitement began to spread. Sutter knew well the value of the discovery, and in a short time, having made hurried arrangements at the fort, he returned with Marshall to Coloma, to see for himself the wonder that had been reported to him.

Two and twenty years have passed over Coloma since the day when James Marshall stood at the end of the tailrace and pondered over that bit of yellow metal. That bit of yellow metal has been multiplied by millions upon millions. The trifling acceleration of the pulse that marked the first emotion of the

Coloma, c. 1850
Courtesy California State Library, Sacramento

discovery has swelled into a wave of maddening excitement, whose roar has re-echoed round the world. The spring struck in that little mountain valley has flowed and spread until mighty cities have been built upon its banks and communities have been refreshed by its waters. From out of that wonderful vale has risen all of good and evil that can affect humanity. At first the center of the swarming adventurers, leaping, as it were, in a moment from the quiet hum-drum of its early settlement into the full glare and crash of a mighty mining excitement, it has passed through the prosperity, the fever, the noise, the hurly-burly, and the slow decline, and has settled at last into the peaceful semblance of some New England village.

Picture it today as a pretty hamlet of some two hundred inhabitants. Its broad single street so overshadowed with stately, heavy foliaged trees that the sidewalks are scarcely visible. Its modest, low-roofed houses, gracefully bedecked with bright flowers and fresh green creepers. Its main thoroughfare silent throughout the day, save when the daily stage dashes gallantly in, and draws up with a rattle and a crash outside the door of the Wells Fargo office—where the courteous agent has also undertaken the duty of telegraph operator.

Upon the hillside the vineyards and the orchards flourish. In the warm summer air the peaches mellow and grow golden, and the great bunches of grapes swell out from behind their leafy screens, and give promise of that "wine that maketh glad the heart of man." Around the modest houses of those few who are content to pass their days in this celebrated yet little known spot, the roses and honeysuckles clamber, and the air at evening is heavy with perfume. Up among the bends of the river some mining is still going on, but there are few claims which now yield high wages. One striking evidence of what the town has been is visible in the rear of the houses nearest the river. Close up to the back doors the bowlders are piled. It is a Titanic beach. The debris of the mining of twelve or thirteen years. Gazing upon these stones, so completely divested of earth, so white, and bare, and ugly, one is tempted to imagine them the bones of the skeleton of Gold, which has here been picked clean by the active fingers of ambitious Man.

And across the river we look in vain for the site of Sutter's mill. Years have passed since the last vestige of that structure was removed by some miner, careless of tradition, but needing timber. Even the man who first found the gold there has to scrutinize the place carefully before he can put his foot down and say: "Here is the spot; it was within a yard of where I stand that the first *chispa* was picked up."[6] So mangled and torn and mined away has the face of nature become in this historic locality, that they who knew the area best would fail to recognize the

[6]*Chispa* "a flake of fire" or "a very small diamond." In California slang it meant nuggets of gold.

scarred and disfigured lineaments. Yet it is Coloma; and the site of the gold discovery can be pointed out. In a few years more, however, the oldest inhabitant will have lost all trace of the spot, and the visitor will be only able to discover that the gold was found "somewhere hereabout." There is need of a monument at Coloma and the site of Sutter's mill should be marked in an enduring manner.[7]

[7] Today, the Marshall Gold Discovery State Historic Park is located on State Highway 49. A statue of Marshall pointing to the discovery site has been erected in Coloma. It was dedicated in May 1890. Today a replica of the original mill has been built approximate to the site by the California State Department of Parks, Beaches and Recreation. Kyle, ed., *Historic Spots in California* p. 72.

VI

The Great Rush and the Fast Life

THE NEWS of the great discovery spread over
the land like wildfire, and wherever it was received, men abandoned business, friends, homes,
everything, tempted by the glittering lure. All that
were poor, disappointed, in debt, in difficulties, or
in dread of the law for offenses committed, at once
prepared to set out for the land of gold. Hundreds
also determined upon the expedition from a pure
love of adventure, tinctured, doubtless, by the hope
which the exaggerated accounts excited. Meanwhile, the resident white population of California
threw itself into the gold quest with characteristic
ardor and energy. The discovery once made that
the precious metal existed, additional revelations
continued to be made in every direction. It seemed
at first as if the prospector had but to sink his pick
into the ground at random, wherever there was a
cañon or a stream, to find gold. The whole country
was revolutionized. It was no longer a struggle
against the difficulties which beset the ordinary pioneer. It was a mad, furious race for wealth, in which
men almost lost their identity. They toiled, strug-
gled, and lived a fierce, riotous, fearfully excited
life, forgetting home and kindred, abandoning old,

steady habits, acquiring all the restlessness, craving for stimulant, unscrupulousness, hardihood, impulsive generosity and lavish activities, which have puzzled the students of human nature who have undertaken to portray or to analyze that extraordinary period. It does not fall within the scope of this work to give a detailed history of those times, but if ever this task is worthily undertaken, the world will listen to a recital so wild, so incredible, so feverish and abnormal, as to remind it rather of the description of a Walpurgis Night than of an era in real life.[1] The state was then invaded by some of the most desperate men in the world. From the Australian gold fields, from the Five Points of New York, from the Seven Dials, St. Giles', and Field Lane, of London, from the slums and dens of vice and crime in every large city, they flocked to the Golden State. Human life was incredibly cheap at that time. Few factual narratives have been recorded concerning the first rush, but there are still a few old-timers and others who have prematurely aged, continuing to live in the mountains, and occasionally to be seen about the What Cheer House in San Francisco, who can tell strange and terrible stories of the crimes

---

[1] *Walpurgisnacht* (Walpurgis Night) is the traditional German witches' sabbath which is celebrated in the Harz Mountains. It was named after Saint Walburga (died c. 779), an English missionary in Germany. She assisted St. Boniface and founded a convent that became a major center of civilization in Germany. *The New Columbia Encyclopedia* (New York, 1975), p. 2918.

committed and never punished in those wild days.[2]

Then arose San Francisco and Sacramento; towns of tents, relieved only by a few wooden shanties, in which every second habitation was a saloon and every saloon a gambling hell. These places were, at once, the focus of business, the principal shipping points for the rapidly developing mines, and the centers of dissipation, profligacy and debauchery. A few weeks or months—sometimes only a few days—sufficed to line the pockets of the adventurer, and if he escaped being murdered by his comrades, or killed in some drunken brawl in the mountains, he usually took a trip to San Francisco or Sacramento, there to dissipate his lightly won gains. There were, let it be understood, many good men in that strange community. But it is true, beyond all question, that the proportion of reckless, desperate, criminal characters, was larger than ever before in any civilized community. The circumstances were altogether peculiar. There were no women, or so few and of such a grade generally, as not to count for much in regard to influence for good upon society. Men had broken loose from all their old ties. Those who had been reared in the land of "steady habits" found

[2]The What Cheer House was opened in 1852. Over the next few years it was enlarged so that by 1856 it contained 400 rooms and could easily handle 800 clients. *Coville's Directory & Gazetter of the City of San Francisco Directory, 1858–1956* (San Francisco, 1956), p. 234; Henry G. Langley, comp., *San Francisco Directory, 1858* (San Francisco, 1858), p. 288.

themselves suddenly transferred to a land of unsteady habits, or rather no habits at all, for society was so new, so incohesive, so inclined to fermentation and change, that no one had time to develop habits. Perhaps the condition of things generally may be described by imagining the possibility of a state of existence in which feverish excitement plus an air of insecurity was continuous. The blare and crash of the band, the dazzling brilliancy of the gas lights, the gaudy trappings of the actors, the heat, the poisonous atmosphere—all combine to stimulate, until the eye deceives the brain, the outside world is forgotten, and the imagination soars into a realm of fiction, the descent from which is alike depressing and repulsive. Perhaps the peculiar, subtle champagne atmosphere of California, had something to do with the strange effects produced upon that cosmopolitan population. It was as if the hidden gold had diffused through the air that swept its burial place with some mysterious emanations which acted upon the well-being of those who came within its reach.

The amount of work done was enormous. Any difficulties, which would have caused ordinary men to despair, were surmounted with a determination that could not be overcome, and reverses were met with a coolness and equanimity that would have brought credit to practiced gamblers.

A growing town today might easily become a mass of ruins tomorrow, but, before the last embers were extinguished, the lumber would be on the ground for new houses, and the smoking timbers would be cleared away to make room for the store, or the saloon, or the gaming house.

Men lived fast in those days. Those who know what the ordinary "fast life" of ordinary cities is, can have no conception of *how* fast the old Californians lived. No man "waited for something to turn up" at that time. Time was money, and plenty of money, too, and he must, indeed, have been a helpless creature who could not find profitable employment at short notice.

But the inevitable consequence of such a congregation of reckless men, and of such a life, soon appeared. The Sydney convict, the London burglar or pickpocket, the New York rough, the adventurer who had wandered over half the earth and marked each resting place by a fresh crime, began to establish a community of interests. For a short time they had worked separately, all being too eager after the main excitement of the day to care for lesser gains. But as population increased, and cities grew up, and wealth in property began to show itself, the worst of the dangerous classes became impatient of the comparatively slow process of acquiring money by earning it, and began to seek out more congenial ways of replenishing their coffers, emptied too frequently by riotous living. Thus it came about that the organization of criminals and bad characters, known as "The Hounds," was established, and, in the fall of

1848, the subject of this sketch came into contact with that body in a very peculiar way.[3]

Marshall had continued to work at the Coloma mill after the discovery of gold, occasionally varying his occupation by prospecting, and had in this manner discovered several rich diggings, which had at once been taken possession of by others who flocked to the neighborhood. Much lawlessness existed in the interior of the state by this time. Robberies from the person had been frequent in and about Coloma and the adjacent mining camps, and several burglaries, unusually daring, had impressed the people with the belief that there was an organized band of robbers in the neighborhood. It was in the month of October, 1848, that Marshall, being on a prospecting expedition, camped one night in a

[3] "The Hounds" was the name given to an organized group, composed mainly of discharged veterans from the New York Regiment, who took it upon themselves to harass San Francisco's Spanish-American residents. They referred to themselves as "Regulators," but, in fact, were a lawless element bent on robbing and terrorizing Latinos. They were abetted in their criminal activities by the "Sydney Ducks," Australian ex-convicts and escapees. Together the two groups practiced arson in order to loot burned buildings. On July 15, 1849, "The Hounds" launched a murderous attack and looting raid on a section of the city called "Little Chile." This provoked outraged citizens to form the Law and Order Party to rid the city of this menace, and they succeeded admirably. Hubert H. Bancroft, *Popular Tribunals* (2 vols. San Francisco, 1877), I: 76–102; Frank Soulé, *et al.*, *The Annals of San Francisco* ... (San Francisco, 1855), pp. 553–61; Stanton A. Coblentz, *Villains and Vigilantes* (New York, 1957), pp. 20–40.

Sutter's Mill

Courtesy California State Library, Sacramento

ravine, called John Town Creek, between Garden Valley and Alabama Flat, about three miles from Coloma. He had selected, as his camping ground, a spot about midway up the sloping side of the ravine, and by the time he had lighted his fire and eaten his supper, night closed in around him. Suddenly, he was startled by hearing a signal from the lower ground, in the direction of the creek. He answered it, and at once it was repeated by someone hidden on the higher ground above him. The suspicions of the old frontiersman were at once aroused, and knowing that honest men would not be lurking in such a place without fires, he determined to reconnoitre. In the first place, he extinguished his fire, lest it should lead the robbers (as he suspected them to be) upon him; and having quietly removed his horse and provisions, and fastened the animal to a tree, he took his trusty rifle and crept softly upward in the direction of the voice he had heard. Carefully making his way through the thick brush and over the fallen timber, with the noiseless stealth taught him by his old backwoods experience, he at length arrived at the trunk of a large tree, which barred his progress, and, as he was preparing to climb over it, his ear caught the sound of whispering voices on the further side. Crouching low, but in such a position that he could see as well as hear, he listened to the dialogue. There were but two men, and one of them was evidently the utterer of the first signal he had heard. They had just met, and the first inquiry that passed between them was— "Who gave the signal from the middle ground?"

Each of them had supposed that he had been answered by another, and on finding that they were not alone in the ravine, they betrayed some uneasiness, but as the fire had disappeared they finally came to the conclusion that they had been mistaken, and once again entered the business which had brought them together. Suffice it to say that his suspicions proved well-founded, and that he overheard enough to convince him that there was an organized band of robbers in the neighborhood, of which one of the men was the lieutenant. He heard them discuss their plans for the future, saw the countersign exchanged between them, and finally recognized the face of the lieutenant as that of a man well-known to him. At last, the robbers moved away, and Marshall rolled himself in his blankets, and was soon asleep.

On returning to Coloma he told some of his friends what had happened, and that he had recognized the lieutenant of the band, but he declined to reveal the names of any of the men, knowing well that if he did so, his life would not be worth a day's purchase. Soon after this, a resident of Placerville (then called Hangtown) named Smith, an active and energetic citizen, determined to raise a posse for the pursuit of the robbers. This action was prompted by the capture of a burglar, a Frenchman, and a member of the gang, who had sought to save himself by becoming an informer. Unfortunately, however, Smith, being unacquainted with the band, and the Frenchman having misinformed him, he enlisted several of the robbers in his posse, and the result was that he failed to find any of the men.

Strong efforts were now made to induce Marshall to disclose the facts he had become possessed of so strangely, but he knew too well the reckless and desperate men with whom he had to deal, and, though he was a good citizen, he did not consider himself bound to sacrifice his life for the benefit of others. He was aware that the law was powerless to protect him. Indeed, it was unsafe even to speak of the robbers in a mixed company. The grocer from whom he bought his provisions, the saloon keeper who mixed his morning cocktail, the hotel keeper who supplied his meals, the blacksmith who mended his tools or shod his horses might be a member of the gang, and might denounce him. No one could guarantee safety against the vengeance of these lawless men, and, knowing this, he concluded that discretion was the better part of valor, and held his peace. In some way, however, it came to the ears of the lieutenant of the gang that Marshall knew him, and from that moment he began to follow and watch the former. This course, at length, became so annoying that Marshall determined to stop it. On one occasion, when he was out on the trail alone, he found that he was being followed. By turning suddenly he confronted his shadow, covering him at the same time with a pistol, and demanding the reason of his conduct. The man was at his mercy, and finding that he must speak, he plainly told him that he had heard that he (Marshall) knew of his connection with the band, and he wanted to know whether he was going to inform against him. Marshall replied that he had no such intention; that he proposed to attend to his own business as long as he was unmolested, but that if he was to be dogged and followed about in this way, he would not answer for what he might do. Upon this the robber said that if nothing more was said in the future than had been in the past, he would never be annoyed by him or any of his men. So the interview terminated, and the robber kept his word, never suffering Marshall to be molested or followed from that time. This gang was commanded by a man named Pete Raymond,[4] who had killed an old sea captain named

[4]Peter Raymond, *alias* Remer, deserted from General Stephen W. Kearny's command at Fort Leavenworth and made his way to California, arriving before the general and his troops. When Kearny did reach Los Angeles, Raymond turned himself in, but the general was not interested. In an effort to redeem himself, he served with Company E of the California Battalion. About October 1, 1848, he murdered John R. von Pfister, an agent for the San Francisco *California Star*, at Murphy's Bar near Coloma. Raymond, while awaiting trial at Sutter's Fort, escaped. He finally got his just desserts when he was executed in Santa Barbara for the murder of John Reed, his wife, a son, a midwife, and a shepherd. San Francisco *Californian*, October 14, p. 2, cl. 2; October 21, 1848, p. 3, cl. 3; Bancroft, *California*, IV: 775; V: 632, 688.

Bonfisto, at Coloma, during a quarrel, and from that time became a desperado of the worst sort. He eventually met a violent death, as nine out of ten of his class have done.

A short time after these events, Marshall was compelled to visit San Francisco on business, and put up at a hotel (or what answered to the name) on Jackson Street, during his stay. While sitting in the reading room one day, he fell into conversation with a certain professor of geology, one of a class of scientific smatterers who came out in early days, convinced that they held the key to all the riches of California, and whose ignorance of practical geology and mineralogy caused serious loss to the miners who confided in their knowledge, until they discovered by bitter experience that theory was untrustworthy. However, after some conversation with this scientist, a game at euchre was proposed, to which Marshall assented. The two men sat down to play, and several others lounged about the table, looking on at the game. Presently, Marshall grew tired of the cards, and surrendering his place to someone else, seated himself alongside one of the on-lookers. This man soon gave him a keen glance, and then, unseen by the others, threw out the signal of the mountain robbers. On the spur of the moment the other answered it, and the stranger then entered into a conversation with him, informing him that he belonged to a city organization, and that they had just effected a junction with the interior gang, to which he supposed Marshall belonged. Hailing him as a brother thief, he then proceeded to unfold the plans of the "Hounds," as they styled themselves, and among other nefarious schemes, told him that they had determined upon a grand operation, to take place in three or four months, which was nothing less than the burning and sacking of San Francisco. He gave his supposed comrade the clue to the headquarters of the "Hounds," instructed him in all the newly arranged grips, passwords, and countersigns, and finally left him, doubtless impressed with the idea that his recent companion was as real and practical a desperado as himself.

Marshall was rendered very uneasy by what he had heard, though he did not place implicit confidence in the robber's story; but the more he reflected the more difficult did his course appear. At length, he resolved to warn a friend of his, who was doing business near the Plaza. He repaired to this man's office, took him out of town, where there was no danger of eavesdroppers, and related all that had happened. In another place and at another time, his narrative would probably have been received with incredulity and ridicule, and he would have been told that some practical joker had played a trick on him, seeing that he was from the country. But the "Hounds" were even then a very serious and palpable organization, and robberies and murders were becoming more and more frequent, and paving the way for that exasperated condition of public senti-

ment which subsequently culminated in the formation of the Vigilance Committee, and the summary
punishment of the most notorious criminals.[5] Marshall's friend, therefore, lent an attentive ear to his
story, and when he had finished, asked, "Surely
you do not mean to keep this to yourself? Why do
you not go and inform the authorities?" To this he
replied, that if anyone would guarantee him a sufficient sum to remunerate him for leaving the state
within twenty-four hours, he would take the risk of
revealing the plot; but as he had only one life, and
as self-preservation was the first law of nature, he
must decline to commit suicide in this way. Besides,
if he was to tell the authorities, in all probability
they would not believe him; and, even if they knew
it to be true, society was in such a demoralized condition that the very men who received his communication might be in league with the robbers. The
risk to be encountered was too great, and the reward was too small. He, however, suggested to his
friend that *he* might inform the authorities, and, as
he was well-known, his statement would be received
with respect. This view did not commend itself
to the listener, and he declined to undertake the
responsibility. Whether the "Hounds" were really
the incendiaries cannot be positively known, but

[5]The Law and Order Party founded by Samuel Brannon
in 1849, became the nucleus for the Vigilance Committee of
1851. Mary F. Williams, *History of the San Francisco Committee of Vigilance of 1851* (Berkeley, 1921; reprint ed., New
York, 1969), pp. 104ff.

it is certain that San Francisco was burned at the time foretold by the robber. The friend, being warned, became prepared, and when the conflagration occurred, he succeeded in saving thirty thousand dollars from the wreck of his property.

No doubt there are many who will blame Marshall for his reticence on this occasion, and will contend that it was his duty to have revealed the conspiracy, no matter what the consequences to himself. Strictly speaking, perhaps this view is correct, but it must be remembered that we are writing the history of a *man*, with human failings, weaknesses, and faults, and not the account of a mere fictional person. And whatever may be said by theorists, we doubt much if a dozen men could be found in San Francisco today who would have acted differently under the circumstances. Marshall knew that this formidable band of cutthroats had ramifications extending to every mining camp in the state. He knew that if he informed against them his life would be sought by hundreds of desperadoes, not one of whom would have thought more of killing him than they would of crushing a spider under foot. He knew that his only chance would have been instant flight, and that he must abandon all that he had been toiling for these many years, while he was man of the world enough to know that there was slight probability that anyone would guarantee him remuneration for his risk and his sacrifice.

VII

Fame is a Curse

IN THE FALL of 1848, Sutter sold his half interest in the Coloma Mills to John Winters and Alden S. Bagley for six thousand dollars which included the privilege of cutting timber for mill purposes but did not affect the title to the land, which rested with Marshall. The same parties, at this time, purchased one-third of Marshall's interest for two thousand dollars, he reserving the pre-emption rights, and only disposing of the timber privilege. What followed was a series of disasters and troubles for the discoverer, which finally ruined him, and left him a broken man in his declining years.

The great discovery, of which he was the instrument, poured wealth upon the world, made millions rich, restored the balance of circulation in the Old World, and stimulated enterprise and industry in the New. Drawing from the ends of the earth a fiercely energetic and desperately adventurous population, it built upon the Pacific Slope a new community, whose vigor and enterprise were destined to become famous, and whose career of prosperity has scarcely yet commenced. But as one who shall strike away with his pick, the barrier which has imprisoned a living stream, whose bright waters rush past him to fertilize and enrich the arid plains below, leaving the agent of their release alone amid the barren solitudes of their birthplace, so the auriferous current swept on its course, enriching and gladdening millions, yet leaving the discoverer poor and desolate, and rather destroying what he possessed before adding to his store. The fate of great discoverers the world over has been melancholy, and Marshall's career has proved no exception to the rule. The importance of the revelation was his downfall, and he paid the penalty by sacrificing his all through persecution, robbery, abuse, slander, and injustice of the basest kind. Henceforth, the history of his life is the record of a series of outrages, which, while they cannot but be humiliating to all who desire to honor the Golden State, yet must be set down, if without malice, not less without extenuation.

Soon after the transfer of Sutter's interest in the mill, the great rush of 1849 commenced, and every steamer leaving New York, and every sailing vessel bound for San Francisco, were crowded with eager adventurers. About the month of March, a large number of newcomers arrived at Coloma for purposes of trade and mining. They knew that the first gold had been discovered there, and they assumed that the richest diggings must be in that neighborhood. Without any inquiry or negotiation, these men at once squatted on the land about the mill, taking possession and starting to prospect with a supreme disregard of the existence of pre-emption or any other law. They recognized no rights in any property holder which they were bound to respect. When their provisions gave out—and they were by no means plentifully supplied—they seized the work oxen belonging to the mill, and when they wanted pack animals to carry their provisions while prospecting, they simply seized Marshall's horses. Oxen and horses were valuable in those days, and the money loss then sustained by Marshall from these raids amounted to no less than six thousand three hundred dollars. He posted many notices and also served the intruders with them, to the effect that he claimed the land as an original settler, but it was all to no purpose. The squatters were absorbed in their fierce quest for gold, and neither law nor justice troubled them.

While these things were occurring, another event transpired which for a time forced him to forget his smaller worries for more serious ones. This event was the massacre at Murderer's Bar.[1] At this time (the spring of 1849), Marshall had a number of the friendly Sutter Indians along with a few white men engaged in making some necessary repairs at the mill. These Indians had been peaceable and industrious, and he had obtained considerable ascendency over the tribe by fair dealing with them on every occasion. While affairs were in this condition, a

[1] Use of the term "Bar" does not mean a tavern, but rather a sandy or gravelly land area in or on the bank of a stream.

party of seven men, who had recently arrived from Oregon, started out on a prospecting expedition up the North Fork of the American River, and having reached a point just above the junction of the North and Middle Forks, looked upon a large rancheria. There was good pasturage in the neighborhood, and they determined to camp there, and give their horses a rest. Having refreshed themselves, and staked out their animals, they went over to the rancheria, and finding some Indian women there, attempted to take improper liberties with them. The cries of the women brought about some of the Indian men, and others attempting to prevent the commission of an outrage. The white men drew their revolvers and shot down three of the Indians. They then, apparently careless of what might follow, started for Murderer's Bar, on the Middle Fork, some three or four miles above the junction, and two of the number went on a prospecting tour, leaving the remaining five in camp. After an absence of a day or two, the prospectors returned and found that their partners had shifted the camp. They followed up the trail and finally arrived at the new camping ground to find that the whole of the party had been murdered by the Indians. The survivors, whose absence had saved them from sharing the fate of their comrades, at once started for Coloma, and on arriving there told their tale, and set about raising a posse to retaliate upon the Indians. A number of the robbers belonging to the band of Mountain Hounds were in

Coloma at the time, and they seized this opportunity to revenge themselves upon the friendly Indians,
one of whom they suspected of having watched
their actions, and given Marshall the information
he possessed concerning them. With this purpose
in view, they joined with the citizens who had collected to pursue the murderers, and induced them
to indulge in a carouse before starting. In a short
time the majority were so intoxicated as to care little whether the Indians they killed were friendly or
unfriendly, and when this point had been reached a
suggestion was made that they seize the Indians at
the mill and punish them. This advice was received
with enthusiasm, and in a short time the mill was
surrounded by a party of half-drunken men, all
armed to the teeth, and swearing vengeance on the
Indians. Previously, however, some of the Hounds
had sent word to several of the Sutter tribe that
Marshall wanted to see them, and thus it happened
that an unusually large number were collected at
the mill when the attack was made upon it. Marshall exerted himself to the utmost to avert the outrage which he saw was contemplated, but his efforts
were useless, since the drunken crew would listen
to no arguments. At first, the leaders said they only
desired to make prisoners of the Indians, but when
they had secured them, the men fell to drinking
again and, rendered furious by bad whisky and the
sinister advice of the scoundrels who had undertaken to mislead them, began an indiscriminate

slaughter of their helpless victims. Marshall strove sturdily for the Indians. He demanded a fair trial for them, and denounced the action of the mob in the strongest terms, and at last, finding all his efforts useless, he called around him the few upon whom he could rely, and told them he was prepared to defend the mill and its inmates with his rifle, if they would stand by him. But his friends saw that resistance would be folly against such a mob, and urged him to save himself, for his bold speech and vigorous denunciation of the cowardly assailants had drawn their anger down on his own head, and already threats had been made that they would serve him as they served the Indians. He was not a man to be easily daunted. His life had been passed amid scenes of peril, and he probably would have accepted the issue, and tried conclusions with them, at the sacrifice of his life, had not his friends forced him to fly, on a horse which one of them had provided. The mob willfully murdered seven friendly Indians on this occasion. There was not a shadow of any justification for the atrocious deed, for the whole of the slaughtered men were constantly employed as mill hands by Marshall and his partners, and therefore could not have had anything to do with the killing of the white men at Murderer's Bar; besides which, they belonged to a different tribe from that of the hostile Indians. This is but one of a number of cases which have been partially and unfairly reported heretofore, and which tend to show

how little justice has often been accorded to Indians by lawless white men. It might be too much to say that this slaughter was the prime cause of the so-called Indian War which followed, and which cost the state three hundred thousand dollars, but it is not too much to say that outrages such as this had very much to do with the subsequent hostility of the natives.

The feeling against Marshall, for attempting to save the lives of his innocent men, was so strong that some time elapsed before he dared to return to Coloma, and the ruse employed by the "Hounds" to entrap the Indians had induced the latter to believe that he was privy to the massacre, and had also drawn their enmity down upon him. When, at length, he returned to his old house, it was to find that the squatters had surveyed the ground about the mill, marked it off into town lots, and distributed it among themselves, utterly ignoring the claims of the real owner.

And now a new form of persecution commenced. The miners had persuaded themselves to believe that since Marshall was the discoverer of gold, he must know where all the rich diggings were located. Absurd and puerile as this idea must seem now, it was a positive belief in those days. They began to regard him as a malignant wizard, who held the key to all the treasures of California, but would not unlock them. If he went out of town, he was followed by crowds, who imagined that he was about to visit some of his secret diggings. If he remained at home, he was watched as closely as though he had been a criminal out on bail, who was known to be meditating an escape. Wherever he went, whatever he was doing, he was beset with questioners, who made no scruple of threatening him if he did not reveal the secrets they supposed him to possess, and who considered themselves aggrieved because he could not tell them what he did not know. This espionage grew more rigorous and irksome as time passed on, and the miners became more convinced that he knew where the gold was, if he could only be forced to confess. No suspected witch in the old, bad days of Matthew Hopkins and his villainous crew was ever watched more closely or jealously than was this unfortunate man.[2] It was utterly useless for him to assure them that he knew no more where the gold was than they did themselves. The more earnest and positive were his disclaimers, the stronger their suspicions became, and finally the day came when, either because they had been drinking more bad whisky than usual, or because their patience was worn out, the whole mining camp rose up, and transforming itself into a crazy mob, started after

[2]Matthew Hopkins earned the sobriquet "Witch Finder General" in southeastern England during late 1644 and 1645 when he mounted and prosecuted a great witch hunt. In all, 153 victims were brought to trial by his efforts, 133 women and 20 men. Richard Deacon, *Matthew Hopkins: Witch Finder General* (London, 1976), pp. 91–92, 133, 136, 154–55, 172–73.

the discoverer, intending to escort him out of town to a spot where a tree grew conveniently, and hang him then and there if he did not tell them where the rich diggings were situated. There can be little doubt that they would have been as good (or as bad) as their word, for Marshall certainly could not comply with the alternative presented to him, had not one of his partners, Mr. John Winters, hearing of the peril he was in, taken measures to engage the attention of the miners, and succeeded in smuggling the threatened man away, directing him to a thicket near the roadside, where a good horse awaited him. Thus was Marshall compelled to fly from his home to save his life for the second time. On the first occasion he was threatened with death because he strove to prevent murder; on the second, because he was not gifted with omniscience.

On this occasion he was compelled to absent himself for nearly six months, so deep was the conviction of the miners that he knew where the rich mining could be found, but that he would not tell. Indeed, some years passed before he ceased to suffer from this strange species of persecution, as will be seen in the course of this history. This may be said to have been the commencement of the failure of the mill business. After the partners had got out the lumber for Sutter's flouring mill at Brighton, the rush became so general, and prices rose so high, that it was almost impossible to get work done. The lawyers came upon the scene, moreover, and what with expensive litigation, arising out of the action of the squatters, and the enormous cost of running the mill, labor being then worth *sixteen dollars a day*, the enterprise became hopeless, and the mill had to be closed.[3] The trouble, however, did not end here, for the same men who had stolen the ground, the cattle, and the horses, belonged to the same establishment that now appropriated the timbers of the mill itself to line shafts and tunnels with, and coolly dismantled the whole building, besides destroying the milldam; and for this damage none of the proprietors ever received compensation even to the value of one cent.

We have spoken of the high prices during that period, and it may be interesting to many of our readers to know *how* high prices were in 1849. Statements have been published in newspapers, and allusions have occasionally been made to the almost fabulous cost of living at that time, but the following extracts from one of the books kept at Sutter's Fort will, perhaps, convey a better idea of the actual state of things. We append a few items at random:

[3]Bagley sold out his one-third interest, June 16, 1849, to Clarkson Dye, for $60,000, who failed to fulfill the terms. It was repossessed on August 9, to little avail. The partners, unable to collect debts for the lumber they sold on credit, pressed with endless lawsuits, compounded by the destruction of the sawmill dam in the 1851 flood, were pushed to the wall. By 1852, only Marshall's share is shown on the county's assessment books and those figures disappear in 1853. The millsite was abandoned to its fate. Gay, *Marshall*, pp. 270–84.

1 Canister of Tea	$13.00
2 White Shirts	40.00
2 Kits of Mackerel	60.00
1 Fine-Tooth Comb	6.00
3 lbs. of Crackers	3.00
1 Barrel Mess Pork	210.00
1 Bottle Lemon Syrup	6.00
4 lbs. of Nails	3.00
1 doz. Sardines	35.00
1 Pair Socks	3.00
1 lb. Powder	10.00
1 Bottle Ale	5.00
1 Bottle Cider	6.00
1 Hat	10.00
1 Pair Shoes	14.00
1 Bottle Pickles	7.00
1 Can of Herrings	30.00
13 lbs. Ham	27.00
1 Bottle Mustard	6.00
2 lbs. Sauerkraut	4.00
55 lbs. Tarred Rope	75.00
1 Tin of Crackers	24.00
1 Candle	3.00
30 lbs. Sugar	18.00
1 Colt's Revolver	75.00
1 Tin Pan	9.00
1 Keg Lard	70.50
1 Pair Blankets	24.00
1 doz. Champagne	40.00
1 lb. Butter	2.50
50 lbs. Beans	25.00
200 lbs. Flour	150.00
13 lbs. Salmon	13.00

VIII

Defamation and Depredation

THE CURSE clung to Marshall. When he returned
to his old home, he found his possessions scattered, his lands occupied by men who scoffed at his
claims, and himself regarded with much of the old
superstitious suspicion which had forced him to
leave the place before. Had he been a keen business-
man, it is possible that he might have compelled
some sort of settlement from those who had plundered him so audaciously. But his frontier experience, though fitting him to undergo the vicissitudes
of pioneer life, and to hold his own against savage
creatures, whether brute or human, had left him ill
prepared to cope with men well versed in the ways
of the world, too often unscrupulous, and prompt
to avail themselves of the advantages which were afforded them by the absence of legal protection or
the laxity and venality of courts. In truth, he fell an
easy prey to such. Naturally of a generous, open-
handed disposition, slow to suspect and prone to
confide, he suffered his adversaries to read his hand
while they carefully concealed their own. Unfortunately for himself, moreover, he did not belong to a
"Ring," for there were "rings" during those days.
The action of these organizations, however, will be

referred to at more length in another place, and at present, their introduction is rather premature.

Marshall at this time returned to his prospecting, during the phases of a business which was becoming more and more hopeless; but when he was poorest, and mostly needing sympathy and help, the curse then hung heaviest upon him. Let us take a single picture of the life he then led. Imagine a gulch or ravine in the mountains, its sides scarped, cut away and laid barren here and there by the miners. A stream, yellow as ochre, glides through the cañon and groups of men are busy digging and washing dirt and arranging flumes and sluice boxes. A solitary figure, bent and worn, less with years than anxiety, but yet showing a broad-shouldered, robust and athletic frame, approaches one of the groups of miners near the head of the cañon, and after examining the ground with a practiced eye, inquires if a certain spot (pointing it out) is taken up. The man addressed replies, scarcely raising his head, in the negative. The stranger then asks if he can borrow a sluice box from the company; and succeeding in this, he repairs to the owner of the water power and arranges for so many inches of water, to be supplied, perhaps, for a couple of days on credit, and paid for out of whatever the claim may contain. This being done, he goes quietly to work in his corner. He has been there but a few hours when some one passing by stops to watch him, and as he rises up to rest his back or wipe the sweat from his brow, recognizes him, and at once says to himself, "Hulloa! there's that Jim Marshall again! he's struck it sure this time!" and off he goes. In an hour or two, twenty or thirty eager men enter the cañon, and at once proceed to use every foot of ground around Marshall's location, coolly driving him away with threats and curses. This is but a single illustration. The same thing was done a score—aye, even three-score of times. He was a marked man wherever he went, until he reached a point where the Coloma influence faded, and where his person, at least, was unrecognized. The fact that he had discovered gold, so far from causing the hearts of those who were enriching themselves by his discovery, to warm towards him—so far from securing for him simple and ordinary justice—served only to raise a steady persecution against him, as against one who was a public enemy. It might be imagined that through these men the innocent agent of the great discovery was being punished for all the evil which the cursed lust of lucre was destined to bring into the world. Few men would have submitted to so much outrage and injustice without resenting it, and without becoming soured and misanthropic. Yet, to show that Marshall never lost his natural warmth of heart and charitable impulses, we may narrate an incident that occurred about this time.

He was out on one of his expeditions, in the summer of 1849, and while proceeding on a certain day along the trail between the Middle and South Forks of the Yuba, he came upon a man lying by the way-side looking near death. Marshall, at once, turned to assist, and having administered some refreshment to the sufferer, succeeded in learning that his name was Jack Abbott; that he had been out prospecting with several comrades and upon becoming ill along the way, his heartless companions had gone off and left him to die. So much has been said and written about the generosity and hospitality of Californians in the early days, that such a story as this may seem almost incredible. However, it would be mere folly to assume that there were no black sheep among the pioneers; and perhaps if the simple truth were told, there would not be found a majority willing to rehearse *all* their actions of those days. Concerning the truth of the present anecdote, however, there can be no question. Having somewhat revived Abbott, Marshall set him on his own horse, and walking beside, carried him to his camp. There he nursed him tenderly and carefully, over-coming the lack of allopathic medicines by using such staples as his earlier Indian experience had taught him. It is fashionable in cities to sneer at Indian medicines, but there are scores of old frontiersmen who will, even to this day, indignantly repel any depreciation of their favorite remedies, and will recite case after case of marvelous cures effected under their own eyes by Indian doctors or Indian medicaments. Anyhow, in this case Marshall's old-fashioned treatment was successful, and through

Marshall's continual care the young man recovered gradually. During his convalescence Marshall did learn that he belonged to a well-to-do family in New York and that his friends were quite wealthy. He had sown his wild oats too prodigally, and had been shipped off to California in the hope that a rough experience there would steady him down. But if it were not for Marshall's discovery of him he would, undoubtedly, have been steady enough before long.

As his strength returned, Marshall was in the habit of lending him his horse to take a short ride everyday, and as time passed on, he extended his rambles, and grew stronger and livelier. When his health appeared to be nearly restored, Marshall one day told him that now he was so well he must do a little light work, and that he had better begin on the morrow. To this, young Abbott cheerfully consented, and mounting, trotted off on his accustomed ride. That was the last time Marshall ever saw him. He vanished completely and utterly, and with him disappeared the horse, saddle, and bridle, lent him by the good Samaritan.

This has always been a sore subject with Marshall. He probably felt it more than the persecution of the miners or the outrages of the squatters. It was so cruel a blow at his faith in human nature, so mean and ignoble a return for a generous and noble deed, that we could almost pardon him for turning into something like a Timon and reviling his fellow

creatures for all of the remaining days of his life.[1]
And yet there is a faint possibility that Abbott did
not voluntarily desert his benefactor. Some time afterwards Marshall was in San Francisco, and there
met by chance one of Abbott's friends, a man who
was well acquainted with his Eastern connections.
This friend, after hearing the story of his disappear-
ance, expressed the belief that Jack had not gone off
as supposed, but that he had fallen a victim to some
accident. This view he fortified by the statement
that several months after Abbott was last seen, the
skeleton of a man and horse—the former sitting on
the ground, and the latter tied to a tree close by—
had been found in a dense wood, not far from the
place where Marshall's camp had been. It would be
infinitely preferable to be able to think of him as
innocent of such base ingratitude as his disappear-
ance seemed to indicate, but Marshall listened to
the story with strong incredulity, and continued to
believe that he had been most basely dealt with,

---

[1] Timon is the leading character in William Shakespeare's
"Timon of Athens" (c. 1607). A generous host and patron
of the arts, finding himself in financial difficulties, he discov-
ers to his dismay that his "so-called friends who had previously fawned on him now refuse to help him." He leaves
Athens cursing his fellowmen and settles in a cave where he
finds a buried treasure of gold. To wreak revenge on Athens,
he finances a military expedition to capture the city. But
through peaceful negotiations, conflict is avoided. Meanwhile Timon dies in his cave, "still inveighing against the
human race." *Benét's Reader's Encyclopedia* (3rd ed., New
York, 1987), pp. 979–80.

and that the skeleton was simply a work of imagination, invented to save the reputation of Abbott by his friend.

Turning from this painful anecdote, we may record a somewhat amusing incident which occurred towards the end of the winter of 1849.

A man named Robinson, a lawyer (who was afterwards concerned in the Lecompton riots in Kansas),[2] had squatted upon a forty-acre lot belonging to Sutter, which was situated on the low, swampy ground which afterwards became the site of the City of Sacramento. Meeting Marshall one day, he offered to sell him a portion of this land, when the following conversation ensued:

Marshall—What title have you got to the land?

Squatter—Oh! That's all right; it's only necessary to have it surveyed and recorded.

Marshall—Humph! Have you got no other title?

Squatter—(Rather sharply.) Other title! No, sir! No other title is necessary.

Marshall—Well, if I wanted to buy, I should want Sutter's title. But now tell me, how long are you expecting to be able to maintain your present position?

[2]The Lecompton riots during the summer of 1857 were provoked by the struggle to make the territory a free or slave state while formulating a constitution to submit to Congress. Lecompton was the seat of the pro-slavery element. Adams, ed., *Dictionary of American History*, III: 259.

Squatter—(Indignantly.) Maintain it, indeed!
  I should like to see the power that would
  try to oust me!

Marshall—Well, what force have you got?

Squatter—I can bring fifty men to back me in
  a few hours.

Marshall—Is that all the force you can find?

Squatter—(Angrily.) No, sir, it is not! In
  three days I can muster five hundred rifles to
  support my claims!

Marshall—(Quietly and aggravatingly.) Is
  that all you can do?

Squatter—(Perfectly frantic.) Yes, sir! And
  enough too! I'd like to see Sutter, or anybody
  else, turn me off this land!

Marshall—(With a quiet chuckle.) Well, sir,
  it 'aint no kind o' use. I'll bet you anything you like that you'll be driven off this
  lot in something less than two months.

The squatter was furious at this prediction, and
boasted of what would happen to anyone who attempted to dispossess him. Marshall heard him out,
and then turned away with a laugh, which seemed
to have the effect of puzzling the other somewhat.

The two months had not expired when the river
rose, and in a few hours the land squatted on by
Robinson was under several feet of water, and he
was paddling his canoe for the high ground, leaving
his shanty submerged. As he neared the shore a
man, who had heard the story narrated above, called

to him with a shout—"Aha! Marshall was right, after all!" The squatter started, and a new light broke
in upon his mind as he asked—"Is *this* what he
meant when he said I should be driven off in less
than two months?" That was exactly what Marshall
had meant. He knew the river well, and was perfectly safe in asserting that neither fifty nor five hundred men would enable the squatter to maintain his
"present position."

IX

The Ohio Diggings

IT WAS IN the summer of 1850 that Marshall went up Antoine Cañon, near the head of the North Branch of the Middle Fork of the American River, and commenced mining there. At this time, men were eagerly watching for new and rich developments, and if a miner was seen to go far from the camp, and on his return was reticent as to what he had found, this was enough to start an excitement. The miners would gather about their favorite saloon, after work was over for the day, and compare notes as to the suspicious conduct of Bill Jones, or Stumpy Jack, or whoever the individual might be; and if they thought there was reason to believe that he had "struck it rich" somewhere up in the mountains, or in a neighboring gulch, expeditions would be fitted out to follow him, and track him to the supposed new diggings. When, as sometimes happened, a strike had really been made, the lucky prospector was compelled to exercise his utmost cunning, and resort to the deepest strategy, to throw his comrades off the scent. The craving after riches develops intense selfishness, and at no time has this been more strongly exhibited than during the excitement of those early days. It is true that the miners were lavish in their expenditures, and that they were often and proverbially generous where the object of their sympathy did not come into competition with them. But there were comparatively few who could put aside the temptation of an opportunity to get an edge on their comrades in securing a rich claim, and there were many who were prepared to perpetrate any crime, if it would enable them to obtain the wealth they sought. Many a dark deed was done in the gloomy gulches and desolate cañons up in the mountains, and many a lonely shanty was the scene of murder, foul and horrible, never discovered until, perhaps, months afterward when some roving prospector, arriving at an apparently deserted cabin, would enter, and find the remains of its former occupant, lying there grim and ghastly, and mutely testifying to the crime, by the mark of bullet or of knife still visible on the decaying form. But of all the black deeds done in those lawless times, none presents more terrible features than that which forms the subject of this chapter.

Before Marshall had been long at work in Antoine Cañon, a great excitement was created by the advent of a party of men hailing from Ohio, who brought with them a large quantity of gold, which they said they had taken from a creek in the neighborhood, the locality of which they refused to disclose. Several parties were soon raised to search for the new strike, which by this time had come to be spoken of as the "Ohio Diggings," from the state whence the supposed discoverers came. The little mining town was alive with rumors and suggestions. Some were confident that the diggings would be found in this, and others in that direction. One man would undertake to guide a party straight to it; but another would be equally certain that he knew the place, and as probably his route was in an opposite direction to that proposed by the first, public opinion was a good deal divided, and the result was that five or six parties started out, all taking different routes. After a short time, two or three of the expeditions returned, weary and worn with climbing rocky trails, forcing their way through heavy brush, clambering precipices, and wading streams, but none of them had succeeded in discovering anyplace that looked even hopeful. At length, Marshall was induced to join a new party, and they set off, like the rest, in quest of the now famous, but hard to find, Ohio Diggings. They spent some weeks in the mountains, and searched carefully and patiently; but at last their supplies became exhausted, and their strength also, so they were compelled to turn their faces once more towards base camp. They had reached a clearing between the north and middle branches of the Middle Fork, when, after pursuing what appeared to be an old Indian trail, though evidently long unused, overgrown, and difficult, they soon came upon a little level opening surrounded by trees so thickly as to darken the place to a dim twilight. A pleasant brook danced merrily over the stones in its bed, and hurried along the center of the little dell, and the grass all around grew thick and green, kept bright and cool by the refreshing moisture and the shade of the tall trees. Marshall was riding ahead, and as he entered this quiet spot, he at once determined that it would be a good place to camp. At first, his eyes, unaccustomed to the dim light, failed to distinguish objects accurately, but by the time he had ridden up to the spring and dismounted, his natural keenness of vision returned. Then he suddenly caught sight of an object that startled even his grim self-possession. A few yards from where he stood lay the skeletons of a horse and mule, the bony back of one still bearing a Spanish saddle, and an *arapejo*,[1] or packsaddle, lying on the remains of the other. Near these was a human skeleton, which was thought to be that of a Spaniard, from the remains of a pair of pantaloons with leather stripes down the legs that were still on the body. Bending over the remains, he at once detected evidence of foul play, a small round hole in the skull of the dead man revealing the manner of his death. By this time the rest of the party had entered the dell, and a shout from one of them announced further discoveries. Some distance away

[1] An *arapejo* is a heavy, leather packsaddle for a horse or mule. "The word derives from the Spanish word *parejo* (level), since it was critical that the load of the saddle be well-balanced lest it should chafe the animal's back." Cornelius C. Smith, Jr., *A Southwestern Vocabulary* (Glendale, CA, 1984), p. 35.

from the first, a second skeleton was found. This man had been shot in the breast. A third was soon after discovered, and it was evident that this one had been struck from behind, as he was in the act of leaping over a log, for when found one foot was caught on the log, and the body was doubled back over it, just as he had then fallen and died. Finally, the skeletons of four more horses were discovered, and this completed the dismal revelation. It was as plain as anything could be that the Spaniards had entered the dell just as this group had entered it, to rest their horses. They had been followed, and were shot down in cold blood as they were in the act of attending to their animals. Men less experienced in frontier life than Marshall and his comrades, might have imagined that the murderers were Indians, but they made no such mistake. One glance at the nature of the wounds, at the indications still remaining of the occupation and business of the victims, satisfied them that the rifles of white men had taken these lives, and that the motive of the deed had been plunder. After the natural exclamations of horror and indignation had been vented by the discoverers, speculations were indulged in, and conjectures made, regarding the murdered men and the murderers. So far nothing seemed clear save that the skeletons were those of Spaniards, and no one was prepared with a plausible theory as to their identity. But while they were conversing and exchanging ideas and suggestions, Marshall, who had been carefully and silently examining the remains, and the surroundings of the place, stepped in front of the party, and raising his hand to secure their attention, waited until silence was obtained, and then uttered this remark:

"Boys! We have struck the Ohio Diggings!"

The men started, looked at one another perplexedly, and then demanded his meaning. The explanation he made, and the story it involves the narration of, were substantially as follows:

Some time before this, three Spaniards who were engaged in mining, struck a rich crevice on Vanfleet Creek, which adjoined and ran parallel with Antoine Creek. They were in the habit of obtaining their supplies from a trader named James Williams, who lived between the two creeks, and when they began to get gold in considerable quantities out of their crevice, they naturally placed it in Williams' care, not feeling that it would be safe in their unprotected cabin. From time to time they came in to the store, depositing gold, and returning to camp with provisions, until they had accumulated sixty-five pounds of the precious metal. At a later time, Williams determined to leave from that neighborhood for some other mining district, and sent word to the Spaniards to come in and take away their gold. Now, there were plenty of men in those days who preferred easy crime to honest work, and who were always on the lookout for an opportunity to plunder the unwary. Several men of this stamp had been in the habit of loafing about Williams' store, appearing to be engaged in prospecting, but rarely visibly occupied in any other kind of employment than playing cards and drinking. This group had watched the Spaniards as they came and went, and had several times asserted that they were bound to find out where the others got their gold from. So, when the day came for the partners to remove their gold, not much attention was excited by the declaration of some of the loafers that they would follow them, and find out their diggings. The Spaniards had, perhaps, half an hour's start of their pursuers, and were traveling at a usual pace, little dreaming of the murderous band that were dogging them, or of the murderous eyes that were watching them. On reaching the dell, it is probable that they determined to stay awhile and rest, though they evidently intended to push on again that day, as the packs were left on the horses and mules. While they were watering their animals, the assassins must have crept up and quietly covered their victims. Apparently, all but one had been killed by the first fire. That one, startled by the sudden volley, made a rush for the shelter of the trees, but a bullet overtook him as he was in the act of leaping over a log, and he died in his tracks, his skeleton, after the flesh had decayed, still remaining in the self-same attitude in which he was when the leaden death struck him. The murderers had taken nothing but the gold, and they had killed the horses and mules lest they might stray to some camp, and, being recognized, suggest a search for their owners. The place where this atrocious crime was committed was so sequestered that no fears were entertained of the discovery of the bodies. The assassins had gone into Bird's Valley with their booty, and as the easiest and most plausible way of accounting for their possession of it, had given out the story about the rich secret diggings which had so excited the camp, and which had set a hundred men on prospecting expeditions, in which they wasted the whole summer. Marshall was right when he said that they had struck the Ohio Diggings. This was the mine which the Ohio men had worked so successfully, and these grim and ghastly figures were the former owners of the claim. All through that summer of 1850, while bands of men were searching every ravine in the mountains round about, and enjoying in imagination the fruits of the discovery they hoped to make, the unhappy men who had located the treasure were rotting in that gloomy dell, there to remain, silent yet imperishable witnesses to the awful crime that lay at the bottom of the Ohio Diggings. The murderers, so far as we know, were never brought to punishment, but it is safe to assert that their ill-gotten wealth secured them neither prosperity nor happiness.

X

Consequences of Secularization

IT CANNOT be said that the Americans, on taking possession of California, established a reckless and bad system of dealing with the Indians, which has since been pursued, though undoubtedly they are to blame for having adopted and continued the pernicious customs which were obtained when they arrived in the country. Long before this, the work of the good Mission Fathers had been neutralized, frustrated, almost annihilated, by the greed and fatuity of the Mexican Governors of the state. During a period of sixty years—embracing the extent of their sway—these Fathers had done, at all events for the native population, what the Americans have never done for any Indians within their possessions.

Twenty-one flourishing missions had been established, and more than thirty thousand Indians had embraced Christianity and found shelter and employment at the hands of the priests. Two hundred thousand horned cattle, three hundred thousand sheep, and sixty thousand horses, belonged to the missions, and the annual slaughter of two hundred thousand oxen produced a revenue of one million dollars to the Church. But the Mexican Congress concluded, in 1835, that it was time to put a stop to this halcyon condition, and so decided to "secularize" the missions. This measure was not carried into effect at that time, but the preliminary measures ruined the missions.[1] The "Pious Fund," which was composed of the proceeds of bequests to the missions by rich, devout Catholics in Old Spain, was first attacked by the avaricious governor, and made to bleed freely. In after years, Santa Anna got hold of it, and most people know how well he was fitted to squeeze a fund or a treasury.[2] In the meantime, the parochial priests who were to take the

[1] These figures are substantially exaggerated. In 1821, at the end of the Spanish period, the missions in their annual reports recorded the following holdings: 149,730 cattle; 193,234 sheep; 19,830 horses. The missions did not produce revenue *per se*. During the Spanish and Mexican periods, the bulk of trade and commerce was carried on by barter. Secularization became effective in 1833 and was carried out between 1834–35. Mission herds and lands were turned over to the local populace. Robert Archibald, *The Economic Aspects of the California Missions* (Washington, D.C., 1978), pp. 179, 181; Gerald J. Geary, *The Secularization of the California Missions (1810–1846)* (Washington, D.C., 1934), *passim*.

[2] The Pious Fund began in 1697 as an endowment to support Jesuit missionization of Baja California. When the Jesuits were expelled from Spain and its possessions in 1768, the crown took over the fund and continued to administer it for missionary activity both in Baja and Alta California. In 1842 President Santa Anna in effect sequestered the endowment. As part of the Treaty of Guadalupe Hidalgo, which ended the Mexican War, it was agreed the Mexican government would pay $719,546 to the U.S. Treasury, which in turn would pass the amount on to the Roman Catholic claimants. Francis J. Weber, "The Final Settlement of the Pious Fund," *Southern California Quarterly*, 51 (June 1969), pp. 97–152.

place of the Mission Fathers were not appointed, and in consequence the secularization was suspended temporarily. The object of this measure was to elevate the natives—to give them additional liberties. Heretofore they had sat at the feet of the Fathers, and had rendered the unquestioning obedience of children. Their religion may not have been comprehensive or intelligent, but it was certainly sincere and faithful. As controversialists, they would, without doubt, have been failures; but as practical illustrations of the good that may be learned from the Gospel, they were unquestionably successful. But the government felt the time had come when they might take another step in advance. From naked savagery and nomadic habits to a state of docility, industry, tranquility and prosperity, the transition had not seemed very difficult. They were now required, however, to abandon their faithful and sure-footed guides, and proceed alone into a new and to them unexplored region. They were to be elevated to the rank of citizens, their missions turned into Indian pueblos, and their churches into parish churches. The experiment was tried, it is true, in a scarcely satisfactory manner, since the aim of the governor seemed to be to secure possession of all Church funds while disregarding what became of the less valuable and important parishioners who were to be affected by this work of secularization. The result, which was generally expected, was the ruin of the missions, the scattering of the Indians and their relapse into barbarism, and the enriching of Flores, Alvarado, and sundry other Mexican potentates, who managed to get their clutches upon the Pious Fund.[3]

All this had happened long before Marshall arrived in California; before Sutter arrived, indeed, and when there were very few settlers in the state who spoke other than the Spanish tongue. And before the conquest of the state by the California Battalion, as heretofore narrated, these thirty thousand Indians were undoubtedly in a very bad condition. While the missions flourished, a calm and peaceful atmosphere had pervaded the country. The influence and example of the missionaries was uniformly benignant, and no licentiousness or depravity could live within their ken. The secularization movement changed all this. Majordomos were appointed to supersede the missionaries in charge of the missions. Parish Priests were not appointed. The new officials were laymen, mostly ignorant, rude, and too often brutal. Religion was neglected. The subtle influence which had curbed and restrained the restless instincts of the Indians, vanished. The mild voices and gentle manners of the old Fathers gave place to the harsh orders and violent demeanor of vaqueros who had been made Majordomos. The Indians were

[3]This is not true. No *Californio* benefited from the Pious Fund since it was sequestered by the Mexican government, however, they enriched themselves through secularization of mission lands and property.

driven from the missions, and they returned to their old haunts, and something worse than their old lives. The administrators of the missions plundered them, and grew wickedly wealthy. The alcaldes, or magistrates, being drawn from the lower classes, were ignorant, and being avaricious, were corrupt. Gambling and drunkenness became general, and while the Indians were forced back into barbarism, their masters seemed bent upon following a similar path, and arriving, as speedily as possible, at the same goal. And as the Californians became more and more degraded, the Indians suffered from their degradation. The few herds left to these latter from the spoliation of the missions were wrested from them; their patches of cultivated land were seized; themselves were abused and ill-treated. The result might have been foreseen. The Indians, having advanced but a little way along the paths of civilization, found no particular difficulty in retracing their steps, and having resumed a savage status, they began to adopt savage methods of retaliation upon their oppressors. The majority of the neophytes returned to their tribes in the Tulare Valley, and made predatory raids upon the settlements and missions, carrying off stock, and sometimes abducting the wives and daughters of the settlers.[4]

[4]This is a bit of an exaggeration. The Indians were not given to the abduction of California women. A number of tribes were addicted to rustling, especially horses, both for transportation and food, for horse meat was highly prized by some Indians.

The settlers in their turn organized expeditions against the natives, and at times surprised and destroyed whole villages, putting the inhabitants to the sword indiscriminately. The action of Governor Micheltorena in bringing into the state a force of three hundred men, composed of the worst desperadoes, taken from the prisons of Mexico, did not mend matters, a large number of these wretches deserting, and forming bands of robbers, who laid the country to waste, and indulged in crime of every conceivable description.

Such was the condition of affairs when the state was conquered by the Americans, and the conquest did not bring about any improvement so far as the Indian tribes were concerned. A large proportion of the adventurers who flocked from all parts of the world into California when the discovery of gold took place, were, as has already been shown, reckless, wild, and unscrupulous, and their rashness was attributable to the disturbance known as the Indian War of 1850. How that war was inaugurated, how it was conducted, and the result to the state, we now propose to show.

In the summer of 1850 four miners left Placerville to move to a neighboring camp. On the way, while crossing the mountains, they fell in with an Indian, accompanied by his woman. One of the miners became violent to the woman. The Indian resented it, and attempted to defend her, where upon the miner drew his pistol and deliberately shot the Indian dead, subsequently ravishing the woman while her husband's corpse lay, still warm, beside her. The Indians had been told that if they were molested by the whites they had but to make a complaint to the nearest magistrate or official, and they would find redress. Not being at that time well versed in the ways of their new rulers, they took the truth of this assurance for granted, and made their complaints accordingly. No notice was taken of their petition. They waited some time, and at last, seeing that there was no hope of redress from the authorities, they took the law into their own hands, and attacking a party of three miners, killed two of them. Of course, this was utterly wrong and unjustifiable, but it should be remembered that the murderers were uncivilized Indians, and that before avenging themselves they had adopted the course prescribed to them, without avail. When the miners heard of the slaughter of their comrades, they at once insisted on speedy retribution, and Colonel William Rogers, then sheriff of El Dorado County, at once proceeded to assemble a force to attack the Indians. Of the so-called war that ensued, which mainly consisted of the killing of peaceable Indians and old women, plus the destruction of deserted rancherias, it does not seem necessary to relate a complete description of events. Two incidents will suffice to convey an idea of the extent and manner of the contest.

Major McKinney rode out one day at the head of

a party of men, all armed to the teeth, in search of Indians. As they were journeying along a mountain trail, they became aware of a peaceable Indian riding some distance ahead of them. Without pausing to inquire whether he was a fit object for their wrath, they raised a wild yell and set off in chase. Seeing that he was pursued, the Indian spurred his horse, but finding himself in danger of being overtaken, leaped from the saddle and commenced running at the top of his speed. The path being rocky and difficult he might have escaped but for Major McKinney, who rode a better animal than his followers, and who finally overtook the fugitive. Finding himself at bay, the Indian turned and fitted an arrow to his bow. Then as the major discharged the contents of his gun into his body, the wounded and dying man sent his arrow up to the feather into the breast of his assailant. Major McKinney died, and his friends gave him a costly and imposing funeral. It is certainly true that he need not have lost his life, for the Indian who killed him did not belong to a hostile tribe, and was pursuing his journey peaceably when attacked. However, an Indian war was in progress, and it was vital that Indian scalps had to be procured.

The other incident to which we alluded was the celebrated attack made by Colonel Rogers upon an Indian rancheria. At the head of a formidable body of eighty sturdy, well-armed men, he descended "like a wolf on the fold" upon an Indian village.

Having reconnoitered in the most approved method of Indian hostility, he stormed the rancheria—a comparatively easy enterprise, considering the fact that its only occupants were one feeble, old, blind woman, and four lank, hungry Indian dogs. The gallant colonel and his no less gallant band made short work of the blind woman and the dogs. They killed them all. And then, at the close of the day, they re-entered Kelsey in triumph, the blind woman's bleeding scalp dangling at the colonel's bridle bits, while the saddles of four of his men were decorated with *the scalps of the dogs.* It was in this manner that the Indian troubles of 1850 came to be called "Bill Rogers' Indian War."

But it must not be supposed that all the expeditions were as bloodless as this. On one occasion the whites attacked a rancheria when the Indians were at home, and a desperate fight ensued. It ended as such affairs almost always do, by demonstrating the superiority of gunpowder and bullets over bows and arrows.

The casualties that occurred in the ranks of the Americans were not numerous, but the bill afterwards presented for medical attendance amounted to twenty thousand dollars, of which the state paid fifteen thousand dollars, finally. This war, so barren of results, so abounding in a species of tragic burlesque, cost the state the princely sum of three hundred thousand dollars, and it has been conjectured that the *whole* of this sum was not expended in military operations against the Indians, or in providing for the wounded.[5]

Frontier life is full of such episodes, and too many of them reach the ears of the dwellers in cities after having been filtered through so many distorting mediums that their tenor is wholly changed. That prompt and repressive counter measures are needed in dealing with Indians cannot be denied. That these tribes have become miserably degraded is a patent fact. That they are treacherous and cruel when they think treachery and cruelty are safe, has been proved, over and over again. That they learn all the worst vices of the white man with wonderful proclivity, and lapse most easily into confirmed thieves, gamblers, drunkards, and loafers, every mining village in the state still testifies.[6] Granting

[5]On November 15, 1850, the governor cut Rogers' "El Dorado expedition" to 100 men and soon thereafter disbanded it. The short-lived conflict cost the state the sum of $72,600. *Journal of the California Legislature, 1851*, pp. 18, 734–35. One historical writer offers this judgment: "Whether, as a matter of fact, the expedition was justified by anything any Indians had done is a matter of doubt. Insofar as they killed whites, it seems likely that they had acted only in retaliation for murders committed against their own people. It was well-known that, among the whites of that region, there were men who boasted of the number of Indians they had killed and declared no redskin should escape them." Theodore H. Hittell, *History of California* (4 vols., San Francisco, 1898), 3:902.

[6]This is a stereotypical view of Indians prevalent at the time. For an understanding of his jaundiced view, see James J. Rawls, *Indians of California: The Changing Image* (Norman, OK, 1984).

all this: admitting all that can be argued from it, we still think that before their present lamentable condition is sweepingly attributed to original sin and innate depravity, justice requires some inquiry into the causes of their decay. And if it should be shown by such inquiry that white men taught them to be treacherous by breaking faith with them; taught them to be cruel by persecuting them; taught them to drink, to steal, to gamble, to loaf, by presenting before them, at every turn, white thieves, drunkards, gamblers, and loafers; taught them to be unchaste by outraging their women and offering a price for dishonor; and taught them to set little value upon human life by taking it, with knife, and pistol, and sudden hemp, in every creek and gulch and flat where mining camps existed; if, we say, these things shall appear to be so upon inquiry, it may seem right and proper to hesitate a little before pronouncing the Indian a forever accursed and reviled people.

XI

A Nightmarish Combination

W E HAVE alluded already to the rude hospitality that existed in those days. Happily it was sufficiently general to make its mark upon the time, though, unfortunately, it could not counteract or conceal the glaring blemishes of that peculiar social condition. Money was lavished on all sides then. Not only were the most extravagant prices charged for every commodity; not only were the services of professional men enormously high, but the miners themselves seemed to be determined to out-Herod Herod, and to cap the climax of the wildest extravagance by meeting all demands with a profuse recklessness that staggered the most extortionate.[1]

As one would expect, these traits were used by all who attempted to sketch the period, and thus the California miner of '49 and '50 has been handed down as a landsman's imitation of the traditional

---

[1] King Herod reigned in Palestine at the time of the birth of Christ. He was famed for his extravagant caprices, indulgences, and taste. For example, he married ten times; later in life, apparently insane, he executed three of his own sons. More importantly, fearful of the prophecy of the Messiah, he ordered the slaying of the innocents, which is recounted in the Gospel of St. Matthew, Chapter 2. *New Columbia Encyclopedia*, p. 1233.

(and theatrical) sailor. The fact that a good many of these miners were old sailors, who deserted their ships in San Francisco, and left them to rot at their moorings while they scampered off to the hills, and plunged into the excitement of gold hunting with all the abandon, ardor, and glee they would have displayed in entering upon a spree ashore after a long voyage, no doubt had much to do with the formation of this peculiar character—which, after all, was no fiction, but a far greater reality than the stage tar, as delineated in the familiar nautical melodrama. In truth, the mixture that produced this society was something the world never witnessed before. Take a sprinkling of sober-eyed, earnest, shrewd, energetic New England businessmen; mingle with them a number of rollicking sailors; a dark band of Australian convicts and cutthroats; a dash of Mexican and frontier desperadoes; a group of hardy backwoodsmen; some professional gamblers, whisky dealers, and general swindlers; then throw in a promiscuous crowd of broken down merchants, disappointed lovers, black sheep, unfledged dry goods clerks, and professional miners from all parts of the world. Now, stir up the mixture, season strongly with gold fever, bad liquors, faro, monte, rouge-et-noir, quarrels, oaths, pistols, knives, dancing and digging, and you have created something that reflected California society in the early days. Of course, in such a community every conceivable shade of human character was represented by turns,

Miners Weighing Their Gold
Courtesy The Huntington Library

and occasionally an instance occurred of a penuri-
ousness so opposed to the general lavish style that
prevailed, as to be worthy of remembrance and narration, if only because of the strong contrast it
formed. Such an instance came under the observation of Marshall in the summer of 1850. He was
then still at Coloma, and was in partnership with
Winters and Bagley, who kept a hotel not far from
the mill. A company of miners arrived in the neighborhood about this time, and located a claim, which
soon gave handsome returns. One of the party falling sick, his comrades applied to Marshall and Winters for accommodation for him, and they allowed
him to occupy an empty shanty belonging to them.
During his sickness, meals were sent to him from
the hotel, at the request of his friends. They also
secured the services of a medical man who was staying at Coloma. The patient grew worse and finally
died, and then his comrades went down to the mill,
borrowed some lumber and nails, and obtained the
services of one of the mill hands to make a coffin.
So far, they themselves had done nothing towards
arranging for the funeral, but they now condescend-
ed to dig a grave, and after the burial of the miner,
they sent a bill to Marshall and Winters, *charging
them three ounces for digging the grave.*

The receipt of such a document as this was what
Dick Swiveller called "an unmitigated staggerer."[2]

[2]Dick Swiveller is a jovial, highly likeable character in
Charles Dickens' novel, *The Old Curiosity Shop.*

Certainly, it was the last straw that broke the camel's back. But it was not ended, by any means, for while the partners were looking perplexedly at one another, the doctor stepped up and presented a little account for four hundred dollars, for attending upon the deceased. This acted as a restorative, and having promptly assured the doctor that he must look elsewhere for his fees, Marshall turned to Winters and exclaimed, "I'll bet an ounce (nobody ever wagered less at that time) that his board is charged to us too!"

The presentiment was well-founded, for on scanning the hotel books it appeared that the friends of the deceased miner had instructed the clerk to "charge it all to Marshall and Winters." It is, perhaps, unnecessary to say that they did not pay for the digging of the grave; but they were out and injured to the extent of the sick man's board and the materials and work on his coffin. The doctor failed to recover his bill, though the men were amply able to pay it, having struck rich diggings.

XII

Gold Field Justice

THE PECULIARITIES attending the administration of justice at this time have been alluded to previously, but as Marshall was eventually a serious sufferer from this cause, it may be well to enter into some details respecting the courts in early times. It must be understood that all courts were not lax in their practice and partial in their decisions. There were many honorable exceptions. But as a specimen of a not uncommon kind, the Tenth District Court, as it appeared in session at Coloma, in the summer of 1850, is worthy of description.

There existed, at this period, a general reluctance among the public to trust to litigation for the redress of injuries, and even in criminal cases, men could not be persuaded to come forward and prefer charges. This unaccountable apathy is referred to in the report of a Grand Jury to the District Court at Coloma, the original of which may be found at page one hundred and two, book A, the minutes of that court. The following extract will convey some idea of the situation:

"Our action has been embarrassed by an inability to obtain the attendance of witnesses in criminal suits, and an apathy on the part of the people to come forward and prefer charges for investigation. We are unable to account for this indifference, unless we attribute it to the transient character of the citizens and their unwillingness to abandon their daily pursuits, or to their want of confidence in the officers of the law and the certainty of public justice being administered. We cannot but think that the charge recently made of the impotency of the laws is unjust in its bearing. That lies with the people, and not with the government."

The last sentence is not a little obscure, nor did the grand jury make it appear very satisfactorily in what particular the charge made was unjust. But it appears clear enough that at this time the people, from *whatever* cause, were strongly opposed to litigation, and that even in criminal cases they were inclined to "rather bear the ills they had, than fly to others that they knew not of." Whether this suspicion of the purity of the courts was well-founded or not will perhaps appear from what we are about to relate, and as every report here presented is drawn directly from the records of the court itself, no question can be raised as to the soundness of the premises, whoever may dissent from the conclusions drawn.

Marshall, we have said, became involved in litigation, and his partners did not escape. It was natural that he should desire to protect his acquired rights to the land which he legally claimed as an original settler, and that he should dispute the authority of strangers to seize and possess themselves of his property, to appropriate his cattle and horses, and to damage and destroy his improvements. Unfortunately for him, however, a great many people in Coloma were interested in defeating his rights. They had squatted on his land and were disposed to keep it. They had interests in common and all their interests were opposed to his. They wielded a large influence in the neighborhood and he was in a minority of one. Colonel William Rogers was then sheriff of the county—he who was the hero of the Indian War. Judge J. S. Thomas occupied the District Bench.[1] What kind of a lawyer he was may be gathered from the fact that he habitually adjourned his court until "tomorrow," never naming the day of the week or month. In a transcript of the minutes of the court now before us, occurs this phrase over and over again: "Ordered, the court adjourned until tomorrow morning, at eight o'clock." Sometimes it stands "tomorrow morning at A.M.," the hour being omitted. Now, if our readers will follow the subjoined record of certain cases tried in this court, they may be enabled better to comprehend why the people were so reluctant to "come forward" and appeal to the legal tribunals for redress.

[1] Judge James S. Thomas of the District Court of El Dorado County was appointed to that post in 1850 when the state legislature passed an act creating nine district courts. The year previous, Thomas tried the first civil suit before a jury of six in Sacramento where he had been appointed to the bench on September 21, 1849. He opened his district court on May 6, 1850, and by October the court docket had a total of 450 civil cases to adjudicate. Bancroft, *California*, VI: 313-14 *note*, 347, 454-55; VII: 192 *note*.

On Wednesday morning, June 5th, 1850, Judge Thomas opened his court as usual, and after disposing of one or two brief cases, came upon a suit in which Marshall and his partners were involved.

ALDEN S. BAGLEY, J. W. MARSHALL
AND WINTERS v. TUNIS V. MOUNT

On motion a jury to be summoned to try this cause. Therefore it is ordered by the court, that the clerk issue a *venire* for the jury. Now comes the sheriff and returned into court the following jurors, to wit: (Here follow the names.) And after being duly sworn, and the arguments of counsel, they retired to their room, and made up and returned into court with the verdict awarding the defendant the sum of three hundred and fifty dollars and ten cents, and plaintiff to pay the costs for each juror. It is therefore ordered by the court that judgment must go *against* the defendant for the like sum.[2]

Such an outcome will probably surprise the reader. After the jury has returned a verdict *for* the defendant, the judge orders the clerk to record a judgment *against* the defendant, "for the like sum." But astounding and bewildering as the above must be to those who happen to be unfamiliar with the "winding ways" of justice in 1850, the disposal of the next case on the docket is far more extraordinary. This was an action to recover a debt, the plaintiff being Marshall's own partner, Winters. The minutes

[2]"There is no record of execution in the case ... They must have paid him but it is not a matter of record." Gay, *Marshall*, p. 276.

of the court bear the following record of the case:

JOHN WINTERS ET AL V. ARNOLD THEILHOVER.

On motion of counsel, it is ordered by the court that a *venire* be issued to the coroner to call a jury of six good and discreet electors to serve as jurors to try this cause. Now comes the coroner and returns into court the following jurors: (Here follow the names.) On motion of plaintiffs' attorney for leave to withdraw his account that was assigned to them, motion sustained. It was, therefore, ordered by the court that leave be granted, and after the jury being duly sworn and the cause submitted to them, after hearing the evidence in the cause, retired to their room, made up their verdict for plaintiff for the total sum of two thousand and fifty-nine dollars and seventy-five cents. It is ordered by the court that judgment go against the plaintiff for a like sum. It is further ordered that the jurors be given three dollars each.[3]

There are two remarkable points in the above case. First, the plaintiff having withdrawn the account, that is, the evidence of the debt, the case is sent to the jury. Second, the jury having found a verdict for the plaintiff, the court orders a judgment to be recorded against him. Thus, a man sues for the recovery of a debt, and obtains a verdict for the amount claimed. Upon which the court decides that the plaintiff creditor must pay to the debtor the sum due from the latter. There is a defiance of law, justice, equity, and common sense, about this decision, that approaches the sublime. The consummate

[3]In this case "execution was issued June 11 and delivered ... on June 17th." *Ibid.*, pp. 276, 492, *note* 24.

coolness with which this judge sets aside juries, shelves their verdicts, and decrees the exact opposite of their conclusion, is actually wonderful. Of course, under such a system litigants became cautious—not to avoid going to law, but to make sure of the judge before they entered court. The term "Justice" ceased to apply to many of these tribunals, and though we have dealt only with the administration of the law in one district, it is not to be supposed that others escaped any better. It would be easy to multiply instances of the recklessness, ignorance, venality, and indifference of some of the justices and judges in those days. In one case that occurred at Placerville, where a miner was charged with assaulting a man who had endeavored to jump his claim, the trial was commenced at eleven o'clock at night, and the labors of all present were lightened by the magnanimous conduct of the judge, who adjourned the court every ten minutes or so, to get a drink. On these occasions His Honor, together with sheriff, deputies, prosecutor, counsel, prisoner, witnesses and jury, swarmed out together and cheerfully fraternized at the bar of one of the neighboring saloons. A constant recourse to these semi-occasional refreshments resulted, as might have been expected, in the complete demoralization of the court, and about five o'clock in the morning, a drunken lawyer addressed a drunken jury on behalf of a drunken prosecutor and an equally drunken defendant; and an intoxicated judge having deliv-

ered an inebriated charge, a fuddled verdict of ac-
quittal was rendered. Upon this His Honor reeled
off the bench, and approaching the defendant, congratulated him warmly on the issue, and ended by
expressing a fervent hope that he had "hit the prosecutor an awful lick."

On another occasion, when an attempt had been
made to jump a claim, a justice of the peace issued
injunction after injunction, restraining the lawful
owners from working their ground, and, as they
paid no attention to his edicts, he fined them again
and again. But there is a good deal of difference between levying a fine and collecting it, for, when the
sheriff appeared on the ground to enforce the order
of the court, he was met by so grim an array of revolvers that he deemed it impolitic to proceed further. Finally, the owner of the claim appeared in
court and told the justice he had better withdraw
the injunctions and remit the fines or there might
be trouble, upon which the justice seeing the force
of this suggestion, courteously acceded to it, and so
the matter ended.

Probably these few examples will be sufficient
to prove that weak or poor suitors had very little
chance of obtaining justice in such courts, and so
Marshall found. Nobody had time, however, to be-
stow a thought upon the evils of the system, or if
they had time they lacked inclination. Time passed
on and brought him no redress. The first residents
near Coloma prospected, gambled, and drank, and

soon departed. Many sold their land to newcomers, and thus Marshall's title was buried deep under fresh deeds, and swept, as it were, out of sight.

His life, from this time on was the life of a hard working miner, seldom successful. He entered one enterprise after another, and though at times making a few hundred dollars, never reinstating himself in his former condition. He retained a small ranch at Coloma—a little patch barely sufficient to supply him with a poor resting place for his old age. Attempts have been made at different times to induce the state to award him a pension, but without success. Slander has often busied itself with his name, and innumerable false statements concerning him and his habits have crept, from time to time, into the press. He has been accused of drunkenness. He has been announced as insane. He has been prematurely killed two or three times. Worthless men have on several occasions assumed his name as a bait for sympathy, and having imposed upon the charitable and been detected, their faults have been shouldered upon him. Those who know him best, however, know that he is neither a drunkard, a lunatic, nor a beggar. Rather, he is full of energy and life, and possesses a memory absolutely wonderful for its capacious retentiveness. He works hard for his living, and is respected through all the country. That he has foibles it would be folly to deny, but that he has any foibles which should alienate from him the sympathy of any good man, or bar his claim to the gratitude and kindly remembrance of all Californians, would be base calumny to assert. The state has recognized the claims of Sutter, but it has ignored the claims of Marshall. Yet the latter was the discoverer of gold in California and is poor. The former only availed himself of the revelation already made, and he is not poor.[4]

It is right and fair that in estimating his title to consideration we should take into account the grand results of his discovery. Gold made California what it is. It built up San Francisco. It erected Sacramento. It placed steamers on the rivers; it brought shipping to the wharves; it filled the cellars of the banks; it created a commerce; it brought population; it developed resources; it brought about internal improvements; it built churches, schools, and

[4]This was hardly the case. Sutter was very hard pressed. He was cheated right and left in Sacramento of his land, of his property and money in trying to defend himself. The last straw was when his Hock Farm on the Feather River was attached for taxes, then burned to the ground in 1865 by a disgruntled employee. He then moved to Washington, D.C. to seek compensation from the Congress. In the meantime, after two failed attempts in the state legislature, a pension bill was finally passed and signed by the governor on April 4, 1864, providing Sutter with $250 a month. The appropriation was renewed three times, but after 1874 no more. The tangled efforts to receive financial reimbursement from Congress for his former land holdings also came to naught. When it appeared prospects had brightened in 1880 only to fail again, the old pioneer, now age seventy-six, could take no more. He collapsed and died June 18, 1880. Allan R. Ottley, ed., *John A. Sutter's Last Days: The Bidwell Letters* (Sacramento, 1986), pp. 4–8.

hospitals. It established a press; it provided education, enlightenment, wealth, prosperity, and happiness. And the man who discovered this wonderful agent sits in his little cabin at Kelsey, up in the mountains, and toils as he toiled two and twenty years ago, glad if he can secure sufficient for the passing hour.

The history of California has not yet been written in detail, but when it is we trust the historian will not have to record that James Marshall, the discoverer of gold, the founder of the state's prosperity, was permitted to sink into a pauper's grave by the people to whom he gave all that they possess.

Editor's Epilogue

MARSHALL'S fame as the discoverer of gold in California was firmly recognized by his contemporaries, both in word and print.[1] Interestingly, it became his lifetime mission to make sure that no one else received the credit due solely to him. However, ironic as it was, he never made a major gold strike, not that he did not try.

By 1857 Marshall began a none too subtle campaign to try to influence the governor and legislature to grant him a lifetime pension to honor and reward his discovery which had brought about so many extraordinary changes in the Golden State. In a rebuff to journalist James M. Hutchings, who was doing a story on his life, Marshall made the point that the profits derived from his discovery netted the nation $600 million, while for himself, "$000,000,000." What really galled Marshall was that Edward Hargraves, an Australian argonaut, who had worked in the mines in 1849, returned to New South Wales the following year and discovered gold there. With little opposition the British

---

[1] As in the Prologue, all biographical details which follow have been drawn from Theresa Gay's thorough biography on Marshall's life.

government rewarded him with "the princely sum of £5,000 (or $25,000), and the Australian government £10,000 (or $50,000), making $75,000." As for Marshall, "his reward from the United States government is, alas! what? Nothing."[2]

Turning from mining, having lost all of his property and the fact that no one would employ him, Marshall took up land near Coloma and planted a vineyard. By 1860 it was producing a goodly crop of various grape varieties. When the harvest became sufficient, he started producing wine, then brandy, both reputedly of good quality. At the same time, a few carpentering jobs came his way. Marshall's reputation as a vineyardist earned him an honorary membership in the California State Agricultural Society in 1866. However, within a few years, due to high taxes levied on wine and brandy producers, along with increased grape-growing competition, Marshall's operation ceased to be profitable. With no recourse, he returned to mining.

It was at this juncture that one of his former partners in a quartz gold mine venture, William Burke, began to develop the idea of a lecture tour where Marshall would describe how he discovered gold and other related events. He made his debut performance in Grass Valley, California on the evening of

---

[2]Marshall to Hutchings, Coloma, September 4, 1857, quoted in Gay, *Marshall*, pp. 317–18. The amount given is incorrect. Hargraves received only £10,000 from the Legislative Council of New South Wales. *Ibid.*, p. 498, *note* 7.

April 17, 1870.[3] A small audience heard a poor, in-experienced speaker whose fluency had never been an attribute. In short, Marshall's career as a lecturer was short-lived. Burke, however had yet another idea—he would persuade George Frederic Parsons, then editor of the Sacramento *Record*, to write Marshall's autobiography. At the outset, Burke gathered basic data from Marshall and then passed it on to Parsons. Later, Parsons interviewed Marshall on a number of occasions to amplify and clarify certain aspects of his life.

The book was available in either late August or early September 1870. Marshall himself distributed a copy to the Sacramento paper which commented on it favorably. He then went to San Francisco to consult a doctor for he was in precarious health. While there, he presented copies to the *Alta California* and *Examiner*, and by mid-September he had returned to Sacramento to sell copies of his book at the State Fair.

With the publication of Marshall's book, Burke developed the idea of a book and lecture tour in the East. Lacking sufficient resources, Marshall asked Leland Stanford, president of Central Pacific Railroad Company and an acquaintance, for free passes, which were readily obtained. Lectures were given in Salt Lake City, Denver, and Kansas City between September 9 and mid-October 1871. In each city,

[3]Grass Valley *Union*, April 16, 1870, p. 3, cl. 1; April 17, 1870, p. 2, cls. 2–3.

Marshall took a copy of his book to the principal newspaper and requested an interview to publicize his forthcoming platform appearance. But it came to little avail. The book failed to attract buyers, and the lectures were sparsely attended. By Kansas City, Marshall abandoned the remaining stops on the lecture circuit and journeyed to Lambertville to spend the winter with his family. It would be his only visit.

Following Marshall's return to California there was a groundswell of support for a state pension. The first such effort had been brought forth in the legislature in March 1860, but died in committee. The second attempt in 1870 was a direct result from the newspaper commentary provoked by Marshall's abortive lecture tour. Partially due to the fact that a parallel bill was being considered for Sutter, the one for Marshall, modified to provide $100 a month for two years, was passed. However, the governor approved the Sutter measure, but pocket-vetoed the one for Marshall. Many newspapers berated the state for failure to provide for him as they had done for Sutter. The Santa Clara *News* waxed eloquent on that subject. One of Marshall's early California friends responded with a letter to the San Jose *Mercury*, sadly noting "that his lecture tour proved a failure for the reason that he is an aged and extremely illiterate man, utterly incapable of pleasing popular fancy." However, he was "a good, simpleminded, honest soul . . . and should receive from every citizen the charity and forebearance due to age and true merit."[4]

Another pension effort was quickly mounted, led by the Sacramento Society of California Pioneers. At the next legislative session, it was proposed to provide Marshall with a pension of $200 a month for two years. In the debates over the provision it is quite clear that many members had read Marshall's story and it had the desired effect. The bill was passed by a large majority, and Governor Newton Booth approved the measure on February 2, 1872. However, when the appropriation ceased, a renewal was introduced to a decidedly hostile legislature. Marshall's pension was renewed but only for $100 a month for two years. On March 3, 1874, Governor Booth again gave his assent. Like success attended the next renewal effort when it became law on April 1, 1876. However, that was the last relief measure to be enacted. From 1878 until 1885 every pension bill introduced thereafter failed to pass. The reason probably concerned Marshall's handling of his money, reputedly appearing drunk in the Assembly to lobby at the 1878 session, whereupon he dropped and shattered a bottle of brandy. That year, the pension measure that failed passage only provided $50 a month, a reflection of the legislators' disapproval for Marshall's lifestyle.

On his return from his family visit to New Jersey,

[4]Letter of William Swasey to the Editor, San Jose *Mercury*, April 28, 1870 excerpted in Gay, *Marshall.*, pp. 350–51.

Marshall once again resumed his permanent residence in the little town of Kelsey, occupying the former Burke house, which he now owned. He vainly continued to work his small mining property with little positive results; it was more a way of life than a livelihood. His state pension certainly eased his plight while it lasted, even though he was imprudent with his limited funds. In addition, litigation concerning title to his mining and household properties proved an added financial burden and drained his meager resources. With the cessation of his state pension, Marshall was well on the road to destitution. Infrequent carpentering jobs provided much needed dollars. His Kelsey neighbors saw to it that he did not go without food. They provided him with hot meals and basic groceries. Perhaps as a way of compensation, in the dimming twilight of his life, he was honored at several special events, especially on California Admission Day when he would be invited to participate in a celebratory parade, or at an early California pioneer's gathering. Thus, a few rays of adulation warmed his declining years and brightened his poverty-stricken existence.

Marshall's health during the last decade and half of his life was fragile, to say the least. He suffered from a variety of illnesses common to the aged, and for which little could be done, medically speaking. Like many others, he wishfully turned to folk remedies to ease his aches and pains and consulted a doctor when he could afford it. His long habit of chewing tobacco and his heavy drinking, common to many old miners, both took their toll on his once robust constitution. It is a wonder he lived to reach the venerable age of seventy-five. Death claimed him on the morning of August 10, 1885. The coroner's jury rendered the verdict—"death from natural causes." The county coroner found $3.60 in Marshall's purse. When probate was complete, his meager estate netted $218.22. With no next of kin on hand to claim his remains, his neighbors decided to bury him on a hilltop overlooking the gold discovery site at Coloma.

Marshall's life had come full circle. His fame was assured: Marshall and Coloma were now one.

The Yankee humorist Josh Billings (pseudonym for Henry W. Shaw) while on a lecture tour met Marshall in Placerville during the winter of 1874. Although his crazy-spelled account of their brief meeting is hardly flattering, he may well have left the perfect epitaph:

Who kan ever compute the splendid fortunes,
the ruined hopes, the intrinsik values, and the
countless woes this vagrant opened to the world?[5]

[5]Quoted in *ibid.*, p. 384.

2

Six Months
in the
Gold Mines

by
Edward Gould Buffum

Going Into It

Making Something

Going Out of It

The Mining Business
Courtesy The Huntington Library

182

Editor's Prologue

LIKE JAMES WILSON MARSHALL, Edward Gould Buffum has earned fame through a single act, the publication of his book which follows. Buffum's life can be fairly well chronicled from the time of his 1846 enlistment in the New York Volunteers until his death at age forty-five, though there are blanks here and there. His biography is like a jigsaw puzzle, made of bits and pieces with some parts missing. His life story thus remains sketchy at best.

We do know that Buffum was the descendant of generations of New England Quakers. The founder of the family, Robert Buffum, immigrated from England to Salem, Massachusetts in 1632. Quakers were known for their staunch adherence to principle and non-compliance to higher authority if it meant a breach of their beliefs. Thus, Robert Buffum's daughter, Deborah, was tied to a cart and publicly whipped for criticizing the local government. A son was imprisoned for a short time, then banished from Salem for voicing his Quaker views. Later, a grandson settled in Rhode Island where he became a prosperous farmer, miller, and cloth manufacturer. His grandson, a famed jurist, won a small niche in history by declining an appointment to the

Rhode Island State Supreme Court because he refused to render a death sentence.[1]

Edward Gould Buffum's father, Arnold (1782–1859), was of like tradition. As a business man, he was very successful as a hat manufacturer. He was also an inventor and had several patents registered in his name. However, he garnered attention for his staunch abolitionist views. He became the first president of the New England Anti-Slavery Society when it was established in 1832. For a time he edited the *Protectionist* in New Garden (now Fountain City), Indiana. He was also a pioneer in early childhood education, an ardent supporter of temperance, and had an active interest in literature.[2]

Edward's sister, Elizabeth, like her father, was not only a dedicated abolitionist, but a militant one. She and her husband, Samuel B. Chace, labored in giving assistance to fugitive slaves who ran away from the bondage of slavery. They were in charge of an Underground Railway station in Valley Falls, Rhode Island, that helped slaves during their flight to freedom in the North and Canada. Because the Quakers were indifferent to the abolition of slavery, Elizabeth and her husband left the fellowship. An

[1] Lillie B. C. Wyman and Arthur C. Wyman, *Elizabeth Buffum Chace, 1806–1899; Her Life and Its Environment* (2 vols., Boston, 1914), I: 3–12.

[2] John G. E. Hopkins, ed., *Concise Dictionary of American Biography* (New York, 1964), p. 121; Allen Johnson and Dumas Malone, eds., *The Dictionary of American Biography* (21 vols., New York, 1928–37), III: 241–42.

extraordinary woman, she was one of the early cru-
saders for women's rights and suffrage as well as an
advocate for temperance and humane penal reform.[3]

Ample evidence underscores the fact that the
Buffums were a deeply religious family, one actively
concerned with the betterment of mankind. They
also prized education and learning. Into this milieu
was born Edward Gould Buffum, the second son of
Arnold and Rebecca Buffum. It was a large family,
five daughters and two sons. Edward was born in
1822 in Springfield, Rhode Island, the exact date
unknown.[4] He received a solid Quaker-school education, but little is known of his boyhood and early
teen years. However, in 1839, he struck out on his
own and went to New York City where he found
employment with William James Bennett's New
York *Herald*. Bennett had founded the penny-a-
day newspaper in 1835, and it became an instant
success because of its thorough as well as enter-
taining reporting. Buffum could not have had a better teacher than Bennett, who was America's first
great editor/publisher.[5] Journalism would be the
young man's profession for the rest of his life,

[3] *Ibid.*, p. 584; Edward T. James, ed., *Notable American Women: A Biography Dictionary* (3 vols., Cambridge, MA, 1971), I: 317–19.

[4] Wyman and Wyman, *Elizabeth Buffum Chace*, I: 7.

[5] Hopkins, *Concise Dictionary of American Biography*, pp. 67–68. The paper still survives in the form of an overseas edition published in conjunction with the Washington *Post* out of Paris, France.

other than the two years he served in the California part of the Mexican War.

On May 13, 1846, the day war was declared, Secretary of War William L. Marcy, with the approval of President Polk, sent a requisition to the Union-aligned states for the recruitment of 50,000 volunteers to serve in the military forces as authorized by Congress. New York State was asked to enroll seven regiments of infantry, totaling some 5,500 men. Governor Silas Wright complied on May 28 and commanded his adjutant general in the state militia to enroll the requested seven regiments by June 15, which proved unrealistic. The governor's general order was printed in the New York City newspapers on May 29 and 30. Apparently like his sister, Buffum had severed his Quaker connection for he came forward to volunteer in response to the appeal. He was elected a second lieutenant in Company B, Seventh Regiment (later renamed the First) New York Volunteers, under the command of Colonel Jonathan D. Stevenson.[6]

Either prior to or shortly after his enlistment, Gould Buffum became engaged to a young New York City resident, Harriet Crowinshield. Unhappily, "she died while he was in California."[7]

On August 1, the regiment with a full complement was mustered into service and posted to Fort

[6]Donald C. Biggs, *Conquer and Colonize: Stevenson's Regiment and California* (San Rafael, CA, 1977), pp. 23–29.

[7]Wyman and Wyman, *Elizabeth Buffum Chace*, I: 100.

Columbus, on Governors Island. By September 24, the regiment was put aboard three ships which would carry them to California. Buffum was aboard the *Thomas H. Perkins* as was Colonel Stevenson.

After a five-month voyage, the *Perkins* was the first vessel of the flotilla to reach San Francisco, dropping anchor on March 6, 1847. The other two ships arrived on March 20 and 22. Shortly after, Company B along with Companies A and F, under command of Lieutenant Colonel Henry S. Burton, were ordered to Santa Barbara where they were posted for occupation duty.[8]

Meanwhile, on January 11, 1847, Secretary of War Marcy pointed out in a dispatch to General Stephen W. Kearny, commander of the United States forces in California, that the government was interested in acquiring both Upper and Lower California. Aware now that Washington desired the conquest of Lower California and with assurances that Upper California was safe from attack, Kearny informed Commodore James Biddle, the naval squadron commander: "I am now prepared to send two companies of New York Volunteers (about 120) now at Santa Barbara if you will furnish a vessel to transport them and remain with or near them."[9]

Now, with Biddle's cooperation secured, Kearny

[8]Biggs *Conquer and Colonize*, pp. 40–42, 74, 93, 96.
[9]Clarke, *Kearny*, p. 318; Kearny to Burton, Monterey, CA, May 30, 1847, House of Representatives, *Executive Document No. 17*, Serial 539, 30th Congress, 2d Session, (Washington, D.C., 1850), p. 245.

ordered Lieutenant Colonel Burton to embark A and B companies for La Paz and San Jose del Cabo in Lower California.[10]

Upon wading ashore at La Paz, Buffum wrote: "I was much ... surprised ... to find the prettiest town I had seen in California. The streets were lined with willow trees, which, meeting overhead, formed an arch, afforded one a delicious shade at midday. The houses were of *adobe*, plastered white, and thatched with the leaves of the palm tree, and were most delightfully cool. The whole beach was lined with palms, date, fig, tamarind, and coconut trees, their delicious fruits hanging upon them in large clusters."

Because "no American force had ever been stationed at La Paz, the inhabitants appeared much pleased" at the Americans' arrival, and manifested no hostility toward them. Under orders "to take possession and hold the country," the volunteers pitched their camp in the plaza, "previous to removing into a large barrack, which was not then completed." After the men had been "fairly barracked, the officers were allowed to live in rooms in the town and select such quarters as they chose." Buffum, for example, "lived in a style of Eastern luxuriance." It proved a once-in-a-lifetime experience, a style of life that possessed "greater per-

[10]Colonel R[ichard] B. Mason to Burton, June 1; Mason to Brigadier General R[oger] Jones, July 21, 1847, *Ibid.*, pp. 324–31.

fection" than he had ever known before or later.[11]

To the north, in and around Mulegé, however, a storm was gathering. Don Manuel Pineda, a captain in the Mexican army, supported by a band of officers and supplies from Guaymas, arrived in late September and began to recruit and organize *Bajacalifornios* to mount resistance to the "neutrality" and "compliance" by Governor Francisco Palacios Miranda to United States' authority. Hostilities broke out in mid-October at Mulegé and San Jose del Cabo. The American garrison at La Paz, 112 strong, was attacked by Pineda's 200-man brigade on November 16. Thrown back, he made another strong assault on November 27, but again was repulsed. Buffum's command faced the enemy "very coolly, and returned their fire with great effect."[12]

Skirmishes and hostile encounters continued to plague the occupation forces. Additional numbers from the New York Volunteers reached La Paz on March 20. Now with his command greatly strengthened to include "217 officers and men," Lieutenant Colonel Burton took to the field on March 26 intent on crushing Pineda once and for all. The following day Pineda was peacefully captured at the village of San Antonio where he had unwittingly lingered too long.

[11] E. Gould Buffum, *Six Months in the Gold Mines*, ed. by John W. Caughey (Los Angeles, 1959), pp. 132–33.
[12] Doyce B. Nunis, Jr., ed., *The Mexican War in Baja California* ... (Los Angeles, 1977), pp. 28–33, 43–44, 167–98.

Pressing on, the American force completely routed the Mexicans in a final showdown at the Battle of Todos Santos on March 30. Hostilities in Baja California were ended. Buffum, however, took no active part in these last military efforts to conquer the peninsula. Ironically, these last endeavors were unnecessary. The Treaty of Guadalupe Hidalgo had been signed on February 2—peace had been restored. The war was over.[13]

On June 13, the American garrison received news of the definitive ratification of the treaty of peace. Because Baja California was to be returned to Mexico the orders were specific: prepare to evacuate troops. This was accomplished on August 31 at La Paz and at San Jose del Cabo on September 6. So ended the last phase of the Mexican War.[14]

Toward the end of his service in La Paz, Buffum ran into trouble. It appears he and a fellow officer were caught gambling with the enlisted men contrary to military regulations. Both were forthwith arrested and dispatched to Monterey under escort. Shortly after their arrival, Governor Mason ordered them to begin duty in Los Angeles on June 16. They reached their new post on July 5. Lieutenant

[13] *Ibid.*, pp. 48–53, 187–98. Also see Bauer, *Surfboats and Horse Marines*, pp. 205–20.

[14] Nunis, ed., *The Mexican War in Baja California*, pp. 59–60, 73; Mason to Commodore Thomas ap Catesby Jones, August 19; Lieutenant William T. Sherman to Commanding Officer, New York Volunteers, August 7, 1848, *Exec. Doc. No. 17*, pp. [5], 97, 633.

John M. Hollingworth, who had long been stationed in Los Angeles, confided to his diary the following day:

> Two officers arrived here from Monterey under arrest
> for gambling with soldiers. Col. Mason thought it best
> to release them and send them to this post to report
> to Col. S[hannon] for duty—until the proper witness-
> es arrived from La Paz. They are worthless fellows.[15]

Buffum and his cohort lucked out. They did not
have to face a court-martial. When Governor Mason
received news of the definitive ratification of the
peace treaty with Mexico, August 6, he ordered the
discharge of all New York Volunteers on August 21.
By mid-September, Buffum once again became a civilian.[16] Already keenly aware of the gold rush and
with his severance pay in his pocket, he headed for
the mines like other ex-volunteers. On October 18,
he reached San Francisco, his land journey taking
almost a month. After procuring some supplies and
clothing, he was "in readiness to start for the *placers.*" He began his odyssey on October 25, 1848. It
is at this point that Buffum's *Six Months in the Gold
Mines* begins.

[15]Mason, Special Order 19, June 16, 1848, Office of the
Adjutant General of the United States, RG 94, Microfilm
182, Reel 1, National Archives, Washington, D.C.; "Journal
of John McHenry Hollingsworth, A Lieutenant in Stevenson's Regiment in California," *California Historical Society
Quarterly*, I (January, 1923), pp. 252–53.

[16]Company Muster-out Roll, October 23, 1848, and Special Order 27, August 21, 1848, RG 94, Microfilm 182, Reel
1, NA.

Author's Introduction

ON THE 26TH of September, 1846, the 1st Regiment of New York State Volunteers, under command of Colonel J. D. Stevenson, sailed from New York harbour under orders from the Secretary of War to proceed at once to Upper California. The objects and operations of the expedition, and the fitting out of which created some sensation, are now too well understood and appreciated to require further explanation.[1] This regiment, in which I had

[1] United States involvement in the War with Mexico provoked a political fire storm throughout the nation, which was reflected in the bitter debates over the declaration of war in the Congress and later. President James K. Polk justified his request on the grounds that Mexican troops had spilled American blood on American soil in the lower Rio Grande Valley. Many Whigs, including freshman Congressman Abraham Lincoln, opposed that justification. The administration countered that the war was a defensive one. That argument carried the day in both Senate and House of Representatives. Later, as various documents were made public, including the appointment of Colonel Jonathan D. Stevenson (1800–94) to command the New York Volunteers, the Whigs increased their attack on the administration, charging that the war was not a defensive one at all, but a war for conquest of Mexican territory. The latter proved to be true. The complexity of the political issues surrounding the conflict are detailed in John H. Schroeder, *Mr. Polk's War: American Opposition and Dissent, 1846-1848* (Madison, Wisc., 1973).

the honour of holding a lieutenant's commission, numbered, rank and file, about seven hundred and twenty men, and sailed from New York in the ships *Loo Choo*, *Susan Drew*, and *Thomas H. Perkins*. After a passage of little more than five months, during which we spent several days pleasantly in Rio de Janeiro, the *Thomas H. Perkins* entered the harbour of San Francisco and dropped anchor off the site of the town, then called Yerba Buena, on the 6th day of March, 1847.[2]

Alta California we found to be in quiet possession of the American land and naval forces—the "Stars and Stripes" floating over the old Mexican *presidios*. There being no immediate service to perform, our regiment was posted in small detachments through the various towns.

The now-famous city of San Francisco, situated near the extreme end of a long and barren peninsular tract of land, which separates the Bay of San Francisco from the ocean, was almost a solitude, there being not more than twelve or fifteen rough houses, and a few temporary buildings for hides, to relieve the view. Where now stands the great commercial metropolis of the Pacific, its bustling streets alive with the hum of trade, were corrals for cattle and unoccupied sandy hills.

[2]The transport fleet of three ships reached San Francisco after a long, trying passage with the prospect of mutiny ripe among the recruits who were not used to the restrictive life at sea. Biggs, *Conquer and Colonize*, pp. 15-92.

San Francisco in 1846
Courtesy National Archives

Following the discovery of gold, a new era in the history of California commences. This event has already changed a comparative wilderness into a flourishing state, and is destined to affect the commercial and political relations of the world.

At the time of the discovery of the *placers*,[3] I was stationed at La Paz, Lower California, however I was soon ordered to Upper California and arrived at Monterey in the middle of June, 1848, about six weeks after the discovery had been made public. The most extravagant stories were then in circulation, but they were mostly viewed as the vagaries of a heated fancy by the good people of Monterey. I was ordered to the Pueblo de los Angeles for duty, and I arrived there on the fourth day of July, and remained with the detachment to which I was connected until it was disbanded, on the 18th day of September, 1848.[4] The day of our disbandment was hailed with joy such as a captive must feel on his

[3] *Placers* is Spanish in origin and refers to gold that has been eroded from rock, then "reduced to a loose condition that has permitted it to be transported and abraded by existing or prehistoric streams, which have finally deposited it on sandbars, in gravel banks, or in 'potholes' in the stream beds. Such gold has long been called '*placer gold*' by miners, and the deposits in which it is found are called '*placers*.'" Rodman M. Paul, *Mining Frontiers of the American West, 1848-1880* (New York, 1963), p. 6.

[4] On June 16, 1848, Colonel Richard B. Mason ordered Buffum to duty in Los Angeles, which he reached on the night of July 5. He was honorably discharged on August 21, 1848. Mason, Special Order 19, June 16, 1848, RG 94, NA; "Journal of. . . . Hollingsworth," p. 252.

release from slavery. For three long months we had anxiously awaited the event. The stories from the mines breathed the spirit of the Arabian tales, and visions of "big lumps" floated before our eyes. In three days *La Ciudad de los Angeles*[5] was deserted by its former occupants, and wagons and horses laden with tin pans, crowbars, iron pots, shovels, pork, and pickaxes, might have been seen on the road to the *placers*. On the 18th of October, I reached San Francisco, where a curious state of things was presented. Gold dust and coin were as plentiful as the seashore sands, and seemed to be thought about as valuable. The town had but little improved since I first saw it, as upon the discovery of the mines it had been nearly deserted by its inhabitants. Real estate had been slowly depreciating for several months, and the idea of San Francisco being a large city within two years had not yet been broached. Merchandise of all descriptions was exceedingly high. Flour was selling at $50 per barrel; dried beef 50 cents per pound; coffee 50 cents; shovels $10 each; tin pans $5; crowbars $10; red flannel shirts $5; common striped shirts $5; common boots $16 per pair; and everything else in proportion. I made a few purchases and held myself in readiness to start for the *placers*.

[5] The Pueblo of Los Angeles was established September 4, 1781. On May 25, 1835, the Mexican Congress raised it to the status of a city (*ciudad*).

I

On to the Mines

Armed with a pickaxe, shovel, hoe, and rifle, and accoutred in a bright flannel shirt, corduroy pants, and heavy boots, and accompanied by two friends, I found myself, on the afternoon of the 25th of October, 1848, wending my way to the only wharf in San Francisco, to take passage for the golden hills of the Sierra Nevada. The scenes that for days had met my eyes, and even as I was stepping on board the launch, might have dampened the ardour of a more adventurous man. Whole launch-loads of miserable victims of fever and ague were arriving daily from the mining region—sallow, weak, emaciated and dispirited—but I had nerved myself for the combat, and doubt not that I would have taken passage when I did and as I did, had the archenemy of mankind himself stood helmsman on the little craft that was to bear me to El Dorado. We had engaged and paid our passage, and such was our eagerness to get a conveyance of some kind, that we had not even looked at the frail bark in which we were to entrust our now more than ever before valuable bodies.

The *Ann* was a little launch of about ten tons, a mere ship's boat, entirely open, filled with barrels and merchandise of every kind, and eight human beings, who, besides ourselves, had taken passage in her. I looked closely at her—there was not room upon her deckless hull to stow a brandy bottle securely. We tried to reason the captain into an idea of the danger of proceeding with so much freight, but the only reply he gave us was, that "he received four dollars a hundred for it." There was no alternative, so in we jumped, and about dusk the boat was under way, and scudding with a fair wind across the Bay of San Francisco.

There was, of course, no room to cook on board, and there was no galley or furnace to cook in; and, indeed, there was nothing to cook, as in our hurry we had neglected to make purchases of any necessary articles of food, and expected to be furnished with our meals among the other accommodations of our boat. The captain generously offered us some cheese and crackers, and after regaling ourselves on these, we commenced instituting a search for sleeping places. It was dark by this time, and black clouds were sweeping over the sky. The wind had changed, and we were beating off and on Angel Island, while the spray was dashing over our boat's sides, which were nearly level with the water from her great load. It augured anything but a pleasant night, and here were eleven of us, with a prospect of rain and spray, forced to find some means of sleeping on the pile of barrels or boxes that loaded the boat or pass a night of sleeplessness.

Sharper-sighted than my companions, I had spied out a box of goods lying aft that rose above the mingled mass around it, and upon which, by doubling myself into a most unnatural and ungentlemanly position, I could repose the upper portion of my body, while my heels rested on the chines of a pork barrel at an angle of about forty-five degrees above my head. With a selfishness peculiar to the human race, I appropriated the whole of this couch to myself, and was already in the land of dreams with bright visions of "big lumps" and bigger piles of gold flitting before my spiritual eyes when I felt myself roughly shaken, and awaking, found Higgins, one of my companions, standing at my side, who coolly informed me that "my time was up, and it was now his turn." It seems that during my absence in the visionary world, a council had been held by all hands in which it was gravely decided and resolved, *First*, "that there was no other feasible sleeping place than the box then occupied by me;" *Secondly*, "that it was contrary to the laws of all human society, that one man should appropriate to his own private and individual use *all* of this world's goods;" and *Thirdly*, "that for the next twenty-four hours, all hands should in rotation take a nap upon the box." When Higgins woke me, the raindrops were pattering upon my *serape*, and half asleep I jumped up, and going forward, found a little place where I could half lie down; and in this manner, with the raindrops and surf dashing upon me, and every roll of the little boat threatening to cast me upon the waters, I passed that night on the Bay of San Francisco—a night which I shall never forget. My companions and fellow sufferers, when not occupying the box, were either catching an occasional wink in a perpendicular position or sitting upon the chines of a barrel, wishing with all their hearts for the arrival of daylight.

Morning came at length, as morning always will, even after the longest night, and the warm sun soon was shining upon us, and drying our wet clothing, and invigorating our dampened spirits. We had passed, during the night, out of the Bay of San Francisco into that of San Pablo. This bay is about ten miles in diameter, its form being nearly circular. Its entrance is about eight miles from the town of San Francisco, and is marked by two rocky islands known as the "Two Brothers," lying a few yards from each other and white with birdlime. The usual channel is on the left of these rocks. From the Bay of San Pablo we entered the Straits of Carquinez, which is about thirty-five miles from San Francisco, and at about noon, we were abreast of the town of Benicia.

The Straits of Carquinez are about one mile in width, and six in length, and connect the Bay of San Pablo with that of Suisun. Near the head of the straits and the entrance to Suisun Bay is placed the city of Benicia. This town was the first laid out among the new towns of California, and many

Early View of Benicia
Courtesy California State Library, Sacramento

months before the discovery of the mines gave a tremendous impetus to town making. Benicia seemed destined to become a great city, and perhaps rival San Francisco in point of commercial importance—possessing many advantages over it.[1] The banks are bold and steep, and sufficient depth of water is found here at all seasons for vessels to lie and discharge their cargoes directly at the bank; while at San Francisco, the tide only serves once in twenty-four hours, and even then all cargoes are obliged to be transported in launches and scows from the ships, which are forced to lie at some distance from the shore, in consequence of the broad flat in front of the town.

Leaving Benicia, we proceeded into the Bay of Suisun, and passing the delta of the San Joaquin, soon entered the magnificent Sacramento River, the Hudson of the western world. The lofty Palisades are not here; but to the lover of the picturesque and

[1] Carquinez Strait was named after the local Karquin Indians who lived in the vicinity. Mariano G. Vallejo and Robert Semple formed a partnership to build a new town on the north shore of the strait on December 23, 1846, tentatively naming it Francisca in honor of Vallejo's wife. On May 19, 1847, Vallejo transferred his interest in the proposed real estate development to Thomas O. Larkin. Hiring Jasper O'Farrell as their surveyor, the townsite was laid out, still using the name Francisca. However, on June 12 Semple restyled the townsite Benecia after another of Señora Vallejo's Christian names, and he made that official on June 19, 1847. Unfortunately, Buffum's prophecy failed to be realized; in no time San Francisco eclipsed the embryonic town. Gudde, *California Place Names*, pp. 26, 55.

beautiful, the tall oak groves, through which the deer, elk, and antelope are bounding, the golden hue of the landscape, the snowy peaks of the distant Sierra, the lofty Mount Diablo, and the calm, broad, and placid stream, present a scene upon the Sacramento River as enchanting as that which broke upon the enraptured vision of old Hendrick Hudson. At the entrance of the river, the land is low and somewhat marshy, being covered with a thick, rank growth of *tule*, a species of rush from which the Indians make baskets, chairs, and many little articles. On the left bank of the entrance to the Sacramento was the wonderous city of Montezuma, consisting of one unfinished house, through which the autumn winds were rattling. This is one of the paper towns laid out some three years before, but abandoned since the discovery of gold brought out more favourable points for location. The Sacramento here is about a mile in width; and to the right, rising up apparently from the end of the *tule* prairie, is the rugged peak of Monte Diablo (Devil's Mountain), four thousand feet in height. The low, alluvial bottom lands along the shore appear to be susceptible for the highest cultivation; and I doubt not, when the gold mania shall have partially ceased, the rich bottoms of the Sacramento will be clothed with well-groomed farmhouses, the abodes of happiness, peace, and plenty, and that the restful music of lowing herds will resound over its spreading prairies.

At the mouth of the river, there is very little timber; but in our progress upward we found the oak and the sycamore growing most luxuriantly. We "tied up" for the night about four miles from the entrance to the river. After building a large fire, we cooked some potatoes and pork which the captain generously furnished us. We then went to sleep around the campfire, and made good ere morning for our previous night's misery, and rested in complete disregard of the wolves and grizzly bears which abound in that region.

The next day, there being no wind, we were obliged to pull for it, and about dusk reached Hala-chum-muck, or, as it is now called, "Suisun," a city under that cognomen having been laid out here.[2] The "city" is on the left bank of the river, and about fifteen miles from its mouth on a bold, high bank and surrounded by a fine growth of oak timber. Hala-chum-muck is an old stopping place on the river; and finding the remains of a house, we "tied up." Then going on shore, and making a fire from the remnants of some boards which had been pulled from the roof of the house, we prepared another supper and slept on the ground, with a small piece of roof over our heads.

[2] The name Suisun first appears in an 1811 diary which refers to an "*estero de los Suisunes*," the name taken from the Indian tribe or village then located on the north shore. *Ibid.*, p. 324. Buffum offers in his narrative a new California place name, Hala-chum-muck, which is not recorded in the literature.

Hala-chum-muck derives its name from an Indian story connected with it. Many years ago, a party of hunters were encamped here for the night, and being attacked by Indians, after a brave resistance were all killed, with the exception of one, who, as he was escaping, was followed with a cry from the Indians of "Hala-chum-muck" (nothing to eat), probably, as he had been forced to throw down his rifle, signifying thereby that they would leave him to die of starvation. The spot has, ever since that time, borne the name of "Hala-chum-muck."

There were three families living here, with a stock of cattle, when the *placers* were discovered, and Hala-chum-muck was bidding fair to becoming a town; but on the reception of the golden news, they deserted their ranchos, and the crews of the launches which stopped here soon killed off the cattle and destroyed the dwellings.

We continued our progress up the river, occasionally stopping and amusing ourselves by firing the woods on either side, and watching the broad flames as they spread and crackled through the underbrush. On the night of the 30th, we hauled up at the rancho of Schwartz—an old German, of whom Bryant speaks as a man who has forgotten his own language, and never acquired any other. He is certainly the most curious specimen of humanity it was ever my lot to witness. He emigrated to California some ten years since, and obtained a grant of six leagues of land, extending along the Sacramento

River; and in the progress of time he will most probably be one of the richest landholders of California. He has built upon the bank of the river a little hut of *tule*, resembling a miserable Indian wigwam; and there he lives, a "manifest destiny" man, with "masterly inactivity" awaiting the march of civilization, and anticipating at some future day the sale of his lands for a princely fortune—a hope in which he will probably not be disappointed. His language is a mixture of his old mother German, English, Spanish, French, and Indian; and it would require an apter linguist than it was ever my good fortune to meet with, to comprehend his "lingua."[3]

I underwent an operation at Schwartz's rancho, that sealed my full connexion and communion with the region to which I was travelling. It was no less than an impromptu baptism in the golden waters of the Sacramento. We had built a fire on shore, and having purchased from Schwartz several pounds of beef at a gold digger's price, *i.e.*, one dollar per pound, had eaten our supper, when I started for the launch, which lay about ten yards from the shore, to get my blankets. The only conveyance was an old

[3] John L. Schwartz arrived with the Bidwell-Bartleson party in 1841. On the rancho property he established a fishing station and built a boat to travel on the Sacramento River and in the delta. Thus, he is frequently mentioned in the records at Sutter's Fort. He died in June 1852. Interestingly, Buffum's description is identical to Edwin Bryant's, *What I Saw in California: Being the Journal of a Tour . . . in the Years 1846, 1847* (New York, 1848), p. 345.

log canoe of Schwartz's; and seating myself in it, in company with one of my companions and an Indian boy he had brought with him, we pushed off. The Indian was seated in the canoe's bow, and was frightened by the oscillating motion given to it when it was first pushed off from the shore. To help balance the roll on one side, he leaned to the other to find an offsetting motion in that direction, he reversed his position, and leaning too far, upset the canoe. I, with heavy overcoat on, and rifle in hand, fell headlong into about fifteen feet of water. I dropped the rifle as though it were boiling lead, and quickly made for the best way to shore. All arrived safely on *terra firma*, and going on board alone in the canoe, I changed my clothing. Telling old Schwartz that I must encroach upon his hospitality, and drinking about a pint of some coloured New England rum, which he assured me was "de tres best clasa de brandy," I stretched my blankets on the mud floor of his wigwam, and awoke in the morning in good health and spirits. I soon engaged the services of a Kanakan to search for my rifle; and after he had brought it up, we got under way.[4]

[4]A Kanakan was a nickname for a Hawaiian Island native. The name Sacramento is derived from the Spanish name for "Holy Sacrament" and appears in 1817 as the name for the river which bore the name before the city was envisioned. In the fall of 1848, John A. Sutter, Jr., and Samuel Brannan, in spite of the displeasure from the senior Sutter, laid out a town at the *embarcadero* of Sutter's Fort, naming it after the river. It was not until 1854 that it became the state capital. Gudde, *California Place Names*, pp. 275–76.

After sleeping another night on the banks of the Sacramento, we reached the *embarcadero*,[5] at what is now Sacramento City, the evening of November 2d. The river here is about eight hundred feet wide.

The beautiful plain on which the thriving and populous city of Sacramento is now located was, when I first landed there, untenanted. There was not a house upon it, the only place of business being an old ship's store laid up upon its bank. Where now, after a lapse of only one year, a flourishing city with a population of twelve thousand stands, I pitched my tent on the edge of a broad prairie.

To complete the party with which we intended going to the mines, we were obliged to wait at the *embarcadero* for three of our disbanded soldiers, who had left the Pueblo de los Angeles about the time we did, and were coming by land through the Tulare valley.

We pitched our tent, cooked our provisions, and anxiously waited the arrival of the men, a prey to the greatest excitement—continually hearing as we did, the most extravagant stories from the mining region. The intense heat of the summer solstice had given way to autumn's cooling breezes, and parties were arriving daily at and leaving the *embarcadero*.

[5]The Spanish word *embarcadero* can be translated as wharf, quay, key, harbor or port. As used here, the word applied to a designated site where one usually took boat passage, in this case, at a site near Sutter's Fort at the confluence of the American and Sacramento Rivers.

II

A Prospecting Expedition

ON THE 7TH of November our party arrived. Their horses, of which they brought five, became jaded because of travel in the mountains, and it was not until the 16th that we were able to make a start. Being entirely ignorant of the best locality in which to proceed, and being all young, strong, and enthusiastic, we determined to strike out on a new path, and go on an exploring expedition in the mountains. It was our hope that fortune would throw our way the biggest of all lumps, and that we might possibly find the fountainhead of El Dorado, where, gushing from the heart of the great Sierra, a stream of molten gold should appear before our enraptured eyes.

Fortune, or rather misfortune, favoured us in this project. We were visited one evening by a man, who informed us that he had recently been on a "prospecting" expedition with a party of three others, and that after nearly reaching the fountainhead of gold, the party was attacked by Indians, and all, with the exception of himself, were killed. He told us the "prospect" was most favourable, and after learning the direction of the mountains in which he had been, we loaded two pack horses with hard bread and dried beef, and six of us started on the evening of November 16th on our quixotic expedition, leaving one with the remainder of our provisions and the tent at the *embarcadero*.

We crossed the Rio de los Americanos about a mile above Sutter's Fort, and, encamping upon its opposite bank, started on the morning of the 17th. The sky threatened a steady rainstorm; nothing daunted, however, we pushed on in the direction of the Bear River settlements, and about noon the sky's predictions were most fully realized. The rain fell in big drops, and soon broke upon us in torrents. The wind blew a hurricane, and we were in the apparent centre of an open prairie, with a row of sheltering trees about four miles distant, mockingly beckoning us to seek protection beneath their thick and wide-spreading branches.

We pushed on, and succeeded in reaching the trees in a little more than an hour, wet to the skin. The little clothing we had brought with us was also wet, and our bread reduced to the consistency of paste. We were dispirited, but managed to build a fire beneath the trees, and remained there throughout the day. The rain ceased at nightfall, and after making a sorry supper from our wet bread and slimy meat, we stretched ourselves on the ground, wrapped in our blankets, and began heartily cursing our folly in travelling out of the beaten track with the hopes of rendering ourselves rich and our names immortal. But tired men will sleep even in wet blankets and on muddy ground, and we were half-compensated in the morning for our previous day's adventures and misfortunes by as bright a sunshine and clear a sky as ever broke upon a prairie. Gathering up our provisions, we made a start, for the purpose of reaching a ravine, where we were to leave the main road and strike for the mountains.

About dusk we reached a dry *arroyo*, which we supposed to be the one indicated on the rough draft of the road we were to travel. We unpacked, built a roaring fire in the centre of the *arroyo*, and placing our wet bread and beef in its immediate vicinity, had them soon in a fair way of drying. We lay down again at night, with a bright starlit sky resting peacefully over us, and hoped for an invigorating rest; but California skies in November are not to be trusted, and so we found to our sorrow, for about twelve o'clock we were all turned out by a tremendous shower of rain. We gathered around the expiring fire, and our sorrows for our bodily sufferings were all soon absorbed in the thought that there lay our poor bread and meat, our sole dependence for support, once half-dried and now suffering a second soaking. There being no indications of a cessation of the rain, we stretched over our provisions a small tent we had brought with us, and for not having previously pitched, we cursed ourselves heartily, and spent the remainder of the night in sleeplessness and wet.

The tantalizing morning again broke fair, and it

was decided to remain where we were throughout the day, and make another attempt at drying our provisions, and at the same time fully decide what to do. Two of the party (myself included) wished either to turn back and try some other part of the "diggins," or proceed along the main road that we had been travelling, which was near to where we were then encamped, directly to the Yuba River, at a distance of about thirty miles. But the go-ahead party was too powerful for us, and, headed by Higgins, a man of the most indomitable perseverance, pictured to us the glorious results we were sure to achieve. We were to go where the track of the white man was yet unseen, and find in the mountain's stony heart a home for the winter, with untold riches lying beneath our feet. We yielded, and the next morning at daylight started again, making a beeline for the mountains, which lay in a northeasterly direction and about twenty-five miles distant. Here we were, setting forth on an unknown track, to go among hostile savages, who we knew had already killed our countrymen, and with provisions for six which consisted of about twenty-five pounds of wet and already moulded hard bread and some miserable jerked beef.

We travelled up the *arroyo* until nearly sunset, when we struck the foothills of the mountains. We had seen no foot tracks, except an occasional bare one of an Indian, and I became fully satisfied that we had taken the wrong *arroyo* as our diverging point. The ground over which we had travelled that day was a miserable stony soil, with here and there a scrubby oak tree growing. As we struck the foot of the mountains, the scene was changed. Rich, verdant, and fertile looking valleys opened out before us, and tall oaks threw a luxuriant, lengthened evening shadow upon the gentle slope of their ascent. We entered the midst of these valleys, and, after proceeding nearly a mile, came to the prettiest camping spot I ever saw. An expansion of the valley formed a circular plain of about a mile in diameter, surrounded on all sides, excepting at its one narrow entrance, with green, tree-covered, and lofty hills. A tall growth of grass and wild oats, interspersed with beautiful blue and yellow autumnal flowers, covered the plain, and meandering through it, with a thousand windings, was a silvery stream, clear as crystal, from which we and our thirsty horses drank our fill, and relished the draught better than the gods ever did their nectar. It was a beautiful scene. The sun was just sinking behind the hills on the western side, and threw a golden stream of light on the opposite slope. Birds of gaudy plumage were carolling their thousand varied notes on the tree branches, and I thought if gold and its allurements could be banished from my thoughts, I could come here and live in this little earthly paradise happily forever.

We selected a gentle slope, beneath a huge rock near the western hillside for our camping ground, and, again building a fire, were about to content ourselves with a supper of mouldy bread, when a jolly son of the Emerald Isle who was one of our party, in diving among the little bags of which our packs consisted, found one of burnt and ground coffee, which we did not know we possessed, and another of sugar, both to be sure a little wet, but nevertheless welcome. Talk of the delights of sipping the decoction of the "brown berry" after a hearty dinner at Delmonico's! That dish of hot coffee, drunk out of my quart tin pot, in which I had boiled it, was a more luxurious beverage to me than the dewdrops in a new blown rose could be to a fairy. I slept delightfully under its influence until midnight, when I was called to stand my turn of guard duty, which, as we were in an Indian region, all knew to be necessary; and I, who so often with my sword belted around me, had commanded guard as their officer, watched post with my old rifle for nearly two hours.

The day broke as clear and beautiful upon our enchanting valley as the previous one had closed. After partaking yet another pot of hot coffee and some mouldy bread, I took a stroll across the little stream, with my rifle for my companion, while the others, more enthusiastic, started in search of gold. I crossed the plain, and found, at the foot of the hill on the other side, a deserted Indian hut, built of bushes and mud. The fire was still burning on the mud hearth, a few gourds filled with water were lying at the entrance, and an ugly dog was growling near it. Within a few feet of the hut was a little circular mound enclosed with a brush paling. It was an Indian's grave, and placed in its centre, as a tombstone, was a long stick stained with a red colouring, which also covered the surface of the mound. Some proud chieftain probably rested here, and as the hut bore evident marks of having been very recently deserted, his descendants had without doubt left his bones to moulder there alone, and fled at the sight of the white man.

Leaving this spot, I returned to camp, and as the gold hunters had not yet come back, still continued to stroll around it. The top of the rock beneath which we had slept was covered with deep and regularly made holes, like those found in the rocks where rapids of rivers have fallen for centuries and worn them out. It was long before I could account for the existence of these, but finally imagined, what I afterwards found to be the fact, that they were made by the continual pounding of Indians mashing their acorns. In the vicinity I observed several groves of a species of white oak, some of them eight feet in diameter and at least eighty feet high. This tree is remarkable for the length of its acorns, several that I picked up measured two inches.

The gold hunters finally returned, and with elongated countenances reported that, though they had diligently searched every little ravine around our camp, the nearest they could come to gold finding

was some beautiful specimens of mica, which John
the Irishman brought in with him, insisting that it
was "pure goold." We camped again in the valley
that night, and the next morning held another
council as to what we should do and whither we
should go. Higgins, as usual, was for going ahead; I
was for backing out; and the little party formed itself into two factions, Higgins at the head of one,
and I of the other. Mounting the rock, I made not
exactly a "stump," but a "rock" speech, in which,
to my own satisfaction, and, as it proved, to that of
the majority of the party, I explained the madness
of the idea of starting into the mountains on foot,
without a guide, and with but about two or three
days' provisions remaining. We had seen but few
deer so far, and knew not whether there were any in
the mountains. I recommended that we should immediately pack up, and strike what we thought to
be the best course for Johnson's rancho, on Bear
River, about fifteen miles from Yuba.[1] I succeeded,
and we packed up and retraced our steps with
somewhat heavy hearts down the little valley. We
left our blessing on the lovely spot, named our
camping ground "Camp Beautiful," and proceeded

[1] In 1845, William Johnson, a native of Boston, purchased
the rancho of five leagues granted to Pablo Gutíerrez in 1844
and was the claimant for some 22,197 acres. One finds frequent mention of him in the Fort Sutter records as well as in
immigrant accounts since his ranch was on their route to San
Francisco. Bancroft, *California*, II: 694; Cowan, *California
Ranchos*, p. 42, Entry No. 214.

on our way, following the base of the mountains.
There was no road, and we knew not whither we
were going, only that we were in the right direction.
The country outside of the mountains was miserably poor and barren, the soil being covered with a
rocky flint. It is entirely destitute of timber, except
on the banks of the *arroyos*, which were dry, and
skirted with magnificent evergreen oaks. We were
travelling in a northwesterly direction, and hoped
to reach Bear River at night; coming, however, to a
little stream, we camped upon its margin, and the
next day started again, refreshed by a good night's
sleep, but dispirited from our ignorance of where
we were, or whither we were going, besides being
footsore from our stepping onto the flinty pebbles.
About noon we saw, at a distance of some three or
four miles, an immense flock of what we took to be
sheep. Elated at the prospect of being near a rancho, we speedily unpacked a horse, and using the
pack lashing for a bridle, I mounted him, and gal-
loped at full speed in the direction of the flock,
hoping to find the rancho to which they belonged
near them. I approached to within three hundred
yards of them before I discovered the mistake under
which I had laboured, when the whole herd went
bounding away. What I had taken for a flock of
sheep was a herd of antelopes, containing nearly a
thousand, and for a supper of one I would have
freely given a month's anticipated labour in the
gold mines. I returned to the party, and dampened

their already disheartened spirits with my report.

We travelled on slowly for we were wearied and heartsick, and at about four o'clock in the afternoon, having traversed a very circuitous route, the horses were unpacked and the small quantity of remaining provisions put in our pockets. Higgins, the owner of one of the horses, mounted his, and John the Irishman, who was suffering with a rheumatic complaint, the other. I was so weary and weak that I could scarcely support myself, and my feet were so covered with blisters, and so swollen, that every step I forced seemed like treading on sharpened spikes. How I wished myself back in "Camp Beautiful," or in Texas, anywhere else but where I was. I was lagging behind the party, when John, turning round, saw me and stopped his horse; as I came up to him he dismounted and forced me to take his place. God bless thee, generous Irishman. Beneath a rough exterior he had a heart which beat with feelings and emotions. How I loaded him with thanks, and only received his unsophisticated reply that I "was tireder than he was." About dark we struck a stream of water, and all but Higgins were ready and glad to camp and eat the last remains of the mouldy bread and beef. The persevering energy of Higgins had not in the least degree failed him, and without getting off his horse, he bade us "goodbye," and assured us that he would never return till he had found Johnson's rancho. After he left us, we built a good fire, and about three hours afterward, while speculating on his return, he came dashing into camp with about a dozen pounds of fresh beef, some bread, and a bottle of fine, old brandy. We welcomed him as we would an angel. My distaste for his desperation changed into an admiration for his energy. It seems he had found a road about forty yards from our camp, and a ride of five miles had brought him to Johnson's rancho. We made a good supper of beef and bread, and revived our fainting spirits with the brandy, and in the fullness of our hearts unanimously voted Higgins excused from guard duty for all that night. Next morning, light-hearted and happy, we started for the rancho, and crossing Bear River reached there about ten o'clock. Johnson is an American, who had obtained a large grant of tillable land on the Bear River, and has been living here for years within fifteen miles of a stream whose banks and bed were filled with incalculable riches.

We procured some provisions here, and started for the Yuba, and without any mishaps reached the camping ground, about three miles from the river, early in the afternoon. We camped, and Higgins and myself started on a hunting expedition to get some game for supper. We made our way into the hills, and were travelling slowly, trailing our rifles, when we stopped suddenly, dumbfounded, before two of the most curious and uncouth looking objects that ever crossed my sight. They were two Indian women engaged in gathering acorns. They were entirely naked, with the exception of a coyote skin extending from the waists to the knees. Their heads were shaved, and the tops of them covered with black tarry paint, and a huge pair of military whiskers were daubed on their cheeks with the same article. They had with them two conical shaped wicker baskets into which they were placing the acorns, which were scattered ankle deep around them. Higgins, with more gallantry than I showed essayed a conversation with them, but made a signal failure, and after listening to a few sentences in Spanish and English, they seized their acorn baskets and ran. The glimpse we had taken of these beauties, and our failure to enter into any conversation with them, determined us to pay a visit to their headquarters, which we knew was nearby. Watching their footsteps in their rapid flight, we espied them, after descending a hill, turn up a ravine, and disappear. We followed in the direction which they had taken, and soon reached the Indian *rancheria.*[2] It was located on both sides of a deep ravine, across

[2] A *rancheria* is Spanish for village or small settlement. The natives encountered by Buffum and his companions were Patwin Indians. The dress and basketry as described, and subsequently their housing, comports to this tribe's cultural pattern. It was traditional for women to shave their heads in time of mourning, but the use of whiskers daubed on the women's cheeks suggests imitation of the vogue then current among male Caucasians. Patti J. Johnson, "Patwin," in *Handbook of North American Indians*, ed. by William C. Sturtevant (20 vols.): Robert F. Heizer, ed., *California* (Washington, D.C., 1978), VIII: 350–60.

Indians Gathering (left) and Grinding (right) Acorns
Courtesy The Huntington Library

which was thrown a large log as a bridge, and consisted of about twenty circular wigwams, built of brush, plastered with mud, and capable of containing three or four persons. As we entered, we soon observed our flying beauties seated on the ground pounding acorns on a large rock indented with holes similar to those which so puzzled me at "Camp Beautiful." We were suddenly surrounded upon our entrance by thirty or forty male Indians, entirely naked, who had their bows and quivers slung over their shoulders, and who stared most suspiciously at us and our rifles. Finding one who spoke Spanish, I entered into a conversation with him. I told him we had only come to pay a visit to the *rancheria*, and, as a token of a peace offering, gave him about two pounds of musty bread and some tobacco which I happened to have in my game bag. This pleased him highly, and from that moment till we left, Pule-u-le, as he informed me his name was, appeared my most intimate and sworn comrade. I apologized to him for the unfortunate fright which we had caused a portion of his household, and assured him that no harm was intended, as I entertained the greatest respect for the ladies of his tribe, whom I considered far superior in point of ornament, taste, and natural beauty to those of any other race of Indians in the country. Pule-u-le exhibited to me the interiors of several wigwams, which were nicely thatched with sprigs of pine and cypress, while a matting of the same material covered the bottom. During our presence our two female attractions had retired into one of the wig-wams, into which Pule-u-le piloted us. It was here we found four or five squaws similarly bepitched and clothed, and who appeared exceedingly fright-ened at our entrance. But Pule-u-le explained that we were friends, and mentioned the high estimation in which I held them, which so pleased them that one of the runaways ran from the wigwam and soon brought me a large piece of bread made of acorns, which to my taste was of a much more excellent fla-vour than musty, hard bread.

Pule-u-le showed us many more bows and arrows, and never have I seen more beautiful specimens of workmanship. The bows were some three feet long, but very elastic, and some of them were beautifully carved, and strung with the intestines of birds. The arrows were about eighteen inches in length, accu-rately feathered, and headed with a perfectly clear and transparent green crystal, of a kind which I had never before seen, notched on the sides, and sharp as a needle at the point. The arrows, of which each Indian had at least twenty, were carried in a quiver made of coyote skin.

I asked Pule-u-le if he had ever known of the ex-istence of gold prior to the entrance of white men into the mines. His reply was that, where he was born, about forty miles higher up the river, he had, when a boy, picked it from the rocks in large pieces, and amused himself by tossing them into the river as he would pebbles. Now, members of the tribe go daily to the Yuba River, and wash out a sufficient amount of gold to purchase a few pounds of flour or some sweetmeats, and return to the *rancheria* at night to share it with their neighbours, who in their turn go the next day, while the others are chasing hare and deer over the hills. There were no signs around them of the slightest attempt to cultivate the soil. Their only furniture consisted of woven baskets and earthen jars, and Pule-u-le told me that in the spring he thought they should all leave and go over the "big mountain," to get from the sight of the white man.

Highly pleased with our visit, and receiving a very earnest invitation to "call again," we left the *rancheria* and proceeded towards our camp. About halfway from the *rancheria*, a loud braying, followed by a fierce growl, attracted our attention, and in a few moments a frightened mule, closely pursued by an enormous grizzly bear, descended the hillside within forty yards of where we stood leaning on our rifles. As the bear reached the road, Higgins, with his quickness and intrepidity, fired, and an unearthly yell from the now infuriated animal told with what effect. The mule in the interval had crossed the road, and was now scampering away over the plains, and Bruin, finding himself robbed of his prey, turned upon us. I levelled my rifle and gave him the contents with hearty goodwill, but the wounds he had received only served to exasperate the monster, who now made towards us with rapid strides. Deeming prudence the better part of valour, we ran with all convenient speed in the direction of the camp, within a hundred yards of which my foot became entangled in the underbrush, and I fell headlong upon the earth. In but another instant I should have fallen a victim to old Bruin's rage, but a well-directed ball from my companion's rifle entered his brain and arrested his career. The whole party now came to our assistance and soon despatched Mr. Grizzly. Dragging him to camp, we made a hearty supper from his fat ribs, and, as I had probably been the more frightened of the two, I claimed as an indemnity his skin, which protected me afterward from the damp ground on many a cold night. He was a monstrous fellow, measuring nearly four feet in height, and six in length, and a stroke from his huge paw would, had he caught us, have entirely dissipated the golden dreams of Higgins and myself.

III

The Upper and Lower Diggings

NEXT MORNING early, in better spirits than we had enjoyed for a week previously, we started for the Yuba River.[1] About a mile from the camping place, we struck into the mountains, the same range at whose base we had been before travelling and which are a portion of the Sierra Nevada. The hills here were steep and rugged, but covered with a magnificent growth of oak and redwood. As we reached the summit of a lofty hill, the Yuba River broke upon our view, winding like a silver thread beneath us, its banks dotted with white tents and fringed with trees and shrubbery.

We had at last reached the "mines," although a very different portion of them than that for which we started. We turned out our tired horses, and immediately set forth on an exploring expedition. As my clothing was all dirty and wet, I concluded to indulge in the luxury of a new shirt, and going

[1]When John A. Sutter took up his Sacramento-area rancho lands in 1841, he became acquainted with the local Indians. He later recorded that at the confluence of the Yuba and Feather Rivers, he found a tribe which called themselves Yubu. "I gave that river the name Yuba, which it has ever since borne." Marysville *Herald*, August 13, 1850, as quoted in Gudde, *California Place Names*, p. 372.

down to the river found a shrewd Yankee in a tent surrounded by a party of naked Indians, and exposing for sale jerked beef at a dollar a pound, flour at a dollar and a half, and for a coarse striped shirt which I picked up with the intention of purchasing, he coolly asked me the moderate price of sixteen dollars! I looked at my dirty shirt, then at the clean new one I held in my hand, and finally at my little gold bag, not yet replenished by digging, and concluded to postpone my purchase until I had struck my pick and crowbar into the bowels of the earth, and extracted therefrom at least a sufficiency to purchase a shirt. The diggings on the Yuba River had at that time been discovered only about three months, and were confined entirely to the "bars," as they are called, extending near a mile each way from where the road strikes the river on both its banks. The principal diggings were then called the upper and the lower diggings, each about half a mile above and below the road. We started off for the upper diggings to "see the elephant," and winding through the hills, for it was impossible to travel all the way on the river's bank, struck the principal bar then wrought on the river.[2] This has since been

[2] During the gold rush era the phrase "seeing the elephant" was widely used in diaries, journals, and letters. It "meant going through a trying and unpleasant experience and getting the best of it, or at least coming out alive. To 'see the elephant' was to graduate from the status of greenhorn." John W. Caughey, ed., *Seeing the Elephant: Letters of R. R. Taylor Forty-niner* (Los Angeles, 1951), frontispiece.

"Seeing the Elephant"
Courtesy The Huntington Library

called Foster's Bar, after an American who was then keeping a store there, and who had a claim on a large portion of the bar.[3] Upon reaching the bar, a curious scene presented itself. About one hundred men were at work, performing the various portions of the labour necessary in digging the earth and working a rocking machine. The apparatus then used upon the Yuba River, and which has always been the favourite assistant of the gold digger, was the common rocker or cradle, constructed in the simplest manner. It consists of nothing more than a wooden box or hollowed log, two sides and one end of which are closed, while the other end is left open. At the end which is closed and called the "mouth" of the machine, a sieve, usually made of a plate of sheet iron, or a piece of rawhide, perforated with holes about half an inch in diameter, is rested upon the sides. A number of "bars" or "rifflers," which are little pieces of board from one to two inches in height, are nailed to the bottom, and extend laterally across it. Of these, there are three or four in the machine, and one at the "tail"—the end

[3] Foster's Bar on the north fork of the Yuba River, now covered by the Bullards Bar Reservoir, was one of the earliest and best-known diggings on the Yuba River. It was named for William McAlister Foster, a survivor of the ill-fated 1846 Donner party. In April 1848, he ran a cattle ranch south of the Yuba River. A few months later he moved to the location named for him, which Buffum so ably describes. Biographical Letter File and Pioneer File, California State Library; Bancroft, *California*, III: 745 (see also II: 770 and IV: 750); Gudde, *California Gold Camps*, p. 120.

where the dirt is washed out. This, with a pair of rockers like those of a child's cradle, and a handle to rock it with, complete the description of the machine, which being placed with the rockers upon two logs, and the "mouth" elevated at a slight angle above the tail, is ready for operation. Modified and improved as this may be, and as in fact it already has been, so long as manual labour is employed for washing gold, the "cradle" is the best agent to use for that purpose. The manner of procuring and washing the golden earth was this. The loose stones and surface earth being removed from any portion of the bar, a hole from four to six feet square was opened, and the earth extracted therefrom was thrown upon a rawhide placed at the side of the machine. One man shovelled the dirt into the sieve, another dipped up water and threw it on, and a third rocked the "cradle." The earth, thrown upon the sieve, is washed through with the water, while the stones and gravel are retained and thrown off.

The steady motion of the machine, and the constant stream of water pouring through it, washes the earth over the various bars or rifflers to the "tail," where it runs out, while the gold, being of greater specific gravity, sinks to the bottom, and is prevented from escaping by the rifflers. When a certain amount of earth has been thus washed (usually about sixty pans full are called "a washing"), the gold, mixed with a heavy black sand, which is always associated with gold in California, is taken

Miners Prospecting with Rocker Box
Courtesy California State Library, Sacramento

out and washed in a tin pan, until nearly all of the sand is washed away. It is then put into a cup or pan, and, when the day's labour is over, is dried before the fire, then the remaining sand is carefully blown out. This is a simple explanation of the process of gold washing in the placers of California. At present, however, instead of dipping and pouring on water by hand, it is usually led on by a hose or forced by a pump, thereby giving a better and more constant stream, and saving the labour of one man.

The excavation is continued until the solid rock is struck or the water rushing in renders it impossible to obtain any more earth, then another place is opened. We found the gold on the Yuba in exceedingly fine particles, and it has always been considered to be of superior quality. We inquired of the washers as to their success, and they, seeing we were "greenhorns," and thinking we might possibly interfere with them, gave us either evasive answers, or in some cases told us direct lies. We understood from them that they were making about twenty dollars per day, while I afterwards learned, from the most positive testimony of two men who were at work there at the time, that one hundred dollars a man was not below what was considered the average estimate of a day's labour.

On this visit to Foster's Bar I made my first attempt at gold digging. I scraped up with my hand my tin cup full of earth, and washed it in the river. How eagerly I strained my eyes as the earth was washing out, and the bottom of the cup was coming in view; and how delighted, when, on reaching the bottom, I discerned about twenty little golden particles sparkling in the sun's rays, and worth probably about fifty cents. I wrapped them carefully in a piece of paper, and preserved them for a long time—but, like much more gold in larger quantities, which it has since been my lot to possess, it has finally come to escape my grasp, and where it now is Heaven only knows.

The labour on the Yuba River appeared very severe, the excavations being sometimes made to a depth of twelve feet before the soil containing the gold, which was a gravelly clay, was reached. We had not brought our tools with us, intending, if our expedition in the mountains had succeeded, that one of our party should return for our remaining stock of provisions and tools. We had no facilities for constructing a machine, and no money to buy one (two hundred dollars being the price for which a mere hollowed pine log was offered us), and besides, all the bars upon which men were then engaged in labour were "claimed," a claim at that time being considered good when the claimant had cleared off the top soil from any portion of the bar. We returned to our camp, and talked over our prospects, in a quandary as to what to do. Little did we then dream that, in less than six months, the Yuba River, then only explored some three miles above where we were, would be successfully wrought for

forty miles above us, and that thousands would find
their fortunes upon it.

We concluded to return to the *embarcadero*, and
take a new start. Accordingly, the next morning we
packed up and set off, leaving at work upon the river nearly two hundred men. Having retraced our
steps, we arrived at Sutter's Fort in safety on the
evening of November 30th, just in time to find the
member of our party whom we had left behind,
packing all our remaining provisions and tools into
a cart so as to be ready to start for the dry diggings on the following morning.[4]

The history of John A. Sutter, and his remarkable settlement on the banks of the Sacramento, has
been one of interest since California first began to
attract attention. Captain Sutter is Swiss by birth
and was formerly an officer in the French army. He
emigrated to the United States, became a naturalized citizen, and resided in Missouri several years.
In the year 1839 he emigrated to what was then the
wilderness of California and obtained a land grant
that approximated nearly eleven leagues, bordering
on the Sacramento River. For a long time he suffered continual attacks and depredations from the
Indians, but finally succeeded, by kind treatment
and good offices, in reducing them to subjection,

[4]The name dry diggings was given to a number of places
which were lacking in water. The miners had to either transport the dirt to a stream for washing or else had to bring
water to the diggings. One of the most famous of these dry
diggings was Placerville, as will be noted later.

and persuading them to enter his settlement, which he called New Helvetia. With their labour he built a large fort of *adobes* or sunburnt bricks, brought a party of his Indians under military discipline, and established a permanent garrison.[5] His wheat fields were very extensive, and his cattle soon numbered five thousand, the entire labour being performed by Indians. These he paid with a species of money made of tin, which was stamped with dots, indicating the number of days' labour for which each one was given; and they were returned to him in exchange for cotton cloth, at a dollar a yard, and trinkets and sweetmeats at corresponding prices. The discovery of the gold mines of California has, however, added more to Sutter's fame than did his bold settlement in the wilderness. This has introduced him to the world as a man of gold, and connected his name forever with the most prized metal upon earth. He is quite "a gentleman of the old school," his manners being very cordial and prepossessing.

[5] John Augustus Sutter (1803–80), German born, was raised partly in Switzerland. Relying on his word, he was an officer in the Swiss army, had an unhappy marriage, and failed in business. He fled to New York in 1834, moved on to St. Louis, then overland to Oregon, by ship to Hawaii, then to California which he reached in 1839. In 1841 he was granted eleven leagues of land that stretched from present-day Nicolaus to Marysville on both sides of the Feather River, which he dubbed Nueva Helvetia (New Switzerland). There he built his famed fort, now an historic monument. Marguerite E. Wilbur, *John Sutter, Rascal and Adventurer* (New York, 1949), pp. 1-132; Cowan, *California Ranchos*, p. 53, Entry No. 284.

Sutter's Fort is a large parallelogram, of *adobe* walls, five hundred feet long by one hundred and fifty broad. Portholes are bored through the walls, and at its corners are bastions on which cannon are mounted. But when I arrived there its hostile appearance was entirely forgotten in the busy scenes of trade which it exhibited. The interior of the fort, which had been used by Sutter for granaries and storehouses, was rented to merchants, the whole at sixty thousand dollars annually, and was converted into stores, where every type of goods was to be purchased at gold mine prices. Flour at $60 per barrel, pork $150 per barrel, sugar 25¢ per pound, and clothing at the most unreasonable rates.[6] The principal trading establishment at this time was that of Samuel Brannan & Co.[7] Mr. Brannan informed me, that since the discovery of gold, he had taken

[6]To put these prices in perspective, wage earnings were proportionally high. Monthly teachers earned $100, housekeepers $40, engineers $100, blacksmiths $100. Hourly bricklayers and masons earned $6, carpenters $5, shoemakers $4. The average miners daily income in 1848 was $20; in 1849 it fell to $16, and by 1850 was $10. Broadside, "Emigration to California!", Huntington Library, San Marino; Rodman W. Paul, *California Gold* (Cambridge, MA, 1947), p. 349.

[7]In 1842 Samuel Brannan (1819–89) converted to Mormonism and established a religious newspaper. In 1846 he published California's first newspaper in San Francisco, January 9, 1847. Subsequently estranged from the Mormons, he arrived early at the mines and built a store at Natoma, Morman Island, May 1, 1848, (*Sutter's Diary*, p. 47). Reva L. Scott, *Sam Brannan and the Golden Fleece, A Biography* (New York, 1944) and Louis J. Stellman, *Sam Brannan, Builder of San Francisco* (New York, 1954), *passim*.

in over seventy-five thousand dollars in gold dust in payment for his wares.

With all our worldly gear packed in an ox wagon, we left Sutter's Fort on the morning of December 1st, and after travelling about twelve miles on the road, set up camp in a beautiful grove of evergreen oak, to give the cattle an opportunity to ingest a sufficient supply of grass and acorns, preparatory to a long march. As we were to remain here during the day, we improved the opportunity by taking our dirty clothing down to banks of the American Fork, about one mile from camp, for the purpose of washing. While we were employed in this laborious but useful occupation, Higgins called my attention to the salmon which were working up the river over a little rapid opposite us. Some sport suggested itself; and more anxious for this than labour, we dropped our half washed shirts and started back to camp for our rifles, which we brought down to the river. In making their way over the bar, the backs of the salmon were exposed some two inches above water; and the instant one appeared, a well-directed rifle-ball perforated his spine. The result was, that by day's end Higgins and myself carried into camp thirty-five splendid salmon, procured by this novel mode of sport. We luxuriated on them, and gave what we could not eat for supper and breakfast to some Indians, who had been employed the whole day in spearing some half dozen each.

Next morning we packed up and made a fresh

start. That night we encamped at Green Springs, about twenty-five miles from Sutter's Fort. These springs are directly upon the road, and bubble up from a muddy black loam, while all around them is the greenest verdure—the surrounding plain being dotted with beautiful groves and magnificent flowers. Their waters are delicious.

As the ox team was a slow traveller, and quarters were to be looked for in our new winter home, on the next morning Higgins and myself were appointed to proceed posthaste to the dry diggings. We started about 10 A.M., and travelled through some beautiful valleys and over lofty hills. As we reached the summit of a high ridge, we paused by common consent to gaze upon the landscape and breathe the delicious air. The broad and fertile valleys of the Sacramento and San Joaquin Rivers lay stretched at our feet like a highly coloured map. The noble rivers which lend their names to these rich valleys were plainly visible, winding like silver threads through dark lines of timber fringing their banks; now plunging amid dense forests, now coming in view sparkling and bright as the riches they contain. Droves of elk, black-tailed deer, and antelope browsed near the mountain sides, on the summit of which the eagle builds his eyry. The surrounding atmosphere, fragrant with delightful odours, was so pure and transparent that objects became visible at great distances, and so elastic and bracing as to create a perceptible effect on our feelings. Far in the distance a massive peak reared its snow-capped head, from within a dense forest, fourteen thousand feet into the sky. We arrived at what was then called Weber's Creek, about dusk.[8] About a dozen log houses, rudely thrown together and plastered with mud, constituted the little town which was to be our winter home, and where we were to be initiated into the mysteries, pleasures, and sufferings of a gold digger's life. A pretty little stream, coursing through lofty oak and pine covered hills, and on whose left bank the settlement had been made, was the river that had borne down the riches which we hoped to appropriate to our private uses. It was a beautiful afternoon when we reached it. The sun was just declining, and, resting upon the crest of the distant Sierra Nevada, seemed to cover it with a golden snow. The miners were returning to their log huts with their implements of labour slung over their shoulders, and their tin pans containing the precious metal from their days work. We learned that the dry diggings, to which we had started, were three miles further into the mountains, that there was a great scarcity of water, and that but very little could be accomplished before

[8]Throughout the several chapters which follow, the original edition uses Weaver or Weaver's Creek. This is incorrect, as Buffum himself points out later. Weaver's Creek is located in Trinity County, some 200–250 miles further northwest. The correct name for the creek Buffum is actually referring to is Weber or Weber's Creek, named for the man who discovered gold there, Charles M. Weber.

the commencement of the rainy season. Finding some old friends here, who generously offered us a "chance" upon the mud floor of their log cabin, we remained with them for the night, and stretching our blankets upon the floor and lighting our pipes, were soon engaged in an interesting conversation on the all-absorbing topic.

Next morning our party arrived with the team, and from the representations of our friends, we concluded to remain at Weber's Creek, and pitched our tent on the banks of the stream. Our teamster's bill was something of an item to men who were not yet accustomed to "gold mine prices." We paid three hundred dollars to transport three barrels of flour, one of pork, and two hundred pounds of small stores about fifty miles. This was the regular price charged by teamsters at that time, and there was no alternative but to pay, which we did, although it exhausted the last dollar belonging to our party. But there before us lay the treasures that were to replenish our pockets, and the sigh for its departure was changed into a hope that our fondest wishes might be realized in our new and exciting occupation.

IV

Work Begins

THE DAY after our arrival, in anticipation of the immediate commencement of the rainy season, we determined to build a log house and were about to commence operations, when we received an offer for the sale of one. We found it to be but a little box of unhewn logs, about twenty feet long by ten wide, which was offered to us at the moderate price of five hundred dollars. The terms seemed quite accommodating, being ten days' credit for the entire amount. With the reasonable expectation that we could own our house by gold digging in less time than it would require to build one, we bought it, and by evening were duly installed in the premises.

Our party now consisted of ten: Higgins and a Marquesas Islander he had picked up somewhere, and who had changed his heathenish appellation of *Pi-pita-tua* to the more Christian and civilized name of "Bob"; five of our disbanded volunteers; a man by the name of Russell, who had persuaded us to allow him to join up;[1] the captain of the little

---

[1] Thomas Russell was an American sailor who landed at San Diego in 1835 to supervise the hide house. He later worked as a carpenter, married a native, and became a naturalized Mexican citizen in 1840 at age thirty-seven.

launch *Ann*, who had determined to leave the sea to try his fortune at gold hunting, and myself. We were a queer looking party. I had thrown aside all the small ornaments of dress and made my best bow before the gold digging public in red flannel and corduroy. Bob was the only member of the concern who retained what he had always in his own land considered his peculiar ornament. He would have been glad to rid himself of it now, poor fellow, but it was too indelibly stamped to allow removal. It was a broad piece of blue tattooing that covered his eye on one side, and the whole cheek on the other, and gave him the appearance of a man looking from behind a blue screen. Our partnership did not extend to a community of labour in gold digging, but only to a sharing of the expenses, trials, and labours of our winter life.

The dry diggings of Weber's Creek could serve as an example of dry diggings in all parts of the mining region. A description of them will give the reader a general idea of the various diggings of the same kind in California. They are called "dry" in contradistinction to the "wet" diggings, or those lying directly on the banks of streams, and where all the gold is procured by washing. As I said before, the stream coursed between lofty tree-clad hills, broken on both sides of the river into little ravines or gorges. In these ravines most of the gold was found. The loose stones and top earth being thrown off, the gravelly clay that followed it was usually laid aside

Prospecting in the Dry Diggings
Courtesy California State Library, Sacramento

for washing, and the digging continued until the
bottom rock of the ravine was reached, commonly
at a depth of from one to six feet. The surface of
this rock was carefully cleared off, and usually
found to contain little crevices and holes, the latter
in miner's parlance called "pockets," and in which
the gold was found concealed, sparkling like the
treasures in the cave of Monte Cristo. A careful examination of the rock being made, and every little
crevice and pocket being searched with a sharp
pointed knife, gold in greater or less quantities invariably made its appearance. I shall never forget
the delight with which I first struck and worked out
a crevice. It was the second day after procuring our
little log hut; the first having been turned over to
what is called "prospecting," or searching for the
most favourable place at which to commence operations. I had slung pick, shovel, and bar upon my
shoulder, and trudged merrily away to a ravine
about a mile from our house. Pick, shovel, and bar
did their duty, and I soon had a large rock in view.
Getting down into the excavation I had made, and
seating myself upon the rock, I commenced a careful search for a crevice, and at last found one extending lengthwise along the rock. It appeared to
be filled with a hard, bluish clay and gravel, which I
took out with my knife, and there at the bottom,
strewn along the whole length of the rock, was
bright, yellow gold in little pieces about the size
and shape of a grain of barley. Eureka! Oh how my

heart beat! I sat still and looked at it some minutes before I touched it, greedily drinking in the pleasure of gazing upon gold that was in my grasp, and feeling a sort of independent bravado in allowing it to remain there. When my eyes became sufficiently feasted, I scooped it out with the point of my knife and an iron spoon, and placing it in my pan, hurried home with it very much delighted. I weighed it, and found that my first day's labour in the mines had made me thirty-one dollars richer than I was in the morning.

The gold, which by some great volcanic eruption, had been scattered upon the soil over an extensive territory, was sunk into the hills by the continual rains of the winter season until it reached either a hard clay which it could not penetrate or a rock on which it rests. The gold in the hills, by the continual rains, has been washing lower and lower, until it reached the ravines. Now, it has washed down the ravines until it has reached the rock base, and thence, it has washed along the bed of the ravines until it has found some little crevice in which it rests, where the water can carry it no farther. Here it gathers, and thus are formed the "pockets" and "nests" of gold, any of which presents such a glowing golden sight to the eye of the miner, and such a field for his imagination to revel. How often, when I have struck one of these, have I fondly wished that it might reach to the centre of the earth, and be filled with pure, bright, yellow gold.

Our party's first day's labour produced one hundred and fifty dollars, I having been the most successful of all. But we were satisfied, although our experience had not fulfilled the golden stories we had heard previous to our reaching the *placers*.[2] Finding the average amount of gold dug on Weber's Creek at that time to be about an ounce per day to a man, we were content so long as we could keep pace with our neighbours. There is a spirit of emulation among miners which prevents them from being ever satisfied with success whilst others around them are more successful. We continued our labours for a week, and found, at the end of that time, our whole party had dug out more than a thousand dollars; and after paying for our house, and settling between ourselves our little private expenses, we were again on a clear track, unencumbered by debt, and in the heart of a region where treasures of unknown wealth were lying hidden in the earth on which we daily trod.

[2]The initial gold discoveries were "fragments that were to be found along the channels of present or former rivers, intermixed with sand, gravel, and stones. The fragments varied in size all the way from fine dust up to masses weighing one hundred pounds. Miners have long classified this type of gold under a word of Spanish origin: *placer* gold." Paul, *California Gold*, p. 41. The Spanish word *placer* means "pleasure, content, rejoicing, amusement, complacence." It also means: "The place near the bank of a river where gold dust is found." Mariano Velázquez de la Cadena, comp., *New Revised Velázquez Spanish and English Dictionary* (Chicago, 1974), p. 520.

About this time, the most extravagant reports reached us from the Middle Fork, about forty miles distant from Weber's Creek in a northerly direction. Parties who had been there described the river as being lined with gold of the finest quality. One and two hundred dollars was not considered a great day's labour, and now was the right time to take advantage of it, while in its pristine richness. The news was too blooming for me to withstand. I threw down my pickaxe, and leaving a half-wrought crevice for some other digger to work out, I packed up and held myself in readiness to proceed by the earliest opportunity, and with the first party ready to go for the Middle Fork. An opportunity soon offered itself, as a party of three who had already been there and returned, were about to go back. We considered it a great act of generosity on their part to allow us to accompany them on their second trip, as during their first exploration on the river they had found a place where no white man had ever before trod, and where gold was said to exist in large pockets and huge, bulky masses. One of my companions and myself determined to go, and if successful we would inform our whole party, who were then to follow.

It was now near the middle of December, and we certainly knew the dreaded rainy season must soon commence. Occasional black clouds dimming the clearness of that mountain sky gave us warning of it; but even though strong in health, and stronger still in hope and determination, we did not wait for any severe warning. Rather, we placed our tools of labour on the backs of two sorry-looking mules, and shouldering our rifles moved away from Weber's Creek on a fine afternoon.

Our road for the first three miles lay across a lofty hill, which formed the dividing line between our little community at Weber's Creek and the Dry Diggings *par excellence* of that vicinity.[3] On descending the hill, we found the Dry Diggings in a pretty little valley surrounded by hills, and forming a town of about fifty log houses. Very little was doing there at that time because the gold was so intermixed with a clayey soil that water was necessary to separate it, and groups of miners were patiently waiting for the rainy season to set in. Many had thrown up huge mountain-like piles of earth, thereby making a large excavation to catch the rain water in which the golden earth was to be washed.

Passing to the northward of the Dry Diggings, we encamped at dusk in a little oak grove about three miles from Sutter's Mill, killed a deer, ate a hearty supper, spread our blankets on the ground, and slept quietly and peacefully beneath a star-studded and cloudless heaven. Next morning we went into Coloma, the Indian name for the territory around

[3]Dry Diggings was located on Weber Creek. After Sutter's Mill and Mormon Island, Weber Creek was blessed with the richest gold deposits. Three of Sutter's employees, William Daylor, Perry McCoon, and Jared Sheldon are credited with the discovery. Gudde, *California Gold Camps*, p. 102.

Sutter's Mill, and here we were to purchase our provisions previous to going to the river.[4] At that time, three stores handled the trade at what is now the great centre of the northern mining region. Now where there are busy streets and long rows of tents and houses, was a beautiful hollow, which, in our romantic version, we named as we were entering it, "The Devil's Punch Bowl." Surrounded on all sides by lofty mountains, its ingress and egress guarded by an ascent and descent through narrow passes, it seemed like a huge bowl which some lofty spirit might seize, and placing it to his lips, quaff the waters of the golden stream that circled through it. Here it was that gold was first discovered in California; this was the locality where was commenced a new era, and where a new page was opened in the history of mankind.

[4] Coloma was where James W. Marshall made the first gold discovery that led to the Gold Rush. The site of the sawmill was on the South Fork of the American River, forty-five miles northeast of Sutter's Fort (now Sacramento). The name was derived from a nearby Southern Maidu Indian village.

V

The Gold Rush Is On

DURING the month of January, 1848, two men, named Marshall and Bennett, were engaged in the erection of a sawmill located by John A. Sutter on the South Fork of the American River, at a point, where oak, pine, cypress, and cedar trees covered the surrounding hills, and where Indian labour was to be procured at a nominal price.[1] These were the motives that prompted Sutter to establish a mill and trading post in this region. Little did Sutter imagine or foresee that he was to be the instrument to disclose to mankind riches of which the

---

[1]One of the first apocryphal stories spawned by the Gold Rush was that Charles Bennett was a co-discoverer of gold with James W. Marshall. That simply is not true. Bennett was hired by Sutter to work on the construction of a sawmill to be located at Coloma. It was Marshall alone who was the discoverer of gold in the millrace on January 24, 1848. This was duly reported to the adjutant general in Washington, D.C. by Colonel Richard B. Mason, military governor of California, following his visit to the gold regions to ascertain the validity of the strikes. Initially printed in the 31st Congress, 1st Session, *House Executive Document 17*, January 24, 1850, pp. 528–36; reprinted in full in Rodman W. Paul, ed., *The California Gold Discovery* ... (Georgetown, CA, 1966), pp. 90–100. The false attribution that Bennett was the co-discoverer appeared in the Monterey *Californian* on August 14, 1848.

most sanguine daydreamer never dreamt, and open caverns in which even the extraordinary lamp of Aladdin would have been dimmed by the surrounding brightness.

One morning Marshall, while examining the tailrace of the mill, discovered, much to his astonishment, some small shining particles in the sand at the bottom of the race, which upon examination he became satisfied were gold. Not content, however, with his own investigations, some specimens which were found throughout the entire race were sent on to San Francisco by Bennett, where an assayer removed all doubt of their nature and purity.[2] The discovery was kept secret while Bennett proceeded to Monterey and tried to obtain a grant of the land on which the gold had been found from Colonel Mason, then Governor of the Territory. Colonel Mason informed him that he had no authority to make any such conveyance, and Bennett returned to San Francisco, where he exhibited his specimens

[2]This is a bit of misinformation. There was no assayer in San Francisco at this time. Unhappily, Sutter chose Bennett to go to Monterey to solicit from Governor Mason a lease to the Coloma site. When Bennett left for San Francisco, he carried with him a pouch of gold. En route he fell in with a group of men at Benecia and told them of the gold strike at Coloma. Eventually reaching San Francisco in late February, Bennett showed off his pouch containing the gold to a number of people, but only one, Isaac Humphrey, went to the goldfields to see for himself. John W. Caughey, *Gold Is the Cornerstone* (Berkeley and Los Angeles, 1948), pp. 1, 17; Gay, *Marshall*, pp. 173–74.

Colonel Richard B. Mason
Courtesy The Huntington Library

to Sam Brannan, a Mr. Hastings, and several others.[3] A number of persons immediately visited the spot and satisfied their curiosity. Captain Sutter himself came to San Francisco, and confirmed the statements of Bennett, and about the 1st of April, the story became public property. Of course, the news spread like wildfire, and in less than one week after the news reached Monterey, one thousand people were on their way to the gold region.[4] The more staid and sensible citizens cautioned the people

[3] After Sam Brannan visited Coloma, he decided to build a store there—a shrewd move, for shopkeepers made more money out of the gold rush than did the average miner. *New Helvetia Diary. A Record of Events Kept by John A. Sutter and His Clerks... September 9, 1845 to May 25, 1848* (San Francisco, 1979), pp. 123, 127, 129–30.

[4] Sutter did not go to San Francisco to verify Bennett's news. As early as March 15, 1848, the first newspaper notice of the gold discovery was announced in the Monterey *Californian*, near the bottom of a column on the inside page! The report headlined: "GOLD MINE FOUND." However, the editor then squelched the story with the remark that "California no doubt is rich in mineral worth." The San Francisco *California Star* followed suit on March 18. It was Sam Brannan who made a decisive impact when he returned to San Francisco with a quinine bottle of gold dust. He bellowed out the news as he walked the town's streets. After all, he was building a store at Coloma and would need customers. The gold rush was on at last! In short order San Francisco had become a ghost town: government and newspapers closed, business and real estate collapsed. Thomas Larkin to Secretary of State, James Buchanan, June 1 and 28, 1848. George P. Hammond, ed., *The Larkin Papers* (10 vols., Berkeley and Los Angeles, 1951–64), VII: 285–87, 301–05, reprinted in Paul, *The California Gold Discovery*, pp. 84–90.

against the fearful reaction that would inevitably ensue. Yet many a man who one day boldly pronounced the discovery as humbug, and the gold hunters little better than maniacs, was seen stealthily wending his way, with a tin pan and shovel concealed beneath his cloak to a launch that would take him up the golden Sacramento River. Before the middle of July, the whole lower country was becoming depopulated. Rancheros left their herds to revel in delightful liberty upon the hills of their ranchos; merchants closed their stores, lawyers left their clients, doctors their patients, soldiers took "French leave." Colonel Mason, then Governor of California, was himself seized with the mania, and taking his adjutant and an escort, started for the mines, "in order to be better able to make a report to the government." The *alcalde* of San Francisco completely stopped the wheels of justice, and left immediately to seek his fortune. Every idler in the country, who could purchase, beg, or steal a horse was off, and by the first of August the main towns were entirely deserted.

In San Francisco, the very headquarters of all the business in California, there were, at this time, but seven male inhabitants, and but one store open. In the meantime the most extravagant stories were in circulation. Hundreds and sometimes even thousands of dollars were spoken of as the reward of a day's labour. Indians were said to pay readily a hundred dollars for a blanket, sixteen for a bottle of grog, and everything else in proportion. In the meantime, new discoveries had been made at Mormon Island,[5] as far north as the Yuba River, and as far south as the Stanislaus; and the mining population had swelled to about three thousand. The stories that had been put into circulation with regard to the richness of the *placers* were in the main true. A few months after their discovery, I spoke with men, in whom I placed the utmost confidence, who assured me that for days in succession they had dug from the bowels of the earth over five hundred dollars a day.

But I have digressed in my narrative, and must now return to Coloma and our own business of prospecting. We purchased from one of the several outfitters two hundred pounds of flour, for which we paid three hundred dollars, one hundred pounds of pork for two hundred dollars, and sugar and coffee at a dollar a pound, amounting to another hundred dollars, making in all six hundred dollars expended for about two months' provisions. With provisions and equipment we crossed the South Fork, and mounting a lofty hill overlooking the river, encamped for the night on its summit. The next day we descended the hill, and passing through a long and watered valley, struck the "divide" or ridge, which overhangs the river at a point three miles above

[5] Information regarding the location of Mormon Island and the gold activity there is provided in the Marshall text—p. 91, footnote 5.

the "Spanish Bar."[6] We again encamped, anxious for a long and invigorating sleep to prepare us for a descent in the morning.

The hill was quite steep, entirely trackless, and covered with such a thick scrubby brush that we abandoned the idea of leading our mules with their packs on down to the river. Instead, the load was distributed; each one took his share of it and commenced the terrible descent into the *canon*. A jolly good fellow named M'Gee, a brother officer of mine in the regiment,[7] had a good-sized buck we had killed in the morning allotted as his burden, and, pioneer like, started ahead; I followed after with a bag of flour, and the remainder variously burdened, brought up the rear. The hill was so steep, and so craggy, that in many places we arrived at jagged rocks where a perpendicular descent was to be made. At one of these, Mac, who was a wild, harum-scarum fellow, had found himself just upon its very edge, from a run or slide he had made above it. He was in a dangerous position, the buck slung over his

---

[6]There were several mining camps named "Spanish Bar," but the one Buffum mentions here was on the Middle Fork of the American River, over the ridge from Spanish Dry Diggings, and about seven miles northwest of Georgetown. Gudde, *California Gold Camps*, p. 329.

[7]John McGee (Bancroft spells it McGhee) was a member of Company B, as was Buffum, in the New York Volunteers. He died in San Francisco on February 23, 1861. Guy J. Giffen, *California Expedition: Stevenson's Regiment of First New York Volunteers* (Oakland, 1951), p. 68; Bancroft, *California*, III: 723.

shoulders, and his only hope was to drop the animal down the crag into a gulf that yawned below. Down went the buck with Mac following as quickly as possible. He found it two or three hundred yards below us, rendered amazingly tender by its voyage. The descent was a terrible and tedious one, and when about halfway down, we first discovered the river, that looked like a little rivulet, winding through its rock-girdled banks. About noon, after two hours of tiresome travel, we reached our campsite on the narrow river bank, and, after depositing our loads, it was necessary for us to go back for the remainder of our provisions.

The banks of the Middle Fork, on which we camped, were rugged and rocky. Awful and mysterious mountains of huge granite boulders towered aloft with solemn grandeur, seemingly piled up on each other as though some destroying angel had stood on the summit of the lofty hills and cast promiscuously these giant rocks headlong down the steep slope.

What a wild scene was before us! A river rapidly coursing through a pile of rocks, and on each side of it hills that seemed to reach the clouds. The mountains that overlook this river are about two miles in height, and are probably as difficult of travel as any in the world.

It puzzled us greatly to find a camping place, although we had no tent to pitch, and only wanted room to spread our blankets on a rock. I searched

the river up and down for fifty yards in this laud-
able endeavour, and finally succeeded in finding a
little triangular crevice, formed by two boulders
resting against each other, into which I crept. I slept
that night with the pleasant anticipation that the
rocks above might possibly give way, in which case
my gold digging dreams would meet with a woeful
denouement by my being crushed to atoms. No
such fate overtook me, however, and the next morning I arose fresh and hearty to commence my first
day's labour on what I hoped would be the golden
banks of the Middle Fork.

We had packed on the back of one of our mules a
sufficient number of boards from Coloma to con-
struct a machine, and the morning after our arrival
placed two of our party at work for this purpose,
while the rest of us were to dig; and, taking our
pans, crowbars, and picks, we commenced operations. Our first attempt was to search around the
base of a lofty boulder, which probably weighed
some twenty tons, in hopes of finding a crevice in
the rock on which it rested and in which a deposit
of gold might be uncovered. And we were successful. Around the base of the rock was a filling-up of
gravel and clay, which we removed with much labour, and our eyes were gladdened with the sight of
gold strewn all over its surface, and intermixed with
a blackish sand. This we gathered up and washed in
our pans, and before night four of us had dug and
washed twenty-six ounces of gold, which was about

four hundred and sixteen dollars. The process of pan washing is the simplest mode of separating the golden particles from the earth with which it is amalgamated. A common sized tin pan is filled with the soil containing the gold. This is taken to the nearest water and sunk until the water overspreads the surface of the pan. The earth is then thoroughly mixed with water and the stones taken out with the hand. A half rotary motion is given to the pan with both hands, and the loose light dirt which rises to the surface washed out until the bottom of the pan is nearly reached. The gold being heavier than the earth, sinks by its own weight to the bottom, and is there mixed with a heavy, black sand. This is placed in a cup or another pan till the day's labour is finished, when the whole is dried before the fire and the sand carefully blown away. The gold which we found the first day was principally procured by washing, although two pieces, one weighing thirteen and the other seventeen dollars, were taken from a little pocket on the rock. We returned to camp exceedingly elated with our first attempt; and after gathering some green branches of trees, built a fire, cooked some venison, crawled into our holes and went to sleep.

The next day, our machine being made ready, we looked for a place to work it, and soon found a little beach, which extended back some five or six yards before it reached the rocks. The upper soil was a light, black sand on the surface of which we could see the particles of shining gold, and could in fact gather them up with our fingers. In digging below this, we struck a red, stony gravel that appeared perfectly alive with gold, shining and pure. We threw off the top earth and commenced our washings with the gravel, which proved so rich, that, excited by curiosity, we weighed the gold extracted from the first washing of fifty pansful of earth and found seventy-five dollars, or nearly five ounces of gold to be the result. We made six washings during the day, and placed in our common purse that night a little over two pounds—about four hundred dollars worth of gold dust.

Our camp was merry that night. Seated on the surface of a huge rock, we cooked and ate our venison, drank our coffee, and revelled in the idea that we had stolen away from the peopled world, and were living in an obscure corner, unseen by its inhabitants with no living being within many miles of us, and in a spot where gold was almost as plentiful as the pebble stones that covered it.

After working three days with the machine, the earth we had been washing began to give out, and it became necessary for us to look for a new place; accordingly, on the fourth morning, we commenced "prospecting." Three of us started down, and three up the river. I sauntered on ahead of the party on the lower expedition until, about three hundred yards from camp, I found a pile of rocks that I thought afforded a reasonable "prospect." I started ·

down to the river bank, and seated myself at the foot of a vast rock to look around. I observed above me, and running in a direct course down the rocky bank, a large crevice, which I carefully searched as high up as I could reach, but found only a very small quantity of gold. Being disappointed in this, I determined to trace the crevice to its outlet, confident that there a deposit of gold must have been made. I traced the crevice down nearly to the edge of the water, where it terminated in a large hole or pocket on the face of a rock which was filled with closely packed gravel. With a knife and spoon I dug this out, and near the bottom of the pocket, I found earth that contained gold. And the last spoonful I took from the pocket was nearly pure gold in little lumpy pieces. I gathered up all the loose gold from the stony bottom of the pocket, which appeared to be pure gold, but upon probing it, I found it to be only a thin covering which by its own weight and the pressure above it, had spread and attached itself to the rock. Crossing the river I continued my search, and, after digging for some time, struck upon a hard, reddish clay, a few feet from the surface. After two hours work, I succeeded in finding a "pocket" out of which I extracted three lumps of pure gold, and one small piece mixed with oxydized quartz. Elated with my good luck, I returned to camp, and after weighing the gold, found the first lot amounted to twelve and a half ounces, or two hundred dollars, and the four lumps last found, to weigh sixteen and three quarter ounces. The largest pieces weighed no less than seven ounces troy. My success this day was, of course, entirely the result of accident; and another of the party had also found a pocket containing about two hundred and seventy dollars, and a place which promised a rich harvest for our machine.

The gold thus found in pockets and crevices upon the river banks is washed from the hills above. I have found small quantities by digging on the hill-tops, and am fully persuaded that the gold is washed by the rains until seeking, as it always does, a permanent bottom, it rests in any pocket or crevice that can prevent it from being washed further, or falls into a stream running at the base of the hills, to find a resting place in its bed, or be again deposited on its banks. If this theory be true, the beds of the rivers whose banks contain gold must be very rich in the precious metal, and recent labours in damming and turning the courses of certain portions of them, have so proved. The richest deposits of gold upon the rivers are found on what are called the "bars." These bars are places where there is an extension of the bank into the river, and round which the stream winds, leaving a greater amount of surface than there is upon the bank generally. They are covered with large rocks deeply imbedded in the soil, which upon most of them is a red gravel, extending to the solid formation of rock beneath.

There are two theories upon which the superior

richness of the bars can be accounted for. The first is, that the river in its annual overflows has made the deposits of gold here, and that being more level and broad than the river's banks, they retain a larger quantity of the gold thus deposited. The other, and the only one that accounts for the formation of the bars themselves, is that where they now are the river formerly ran, and that they were once the river's bed, but from some natural cause, the channel has been changed and a new one made. The old channel is left dry, but annually receives fresh deposits of gold from it during its overflows.

We were all ready to commence operations on our new place in the morning, however, upon waking, we found the sky hazy, and soon after breakfast, a severe rain set in. We crept into our holes and remained there through the day, hoping for a cessation of the rain, but it continued pouring in torrents. Never have I seen rain come down as it did then and there; not only the "windows" but the very floodgates of heaven seemed to open upon us, and through that doleful night we lay upon our blanketed rocks, listening to the solemn music of the swollen river rushing rapidly by us, and the big rain torrents pouring upon its breast. In the morning we found that the river had risen four feet, and observing, high above our camp, the marks of the height to which it had risen during previous seasons, we judged it prudent to be looking for higher quarters. The torrents continued raising the river through the second and third days, nearly three feet more, until it nearly reached our rock couches. We talked the matter over, and determined to leave the next day, and return to our tiny winter quarters on Weber's Creek. We felt, of course, a profound sorrow to leave our rich spot, after having satisfied ourselves that a few months' labour would make us all wealthy men. But the dreaded rainy season we knew had commenced, and rosy health was better than the brightest gold, so we stowed away our provisions with the exception of what we supposed would be requisite for our journey homeward, and on the fourth morning after the rain commenced, took our line of march up the formidable hill.

VI

Hurry Before the Winter Break

THE BANKS of the Middle Fork have proved richer than any other tributary of the Sacramento River. The fork is the central one of three streams which rise in the Sierra Nevada and course their way to the American Fork, a large branch of the Sacramento, into which they empty. The first exploration of the Middle Fork was made in the latter part of June 1848 by a party of Mormons who had been working on the South Fork, and had left for the hills to search for richer deposits. The first diggings were made at the Spanish Bar, which is about twelve miles from Sutter's Mill, and has yielded at least a million dollars. The Middle Fork has now been explored to its very source in the Sierras, and has been found to be richer below than nearer its source. Since my first trip there, I have travelled for thirty miles on both its banks and never yet washed a pan of its earth without finding gold in it. When the immense tide of emigration began to pour in from the United States, the Middle Fork was the grand headquarters of the enthusiastic gold hunters, and its banks have been torn to their very bottoms, and incalculable treasures taken from them. Within the past summer and fall, about ten thousand people

have been at work upon this river, and at the fair
average of one ounce, or even ten dollars per day
to a man, more than ten million dollars worth of
gold dust have been extracted from this river fork.
After its banks ceased to furnish large amounts of
gold, the river itself has, in many places, been di-
verted from its wonted course. A new channel was
dug through a bar, and its former bed yielded an
immense quantity of the precious metal. This is
now about the only profitable labour that can be
performed here, as the banks of the stream have
been completely riddled; but when companies with
capital and scientific mining apparatus shall commence operations here, a rich harvest will follow.

About ten miles beyond the Middle Fork, and
coursing in the same direction, is another stream,
the North Fork, whose banks have proved nearly
equal in richness to those of the Middle Fork. Within the past spring and summer some fifteen points
along this river have been dammed, the channel
turned, and the bed of the river dug. In one case, a
party of five dammed the river near what is now
called "Smith's Bar."[1] The time employed in damming off a space of some thirty feet was about two
weeks, after which from one to two thousand dollars a day were taken out by the party within the

[1]Smith's Bar, named for a local store owner, was located
on the west side of the North Fork of the American River
between two mining camps, Horseshoe Bar and Long Bar.
The site in El Dorado County is now covered by Folsom
Lake. Gudde, *California Gold Camps*, p. 324.

space of ten days. Another party above them made
another dam, and in one week took out five thousand dollars. In other cases, where unfavourable
points in the river were selected, little or no gold
was found; and a fair average of the amount taken
out from those parts of the river which were dammed brought about fifty dollars per day to a man.

Here is an immense field for a combination of
capital and labour. As yet no scientific apparatus
has been introduced, and severe manual labour
alone has produced such golden results. When
steam and money are united for the purpose, I
doubt not that the whole waters of the North and
Middle Forks will be turned from their channels
and immense canals dug through the rugged mountains to bear them off. There are placers upon the
Middle Fork, where, within a space of twenty-five
square feet, are lying undisturbed pounds of gold.
This may appear startling, but facts and experience
have led me to an analogical mode of reasoning
which has proved it to my own mind conclusively.
A Frenchman and his boy, who were working on
the Middle Fork in November 1848 found a place in
the river where they could scrape from the bottom
the sands which had gathered in the crevices and
pockets of the rocks. These were washed in a machine, and in four days the father and son had taken
from the riverbed three thousand dollars, and this
with nothing but a hoe and spade. Two men on Kelsey's Bar, on the Middle Fork, adopted the same

process, and in two days washed from the earth fifty pounds of gold, amounting to nearly ten thousand dollars.[2] The great difficulty in this way of labouring is because there are very few places where the water is sufficiently shallow to permit it, and the river bed is so rocky and the current so strong that in only a few places it becomes a pool of still water where soil can be taken from its bottom.

The width of the Middle Fork is in most places about thirty feet, and that of the North a little less. The current of both rivers is very strong, being at the rate of five or six miles an hour. The beds of these rivers are composed of huge rocks, tumbled together as they are upon the banks; and it is in the crevices and pockets of these rocks that the nuggets have fallen. Where the stream is narrow and the current strong, the probability is that there is little gold; but where it expands, and the water becomes more quiet, the gold has settled peacefully, there to remain till the hand of some irreverent Yankee shall remove it from its hiding place.

During the months of September, October, and November, and sometimes a part of December, the

[2]Kelsey's Bar is on the North Fork of the American River next to Clinton Bar. The name is derived from Kelsey's Diggings, located in the same area in Kelsey Canyon, and named for Benjamin Kelsey, who came overland in the Bidwell-Bartleson party. *Ibid.*, pp. 183–84; Mrs. Eugene Fountain, "The Four Kelsey Brothers," *Sonoma County Historical Society Journal*, II (June 1963), p. 13; III (March 1964), pp. 5–8; III (June 1965), p. 708; III (September 1965), p. 8.

rivers are at their lowest ebb, when the water is from three to seven feet deep in the Middle and North Forks. In the latter part of December or the early part of January, when the yearly rains commence, the rivers become swollen, sometimes rising eight or ten feet in the course of a week's rain. During the winter the rivers are continually rising and falling, as the rains cease or commence again. About the first of March, the snows which have fallen during the winter begin to melt on the mountains, and flow in little streams down the mountain sides. Every warm day raises the rivers perceptibly, sometimes to the extent of four feet in a single day, so that in the heat of summer they are fifteen feet higher than in the fall. It should be noted that the only practicable time for damming is in the fall, or early in the spring.

When I dropped the thread of this narrative, I left myself about to start up the hill on my return with the remainder of the party to Weber's Creek. We found the journey up more toilsome than it had been before, as the soil was reduced to a pasty consistency, into which we sank ankle-deep at every step, and the rocks were rendered so slimy and slippery by the rain, that it was with great difficulty we could maintain our foothold when climbing over them. After a tedious three hour struggle, however, we succeeded in reaching the top, where we encamped again, and the next day travelled to the summit of the hill which overlooks Coloma. There we again encamped, and on the following morning entered the settlement. The country between the mill and the Middle Fork is made up of a succession of hills, covered with oak trees and interspersed with beautifully watered valleys. In these valleys the soil is a rich, black loam, while the hills are barren, and of a red, gravelly soil. As yet no attempts at agriculture have been made in this region, however, I am satisfied that sometime in the not too far distant future, the valleys would produce the common field crops in great profusion.

We reached the mill about nine o'clock in the morning, a little too late to get a breakfast at one of the stores, where sometimes the proprietor was sufficiently generous to accommodate a traveller with a meal for the moderate price of five dollars. The only resource was to lay a cloth on the storekeeper's counter, and make a breakfast on crackers, cheese, and sardines. In order not to make a rush upon the trade, we divided ourselves into three parties, each going to a different store. Mac and myself went together, and made a breakfast from the following items: one box of sardines, one pound of sea biscuit, one pound of butter, a half-pound of cheese, and two bottles of ale. We ate and drank with great gusto, and when our meal was concluded, we called for the bill. It was such a curiosity in the annals of a retail grocery business that I preserved it, and here are the items. It may remind some readers of Falstaff's famous bill for bread and sack.

One box of sardines	. . . . . .	$16.00
One pound of hard bread	. . . . . .	2.00
One pound of butter	. . . . . .	6.00
A half-pound of cheese	. . . . . .	3.00
Two bottles of ale	. . . .	16.00
Total	. . . .	$43.00

A pretty expensive breakfast, thought we! If I ever get out of these hills and sit and sip my coffee while eating an omelet at a nominal expense in a marble palace with a hundred waiters at my back, I shall send back a glance of memory at the breakfast I ate at the Coloma sawmill.

We laid over at the mill during the day, and prospected a mile or two up and down the South Fork. It appeared remarkable that here, where the gold was first discovered, and while hundreds and thousands were crowding to the mines, not a single man was at work upon the South Fork. But very little digging has ever been done at the mill, although I doubt not there will yet be found vast deposits of gold on the banks of the South Fork. We tried several places, and invariably found gold, but in such small quantities that we thought it would not be profitable to work there; and the day after, as the rain had ceased, we went to Weber's Creek with a huge load of blankets on our backs while sweating under a broiling sun.

We found our companions there, anxiously waiting for our return and eager to listen to the glowing report we made of our early success, but almost as disappointed as we were at the unfortunate ending of the affair. We determined to settle down quietly for the rest of the winter in our log house, and take our chance among the dry diggings.

It had by this time started to snow, and from the first until the fifteenth of January it continued falling heavily, so that by the middle of January it was about four feet deep on a level. All labour was, of course, suspended, and we amused ourselves by playing cards, reading, washing our clothing, and speculating on the future results of gold digging. By the middle of January the snow ceased and the rain again commenced falling; and a few days later, the snow having been entirely washed off the surface, we anticipated being soon able to recommence mining operations.

A scene occurred about this time that exhibits in a striking light, the manner in which "justice" is dispensed in a community where there are no legal tribunals. We received a report on the afternoon of January 20th that five men had been arrested at the dry diggings, and were put on trial for a robbery. The circumstances were these: A Mexican gambler, named Lopez, who had in his possession a large amount of money, retired to his room and was surprised about midnight by five men rushing into his apartment, one of whom applied a pistol to his head, while the others barred the door and proceeded to rifle his trunk. After an alarm was given, some citizens rushed in and arrested the whole party.

The next day they were tried by a jury chosen from among the citizens and each was sentenced to receive thirty-nine lashes on the following morning. Never having witnessed a punishment inflicted by Lynch law, I went over to the dry diggings on a clear Sunday morning and found a large crowd collected around an oak tree to which was lashed a man with a bared back while another was applying a raw cowhide to his already gored flesh. A guard of a dozen men, with loaded rifles pointed at the prisoners, stood ready to fire in case of an attempt to escape. After the five had been flogged, some fresh charges were preferred against three of the men— two Frenchmen named Garcia and Bissi, and a Chileno named Manuel. These three were charged with robbery and attempt to murder, on the Stanislaus River, during the previous fall. The unhappy men were taken to a neighbouring house, and being so weak from their punishment as to be unable to stand, were laid stretched upon the floor. As it was not possible for them to attend, they were tried in the open air by a crowd of some two hundred men, who had organized themselves into a jury and appointed a *pro tempore* judge. The charges against them were very well substantiated, but amounted to nothing more than a feeble attempt at robbery and murder; no overt act being even alleged. They were known to be bad men, however, and the general sentiment seemed to prevail in the crowd that they ought to be put away. At the close of the trial, which lasted some thirty minutes, the judge put to vote the question as to whether or not they were guilty. A universal affirmative was the response, and then the question, "What punishment shall be inflicted?" A sinister looking fellow in the crowd cried out, "hang them." The proposition was seconded and met with almost universal approbation.

I quickly jumped up on a stump, and in the name of God, humanity, and law protested against such a course of proceeding, but the crowd, excited by frequent and deep potations of liquor from a neighbouring groggery, would hear of nothing contrary to their brutal desires, and even threatened to hang me if I did not immediately desist from any further remarks. Somewhat fearful that such might be my fate, and sensing the uselessness of further argument, I stepped down and prepared to witness the horrible tragedy. Thirty minutes only were allowed the unhappy victims to prepare themselves to enter into eternity. Three ropes were procured, and attached to the limb of a tree. The prisoners were marched out, placed upon a wagon, and the ropes put round their necks. No time was given them for explanation. They vainly tried to speak, but since none of them understood English, they were obliged to employ their native tongues, which only a few of those assembled understood. Vainly they called for an interpreter, but their cries were drowned by the yells of a now infuriated mob. A black handkerchief was bound around the eyes of each; their arms were pinioned, and at a given signal, without priest or prayer book, the wagon was drawn from under them, and they were launched into eternity. Their graves were dug ready to receive them, and when life was entirely extinct, they were cut down and buried in their blankets. This was the first execution I ever witnessed, God grant that it may be the last![3]

The bad weather had cleared off, and our gold digging life was again commenced. The little ravines that ran down from the hillsides afforded us an ample field for labour. The regularity and extent with which the gold is scattered in California is remarkable. When wearied with our continual labour in the immediate vicinity of our cabin, we would sometimes start on a prospecting expedition some five or six miles distant. During all these searches I have never yet struck a pickaxe into a ravine without uncovering gold, but usually in such small quantities as not to warrant the expenditure of manual labour. All throughout this territory gold is scattered everywhere, as plentifully as the rich blessings

[3]Dry Diggings was the first name for what would later be called Placerville by 1850. The site was one of those mined by William Daylor, Charles M. Weber, and Jared Sheldon and in 1849 was restyled Old Dry Diggings to distinguish it from a new Dry Diggings. Because of the hanging on January 20, 1849, so graphically recounted by Buffum, an eyewitness, it was nicknamed Hangtown. The latter name survives for a nearby stream, which is a tributary to Weber Creek, and is still called Hangtown Creek. Gudde, *California Gold Camps*, pp. 150, 269–70.

of the Providence that created it. Our labours usually yielded us sixteen dollars per day to each man throughout the whole winter.

There have been the various speculations as to the manner in which the gold became distributed in the gold region of California. Some have supposed that, like the stones that cover the earth's surface, it was always there, while others believe that it sprung from some great fountainhead, and by a tremendous volcanic eruption, was scattered over an extensive territory. With the latter I agree; and observation and experience have proved to me the truth of this theory. The gold found in every placer in California bears the most indubitable marks of having, at some time, been in a molten state. In many parts it is closely intermixed with quartz, into which it has evidently been injected while in a state of fusion; and I have myself seen many pieces of gold completely coated with a black cement that resembled the lava of a volcano. The variety of form, which the gold of California has assumed, is sufficient evidence of the fact that it has been thrown over the surface while in a melted state. The earliest comparisons of the California gold were to pieces of molten lead dropped into water. The whole territory of the gold region bears the plainest and most distinct marks of being volcanic. The soil is of a red, brick colour, in many places entirely barren, and covered with a flinty rock or pebble, entirely parched in the summer, and during the rainy season becoming a perfect mire. The formation of the hills, the succession of gorges, the entire absence of fertility in many portions, distinctly exhibit the result of a great upheaving during past times. But there is one phenomenon in the mining region which seems to defy all geological research founded upon any other premises than volcanic formation. Throughout the whole territory, so generally that it has become an indication of the presence of gold, a white slate rock is found, and is the principal kind of rock in the mining region. This rock, instead of lying, as slate rock does in other portions of the earth, in horizontal strata, is perpendicular, or nearly so; seeming to have been torn up from its very bed and left in this position. On the banks of the Middle Fork are several excavations, which can only be accounted for upon the supposition that they were at some time volcanic craters. There is one of these on the mountain side, about five miles below the "Big Bar," from which, running down to the base of the mountains, is a wide gorge entirely destitute of verdure, while the earth all around it is filled with shrubbery. This, I am fully convinced, was the bed of the lava stream that was thrown up from the crater; and in searching for gold at the foot of it, I found several pieces entirely covered with the black cement or lava. From all these evidences, I am now fully satisfied that at an early date in the world's history, by some tremendous volcanic eruption, or by a succession of them, gold, which was existing in the form of ore, mixed with quartz rock, was fused and separated from its surrounding substances, and scattered through every plain, hill, and valley, over an immense territory. By its own gravity, and the continual washing of the rains, it sank into the earth until it reached either rock or hard, impenetrable clay. It continued washing and sliding down the hillsides, until it reached the rivers or ravines, and in the former was washed along with its current until it settled in some secure place in their beds, or was deposited within crevices of rocks along their banks.

VII

Rigors of Gold Mining

OUR LIFE at Weber's Creek became exceedingly monotonous. There were about three hundred people working at this point, and whenever a new ravine was opened, everybody swarmed to it, and in a few days it was "dug out." Moreover, dry digging is exceedingly uncertain. Where it is necessary to search among the crevices of rocks to find the gold deposits, one may at times dig and delve through the whole day without striking a single deposit of gold. In this respect they are entirely different and far inferior in point of certainty to the wet diggings upon the banks of rivers. In the latter, where the gold is nearly equally distributed among the earth, a certain amount of labour will produce a certain reward; while in the former, success may not attend the operations of the gold digger. There is a remarkable peculiarity in the gold from all dry diggings, which is, that the formation of gold in every ravine is different, so much so that one acquainted with the character of the gold in any certain region can easily tell by a glance at a piece of gold from what ravine it was extracted. This can only be accounted for on the theory that in a narrow and deep ravine, where the water flows swiftly during the rainy season, the gold courses further over the rocks and is more thoroughly washed, while in a shallow and wide ravine, where but little water runs, it settles upon the first rock on which it strikes allowing it to retain its distinctive marks.

Tired of the old ravines, I started one morning into the hills with the determination of finding a new place, where I could labour without being disturbed by the clang of picks and shovels around me. Striking in an easterly direction, I crossed a number of hills and gorges until I found a little ravine about thirty feet in length embosomed amid low undulating hills. It attracted my attention, I know not why, and clearing off a place about a yard in length, I struck the soil which contained the gold. The earth on the top was a light black gravel filled with pebbly stones, which apparently contained no gold. Below this was another gravel of a reddish colour in which the fine particles of gold were so mingled that they shone and sparkled through all of it. A little pool of water, which the rains had formed just below me, afforded a favourable place to test the earth, and scooping up a panful, I took it down and washed it, and it was worth about two dollars. I continued digging and washing until I reached a slate rock, wherein the crevices I found many little nests or clusters of gold, some of them containing eight or ten dollars. However, these clusters were mixed with a heavy, red clay from which the gold was almost inseparable. The gold was of the finest quality, both in size and richness, and I flattered myself that I had here, at last, found a quiet place, where I could labour alone and undisturbed, and appropriate to myself the entire riches of the ravine. When I reached and had explored the surface of the slate rock, I tried the experiment of breaking the rock itself into small pieces and washing it. This proved as rich as the red gravel, turning out two dollars to a panful. The results of that day's labour were one hundred and ninety dollars worth of gold dust, and I returned to the cabin with a profound secrecy resting on my countenance, and took good care not to expose to my companions the good luck I had experienced. But either my eyes betrayed me or some prying individual had watched me, for the next morning, when busily at work in my ravine, I found myself suddenly surrounded by twenty good, stout fellows, all equipped with their implements of labour. I could not say or do a thing. Preemption rights are unknown here, and the result of the matter was that in three days the little ravine, which I had so fondly hoped would be my own property, was turned completely upside down. About ten thousand dollars worth of gold dust was extracted from it, from which I realized a little over a thousand. Merely the body of the ravine, however, was dug, and after it was entirely deserted, many a day I went to it, solitary and alone, and took from one to three ounces out of its banks. In the early discovery of the mines, and during the first working of the dry diggings, it was felt that the gold lay only in the beds of the ravines. But since a more philosophical idea concerning the cause of gold deposits has been entertained, it is found that, depending upon the character of the soil, the banks on each side prove richer in gold than the ravines themselves. The gold having washed down from the hillsides, should it before reaching the ravine strike a rocky gravel or hard clay, will remain there instead of descending farther. When we first came upon Weber's Creek, we found a ravine which appeared to have been completely "dug out;" so much, in fact, that it would not yield five dollars a day to a man. Reports concluded that nearly one hundred thousand dollars had been taken from it since the time of its discovery, and it was supposed there was little or no gold remaining. One day, however, an ignorant Irishman sank a hole about six feet deep on the bank, twelve feet from the bed of the ravine. He struck a hard, solid white clay, through which gold could scarcely penetrate, and by washing it, took out the first day nearly one hundred dollars worth of gold. This, of course, attracted crowds to the old ravine, and before a week was completed, nearly fifteen thousand dollars had been taken from the place which was supposed to be entirely worthless. Among the prizes was one piece weighing twenty-eight ounces and valued at four hundred and forty dollars; and I have no doubt that even to this day the banks of many of the ravines are as rich in the pure metal as were their beds on the first discovery.

The diggings at Weber's Creek were first wrought by a German, Charles M. Weber, a *ranchero* on the San Joaquin River.[1] He carried with him articles of trade, and soon gathered around him a thousand Indians, who worked for him in consideration of the necessaries of life and of little trinkets that so win an Indian's heart. He was soon joined by William Dalor, a *ranchero* located near Sutter's Fort, and the two, together with the labour of the Indians, soon realized more than fifty thousand dollars.[2] By this time, individual labourers began to come in, and one of Dalor's men started into the hills for fresher diggings. He struck what was formerly called the dry diggings, but which now goes by the

[1]Charles M. Weber (1814–81), a German, emigrated to the U.S. in 1836. In 1841 he came overland with the Bidwell-Bartleson party, then became a Mexican citizen in order to obtain the eleven-league Rancho Campo de los Franceses including the town of Tuleburg, which became the present-day Stockton. George P. Hammond and Dale L. Morgan, *Charles M. Weber, Pioneer of San Joaquin and Founder of Stockton, California* (Berkeley, 1966), pp. 1–27.

[2]William Daylor (sometimes Dalor) was born c. 1810 and was an English sailor who jumped ship in California in 1835(?). He became a Sutter employee in 1840–41 and settled on the Cosumnes River with his brother-in-law, Jared Sheldon, around 1844. Later, he and Sheldon were two of the three discoverers of the fabulous Mormon Island strike. He died in July 1850, a cholera victim, leaving his widow, Sarah Rhoads. In 1851 she married William R. Grimshaw, who supplied Bancroft with his *Narrative*, a manuscript that details Daylor's life (Bancroft Library). Bancroft, *California*, II: 773; Biographical Letter File, California State Library.

euphonious name of Hangtown, because of the circumstance I have previously related.[3]

Indians still frequent this vicinity in considerable numbers, having acquired a taste for the luxuries of mouldy bread, putrescent codfish, and jerked beef, which form so large a portion of the stock in trade of the provision dealers who supply the miners. I have often been amused to witness the manner in which they make their purchases. When gold was first discovered, they had very little conception of its value, and would readily exchange handfuls of it for any article of food they might desire, or any old garment gaudy enough to tickle their fancy. Later they became more careful, and now they exhibit an understanding of the worth of the precious metal. When they desire to make a purchase from a dealer, they usually go in a party of from ten to twelve and arrange themselves in a circle, sitting only a few yards distant from the shop. Then in a certain order of precedence, they proceed to the counter in

[3]Gold deposits found primarily on Hangtown Creek and Cedar Ravine were dubbed Dry Diggings. Later the word "Old" was added to differentiate it from a new strike. In 1850 the place was officially renamed Placerville. Amazingly, the town spawned four millionaires: J. M. Studebaker, the automobile tycoon, worked there in the early days as a blacksmith making wheelbarrows, which he sold for ten dollars cash. Philip D. Armour was a butcher in town from 1852 to 1854, earning enough to return to Chicago to found his famous packing firm. Abe and Rudolph Seligman, who later founded the famous banking firm in London and New York, operated a clothing store there. Gudde, *California Gold Camps*, p. 270.

Charles M. Weber

Placerville (or Hangtown) at the Time of the Gold Rush
Courtesy California State Library, Sacramento

rotation, and make their purchases, as follows: they first place on the palm of the hand a small leaf or piece of paper upon which is perhaps a teaspoonful of gold dust, then the Indian stalks up to the dealer, and pointing first at his *dust* in hand and then at whatever article he may desire, gives a peculiar grunt—*Ugh!*—which is understood to mean an offer. If the dealer shakes his head, the Indian retires, and usually returns with a little more gold dust, going through the same ceremony continually until a sufficient amount is offered, when the dealer takes it and hands over the coveted article. The only objection of this mode of proceeding is that the unfortunates have been frequently plundered, and are afraid to find themselves all alone with a white man with too much gold upon their persons. Another peculiarity is, that if they should purchase half dozen hard biscuits for a teaspoonful of gold, and want several dozen, they will return with one teaspoonful more, obtain six biscuits and retire, and then return again until they have obtained the desired quantity.

About the first of February, the rains and snows commenced again with much vigour, and continued through the whole month with little or no interruption. Inured, however, by our previous experience, and stimulated by an ambition that will carry men through dangers and difficulties, we continued our labours in earnest, and returned many a night to our log hut drenched with the rains that had been pouring on us throughout the day. A blazing log fire and a pipe of tobacco compensated us for the hardships we had endured, and we were ready the next morning, to toil again. One morning, after a severe rainstorm and swell of the river, I was gazing earnestly upon its banks when my attention was suddenly arrested by the sight of gold lying scattered over the surface of the shore. I commenced gathering it up, and soon had exhausted it. How it came there I was never able to satisfactorily determine. Some of the pieces, to the weight of two and three dollars, were lying ten feet above the edge of the river's bank. The first day I picked up about four ounces, and waited for another rain. It came that night, and the next morning I found gold there again as plentiful as it had been the day before. In addition to this I observed, in the crevice of a rock nearly in the centre of the stream, a large deposit; and though it was cold and wintry weather, I bared my limbs, and waded in to get it. With my knife I tore it from the crevice in a very few minutes, and hurried home to dry myself and learn the extent of my good fortune. I found that the gold I had taken from the river bed weighed nearly three ounces. For several days I continued to find gold scattered over the surface of the bank, but it suddenly disappeared and I never saw more of it. How it came there was a mystery which I have never been able to fathom. It was either rained down from the clouds, thrown up by the river in its course, or was washed by the rains from the banks.

A town, with the name of Weberville,[4] has now been formed upon the direct site of the original settlement. Surely there are miles of creek banks which are rich in gold, and will one day provide as great a fortune as already has the site of the present town of Weberville.

Among the peculiarities consequent upon the extraction of gold may be mentioned the fact that in Weber's Creek, during the whole winter of 1848, the price paid in silver or gold coin for gold dust was from six to eight dollars per ounce. I, myself, bought some hundred ounces from a Mexican for six dollars and a half. The only object in selling gold for coin was to procure specie for gambling purposes—and gambling was the life of two-thirds of the residents there at that period. At the same time, communication with San Francisco and Sacramento City having been closed by the rains, provisions were priced enormously high. A few items will provide an idea of gold mine prices. Flour was

[4]As noted previously in Chapter 3, *note* 8, Buffum uses the name "Weaverville" instead of "Weberville." The latter was founded in El Dorado County on Weber Creek and was first mined by Charles M. Weber and William Daylor, his partner. Together they made fifty thousand dollars in a short time. Governor Mason visited the camp in July 1848 and left a glowing account of it. In October 1849, the Royce family arrived and stayed two months. Mrs. Sarah E. Royce left an account of Weberville in her book, *Frontier Lady; Recollections of the Gold Rush and Early California* (New Haven, 1932), pp. 82 ff. The town has long since vanished. Gudde, *California Gold Camps*, p. 366.

selling at one dollar per pound, dried beef at two
dollars, sugar at a dollar, coffee seventy-five cents,
molasses four dollars per gallon, pork two dollars
per pound, awful New England rum at fifty cents
per glass or eight dollars per bottle, and tobacco at
two dollars per pound. At these prices, the trader
and transporter realized a greater profit from the
miner's labour than the miner himself; but provisions must be had, and no price, however great,
could deter the ordinary labourer from purchasing
the necessaries of life.

About the first of March, the long and difficult
winter broke up, and, tired of our winter quarters,
our party divided up the remaining provisions and
cooking utensils, broke up housekeeping, and most
of us started out for the Middle Fork. Our travel
was not diversified by anything new or strange, and,
upon striking the river, we proceeded up it about
eighteen miles above the Spanish Bar to a bar opposite the Big Bar, where we pitched our camp,
built a machine, and started operations.[5]

The soil on this bar was exceedingly sandy, and
the surface was covered with huge imbedded rocks,
which required an extra amount of manual labour
to remove. Below this was red gravel, which was
united with gold, the washing of which turned out

[5]Spanish Bar on the Middle Fork of the American River
was located near Spanish Dry Diggings, which in turn was
five miles northwest of Georgetown. Big Bar was just below
Volcano Bar, which was opposite the mouth of Volcano
Creek. Gudde, *California Gold Camps*, pp. 34–35, 329, 362.

about four ounces per day to each man. I was once again dreaming of good fortune and success when my hopes were blasted by an attack of a terrible scourge that wrought destruction throughout the northern mines during the winter of 1848. I refer to what was known as the land scurvy. The exposed and unaccustomed life of two-thirds of the miners, and their entire subsistence upon salted meat, without any mixture of vegetable matter, had produced this disease, which was experienced by at least half of the miners within my knowledge. It was first noticed in the Dry Diggings, where, about the middle of February, many persons were rendered unable to walk by swellings and severe pain in the lower limbs. It was at first supposed to be rheumatism, and was treated as such. But it withstood the most powerful applications used in that complaint, and was finally decided to be scurvy. So long as the circumstances which caused it continued, the disease made rapid progress. Many, who could obtain no vegetables, or vegetable acids, lingered out a miserable existence and died, while others, fortunate enough to reach the settlements where potatoes and acids could be procured, did recover. I noticed its first attack upon myself by swelling and bleeding of the gums, which was followed by a swelling of both legs below the knee, which rendered me unable to walk, and for three weeks I was laid up in my tent, obliged to feed upon the very food items that had caused the disease. I was growing weaker daily, without any reasonable prospect of relief. There were, at that time, about eight hundred miners at work along the river hoping to get some medicine. One morning I dispatched one of my companions with instructions to procure for me, if possible, a dose of salts, and to pay any price that should be asked. He returned that night with the consoling news that he had failed, having found only two persons who had brought the article with them, and they refused to sell at any price.

I was almost in despair: with only a blanket between myself and the damp, cold earth, and a thin canvass to protect me from the burning sun by day, and the heavy dews by night. I lay day after day enduring the most intense suffering from pain in my limbs, which were now becoming more swollen, and were turning completely black. Above me rose those formidable hills which I must ascend before I could obtain relief. I believe I should have died, had I not by accident discovered the best remedy that could have been produced. In the second week of my illness, one of our party, descending the hill on which he had been deer hunting, found near its base, and strewn along the footpath, a quantity of beans which sprouted from the ground and were in leaf. Someone, in descending the hill with a bag of them on his back, had probably dropped them. My companion gathered a quantity and brought them into camp. I had them boiled and lived on them for several days, at the same time using a decoction of

the bark of the spruce tree. These seemed to operate magically, and in a week after commencing the
use of them, I found myself able to walk, and as
soon as my strength was partially restored, I ascend-
ed the hill, and with two companions walked into
Coloma. By living principally on a vegetable diet,
which I procured by paying three dollars per pound
for potatoes, I recovered in a very short time.

I found matters very much changed at Coloma;
the little settlement of three houses had grown into
a large town. Buildings were being erected in all
parts of it, and hundreds of tents whitened the
plain. The steamer *Oregon* had just arrived at San
Francisco on her maiden trip from Panama, and the
vast fleet of sailing vessels loaded with passengers
attracted by the report of the gold discovery had
begun to arrive.[6] All sorts of people, from the pol-
ished Broadway dandy, who never handled an instrument heavier than a whalebone walking stick, to
the sturdy labourer who had spent his life in wield-
ing the pickaxe and the shovel, had come to California for one common object—to dig gold; and one
class was as enthusiastic and anticipated as good
success as the other. Since there were no such accommodations as hotels at Coloma, everybody was

[6]The *Oregon*, 1,099 tons, Captain R. H. Pearson, master,
was the first steamship to reach California. It sailed from
New York on December 9, 1848 and reached San Francisco
on April 1, 1849 with 250 passengers on board. *The Key to
the Goodman Encyclopedia of the California Gold Rush Fleet*
(Los Angeles, 1992), Sheet 12, Entry No. 526.

living in tents, cooking their own provisions, and getting ready to pack up and move to the Middle Fork. Some of them had commenced working on the banks of the South Fork in the immediate vicinity of the mill, and the miners could be daily seen sweating (for the weather by this time had become exceedingly warm) under a load of tools sufficient to dig a whole canal, on their way to, or coming from their places of labour. As I have said before, very little gold has been found in the vicinity of the mill, and the gold diggers there were rewarded by not more than five dollars per day.

Most of them had brought with them one of the many newfangled machines that were manufactured in the United States, after reports of the gold discovery were announced. They were of all imaginable shapes and sizes, some of them appearing most admirably adapted to the churning of butter. These were tried and found to fail, and have been abandoned for the rocker, which is, as I have said before, the best machine to be used in connection with manual labour. Many of the newcomers were most woefully disappointed at the appearance of things, finding that gold, instead of lying scattered in "big lumps" over the earth's surface, was only to be obtained by the most severe toil.

About this time, reports were arriving daily at the settlements of outrages committed by Indians upon argonauts in the vicinity of the North and Middle Forks. A summary which afterwards proved to be

Steamship "Oregon"
Courtesy California State Library, Sacramento

strictly correct came to the mill that a party of Indians had descended into the campsite of five men on the North Fork, while the latter were engaged in labour, had broken the locks of their rifles which were in their tents, and then fallen upon and cruelly beaten and murdered them. A large party, headed by John Greenwood, a son of the celebrated mountaineer, was immediately mustered at the mill, and started in pursuit of the Indians and tracked them to a large Indian *rancheria* on Weber's Creek.[7] This they attacked, and after killing about twenty of them, took thirty prisoners and marched to the mill. Here they underwent a trial, and six of them, having been proved to have been connected with the party who killed the miners, were sentenced to be shot. They were taken out the afternoon after their arrival, followed by a strong guard, and, as was anticipated, a little distance ahead being allowed them, they ran. They had no sooner started than the unerring salvo of twenty mountaineers' rifles

[7] John Greenwood was the son of Caleb Greenwood, famed trapper and mountaineer, whose mother was a Crow. His father guided the 1844 Stevens party overland and rendered like service to various parties in 1845–48. John served in the California Battalion during the Mexican War and in 1848 had a trading post in Long Valley. After gold was discovered in the area, a town and nearby creek bore the family name. Greenwood was an important mining center while the bonanza lasted. John moved to Bolinas in 1850 and in 1859 killed himself from heavy drinking. Gudde, *California Gold Camps*, pp. 145-46 and *California Place Names*, p. 128; *History of Marin County, California* (San Francisco, 1880; reprint ed., 1972), p. 268.

was upon them, and the next moment five of the six lay weltering in their blood. Shortly after this, several expeditions were fitted out, who scoured the country in quest of Indians, and now an Indian is scarcely ever seen in the inhabited portion of the northern mining region.

After having remained some time at the mill, I returned to my first residence at Weber's Creek. I found it deserted; the opening of the warm spring weather had drawn away the entire population, both of our settlement and the Dry Diggings, to the richer *placers* of the golden rivers. I remained but a few days, when I proceeded to Sacramento City.

VIII

Back from the Mines

THE GOLD region of Upper California is embraced in the western slope of the Sierra Nevada Mountains, and extends over a space of six hundred miles. Within the last six months explorations have been made as far south as Kings River, which flows into the Great Tulare Lake. Above this are the Stanislaus, Mokelumne, Tuolumne, and Mariposa Rivers, all tributaries of the San Joaquin, and from all of which gold has been taken. The two great streams, with their tributaries, that fence in the present gold region, are the Sacramento and San Joaquin. The most probable theory, regarding the extent of the gold region, is that it is in the whole range of mountains, extending from the Sierra Nevada through Upper California, Mexico, Peru, and Chile, although it is positive that there are nowhere in the course of the range such extensive and rich gold washings as are found between the Sacramento and San Joaquin Rivers. Many years before the discovery of gold at Sutter's Mill, a *placer* had been wrought at San Bernadino, about thirty miles southeast of the town of Santa Barbara. The gold was of the same character as that of the upper region, although found in much smaller quantities, and it is well-known that for many years gold *placers* have been wrought in the province of Sonora, one of the northern departments of Mexico.[1]

Throughout this entire region there is not a stream, valley, hill, or plain in which gold does not exist. It seems to be the natural product of the soil, and is borne like the sand along the river courses. In travelling over some three hundred miles of this territory, I have never yet struck a pick or a knife into a spot where gold would likely be deposited, without finding it in greater or lesser quantities. Until lately, it was supposed that the gold existed only in the ranges of the Sierra Nevada, and that what is known as the Coast Range, bordering the whole coast of California, was destitute of it. But experience has already proved the incorrectness of this theory. A party headed by Major P. B. Reading in the spring of 1849, struck into the Coast Range of mountains about two hundred miles north of

[1]Buffum's statement is incorrect. The first gold discovery in California was in March 1842 when Francisco López, a native son, made a purely accidental strike at a place called San Francisquito in Placerita Canyon, some thirty-five miles northwest of Los Angeles. López, who was resting his horse, dug up some wild onions, and in the dirt discovered a piece of gold. Searching further, he found some more and a short-lived rush ensued. When Alfred Robinson (1807–95) returned east in the fall of 1842, he took with him "the first parcel of California gold dust received at the United States mint in Philadelphia." James M. Guinn, *A History of California and an Extended History of Los Angeles* (2 vols., Los Angeles, 1915), I: 155–56; Douglas E. Kyle, *Historic Spots in California* (Rev. ed.; Stanford, CA, 1990), p. 159.

Sacramento City, and is still labouring there very successfully, having found gold not only in quantities, but in large pieces and of the finest quality.[2] Certainly I doubt not that when the *placers* at the base of the Sierra Nevada shall have become partially exhausted, labour will be performed in various portions of the Coast Range with as good success as has already crowned the efforts of the diggers in the present gold region.

I do not believe, as was first supposed, that the gold washings of northern California are inexhaustible. Experience has proved, in the workings of other placers, that the rich deposits of pure gold found near the surface of the earth have been speedily displaced, and that with an immense influx of labouring population they have totally disappeared. Thus

[2]Pierson B. Reading (1816–68) was employed by Sutter in 1843 as chief of his fur trappers. In 1844 he received six leagues of land (26,632 acres) in present-day Shasta County, the Rancho San Buenaventura. He was an active participant in the Bear Flag Revolt and was a member of the California Battalion during the war with Mexico. He made a major gold discovery on the Trinity River. Using sixty-five Indians to work the strike, Reading had to forego the Indians' labor due to the objections raised by Oregon prospectors. He netted some $80,000 by use of pan and rocker at a site dubbed Reading's Bar. In 1849 he opened a store in Sacramento, and took an active part in politics. He came close to being elected governor of the state in the 1851 election, and thereafter devoted his energies to agriculture. He founded the town of Redding, originally called Reading, in 1862. Bancroft, *California*, V: 689; Cowan, *Ranchos of California*, p. 75; Helen S. Griffen has authored his biography, *Man of Destiny, Pierson Barton Reading* (Redding, CA, 1985).

in Sonora, where many years ago fifteen, twenty, and even fifty dollars per day were the rewards of labour, it is now found difficult with the common implements to dig and wash from the ground more than from fifty cents to two dollars per day to a man. When first discovered, before the soil was molested by the pick and the shovel, every little rock crevice and every river bank was blooming with golden fruits, and those who first struck them, without much severe labour, extracted the deposits. As the tide of emigration began to flow into the mining region, the lucky hits upon rich deposits, of course, began to grow scarcer, until, when an immense population was scattered throughout the whole golden country, the success of the mining operations began to depend more upon the amount of labour performed than upon the good fortune to strike into an unfurrowed soil that was rich in gold. When I first came to the mines, only six months after they were founded, and when not more than three thousand people were scattered over the immense territory, many ravines extending for miles along the mountains were turned completely upside down, and portions of the river's banks resembled huge canals that had been excavated. And now, after two years have elapsed and a population of over one hundred thousand have expended so great an amount of manual labour, the old ravines and river banks, which were abandoned when there were new and unwrought placers to go to, have been wrought and re-wrought, and some of them with good success. Two years have entirely changed the character of the whole mining region.

That the mere washings of pure gold will at some day become exhausted is not to be doubted, although for fifty years at least, they will be wrought to a greater or less extent. In the ravines of dry diggings that have been, in mining parlance entirely dug out, any man with a mere sheath knife and crowbar can extract five dollars a day. The earth here has been thrown up from the body of the ravines, and in other places the ground has merely been skimmed over and many parts of the ravine left untouched. Upon the river banks the very earth that has been thrown aside as useless, and even that which has been once washed, will still, with careful washing in a pan, turn out from three to ten dollars per day.

Upon my return from the gold fields, the city of Sacramento had taken on quite a different aspect from that which it exhibited when I previously left it. Where the old store ship used to be on the banks of the Sacramento, tall masted ships were moored, and the extensive plain on which I pitched my tent was now dotted with houses. Around the fort itself, which is nearly two miles from the bank of the river, houses had begun to spring up. Building lots which, four months previous had sold from fifty to two hundred dollars, were now held by their owners at from one to three thousand. I looked on with astonishment at the remarkable progress, and did not think that the ensuing six months would develop a growth, both in size and prices, which would entirely outstrip what I then witnessed.

Getting on board a launch, I spent a weary five days in sailing down the Sacramento and arrived at San Francisco in the early part of May. What a change had occurred in six months! San Francisco, when I saw it before, was almost entirely deserted, everybody having departed to the mines. Now it was being daily visited by the arrival of visitors across the plains, by vessels around Cape Horn, by Sandwich Islanders, Chinese, French, English, and Mexicans. The age of speculation had commenced. The building lots which, when I landed in San Francisco, were granted by the alcaldes for the sum of fifteen dollars, and in the autumn before were worth but five hundred, had now risen in value to from three to five thousand. Hundreds and thousands of men with capital were arriving, who readily seized upon the opportunities for speculating. Houses were going up on the vacant lots, and the town was beginning to assume an air of business. Goods of all kinds had fallen in price, owing to the arrival of fleets of loaded ships from all parts of the world, and in some cases from willful neglect on the part of consignees. Large hotels had been erected, and life began to be rendered comfortable. Gambling in all its forms was carried on to an enormous extent, and money, as before, was most plentiful.

Sacramento, c. 1849
Courtesy California State Library, Sacramento

San Francisco, c. 1849
Courtesy The Huntington Library

IX

Changes in Government

WHEN I ARRIVED in San Francisco, a basis for an Americanized state government had already been set in operation. As the town of San Francisco began to fill with American citizens, it was thought that a better form of town government than then existed was needed to secure the rights of person and property. Thus far the old Mexican system of *alcaldes* or chief justices, and *ayuntamientos* or town councils, had been retained,[1] however, the people were living under laws which they did not understand, and were being abused by those who did. It was determined that the system should be changed, and one which was understood be substituted. In

[1] *Alcaldes* were not "chief justices," rather they were justices of the peace. They were by far "the most important single officer in the administration of local government in California, both before and after the American conquest." *Alcaldes* were also charged with executing all actions of the *ayuntamiento* (town council). Thus they acted as the mayor of the community. With the American occupation of California in July 1846, the military governors of California simply retained the existing local government system, with one exception: Americans replaced *Californios* as *alcaldes* and members of the *ayuntamientos*. This system prevailed until the 1849 constitution was ratified. Theodore Grivas, *Military Governments in California 1846–1850* (Glendale, CA, 1963), pp. 151–84.

compliance with a call signed by a large number of
respectable citizens of the town, a mass meeting was
planned in Portsmouth Square on the afternoon of
February 12th, 1849. After organizing in the usual
form, and hearing the speeches given by several
gentlemen, a series of resolutions were offered and
unanimously carried, from which it was determined
to form, for the government of the district of San
Francisco, a legislative assembly, which should en-
act laws, and that three judges and other necessary
officers should be elected to administer them.[2]

[2] Buffum's account is a bit confused, though fairly accurate.
First of all, an election was held in San Francisco on December 27, 1848, to choose the town council for 1849. The old
ayuntamiento invalidated the returns, rejecting the results
because of the large number of unqualified voters who participated in it. A second election was held on January 14,
1849, and the council was elected by a comparatively small
turnout—only one fourth of the number that cast ballots in
the invalidated election. Thus, San Francisco had what appeared to be three councils, each claiming to be the legiti-
mate one. Each refuted the others' authority until the first
council's term expired on January 15, 1849, leaving only
two to contest for power.

This complicated situation worsened by the holding of a
public mass meeting in Portsmouth Square on February 12,
1849, which, in effect, asserted popular sovereignty. The
gathering gave its approval to a plan presented by George
Hyde. In essence, the crowd endorsed a constitution and
laws for the city of San Francisco "not repugnant to the
Constitution of the United States and common law." It also
provided for a "Legislative Assembly of the District of San
Francisco." San Francisco *Alta California*, January 18, p. 3,
cl. 1, and January 25, 1849, p. 2, cl. 2; Grivas, *Military Governments in California*, pp. 138–39; Ellison, *A Self-Governing Dominion*, p. 18.

Portsmouth Square, San Francisco
Courtesy California State Library, Sacramento

319

On the 21st day of February, an election was held in compliance with the above resolutions, and a legislative assembly consisting of fifteen members and three judges were elected. One of the initial acts of the Legislative Assembly, which only claimed authority over the district of San Francisco, was to abolish the office of *alcalde*, considering it not only unnecessary, but incompatible with American institutions; and in compliance with the act of the Assembly, Myron Norton, chief magistrate, directed a note to T. M. Leavenworth, late *alcalde*, requesting him to deliver to the new government the records of the town.[3] To this note Mr. Leavenworth made no

[3] Myron Norton arrived in San Francisco in October 1848 and became a point man in the struggle for self-government. He was a prime mover in the calling of the 1848 constitution convention and was a major participant in its deliberations, chairing the Judiciary Committee. He was San Francisco's first Justice of the Peace and then its first Superior Court Judge. He held the rank of lieutenant in the City Guards and organized the city's first police force. Harris Newmark, *Sixty Years in Southern California* (4th rev. ed., Los Angeles, 1970), pp. 47–48; Bancroft, *California*, IV: 755; Los Angeles *Daily Herald*, April 17, 1886, p. 6.

Thaddeus M. Leavenworth was both a physician and clergyman. He came to California with the Stevenson regiment of New York Volunteers. He was appointed San Francisco's second *alcalde* in 1847 and was elected first *alcalde* in 1848. He was suspended in May 1849, but was later reinstated by Governor Bennet Riley after an investigation of charges of wrong-doing in the matter of city lands and political favoritism proved untrue, but resigned his post on June 5, 1849. W. F. Swasey, *The Early Days and Men of California* (Oakland, CA, 1891), pp. 48–49; Biggs, *Conquer and Colonize*, pp. 107, 171; Giffen, *California Expedition*, p. 63.

reply, and another one of the same tenor was sent by Mr. Norton. This received the same treatment as the first. Trouble appeared to be brewing, and, as is usual in such cases, many, who had been the first to propose and aid the new movement, were found at this time most woefully wanting. A series of laws had already been established by the Assembly, and the wheels of the new local government were ready to be put into operation, when it was found very difficult to procure a quorum to handle business at meetings of the Legislative Assembly, and it was decided that additional members should be added thereto. On the 11th of May, another election was held, at which time a large and respectable vote was cast, and ten new members of the Assembly were chosen. Among those newly-elected was Peter H. Burnett, governor of the new state of California.[4]

[4]Peter H. Burnett (1807–95) served as the first governor of the state of California. He became a lawyer in 1838, moved to Oregon in 1843, and played a prominent role in establishing its territorial government. In 1848, he set out for California in the first company of gold seekers, but soon tired of the mines. Although adamantly opposed to military rule, he accepted appointment to the Superior Tribunal—the appellate court—when the post was offered to him by Military Governor General Bennet Riley. He was appointed to the State Supreme Court, January 13, 1857 and served until October 2, 1858. In 1863 he became president of the Pacific Bank in San Francisco and retired in 1880 a very wealthy man. J. Edward Johnson, *History of the Supreme Court Justices of California, 1850–1960* (2 vols., San Francisco, 1963), I: 62–64; H. Brett Melendy and Benjamin F. Gilbert, *The Governors of California* (Georgetown, CA, 1965), pp. 24–37.

T. M. Leavenworth

General Bennet Riley
Courtesy California State Library, Sacramento

323

Previous to this election a letter had been addressed by a committee of the Assembly to General Persifor F. Smith, who was at the time principal military commander in California, to which was received a decidedly noncommittal reply. But it was understood that Brevet Brigadier General Bennet Riley, who had assumed the civil government of the territory, would support the old authorities, and, if possible, crush the Legislative Assembly.[5]

---

[5] Brigadier General Bennet Riley was California's last military governor, and served until December 20 when the newly adopted state constitution was implemented with the election of Peter H. Burnett as the first state governor (even though California was not legally a state!).

General Persifor F. Smith had a distinguished military career as an officer in the Seminole and Mexican Wars, serving as military governor of Mexico City. President Taylor had decided to split the military in California into two separate roles, placing Smith in military command of the territory while civil government was delegated to Riley. Thus, Smith was Riley's superior, but had no say in civil affairs.

The Legislative Assembly argued the brief that the military government's role had ceased with peace. Furthermore, Governor Mason had withdrawn from the political affairs of the territory with the ratification of the peace treaty. Riley replied on March 27 that even establishing the best possible government on a false premise would lead to endless litigation. However, he thought that each district could make its own regulations for police and security and promised aid in that respect. General Smith advised the adjutant general that he had no intentions of using military force to challenge the growing "usurpations" of civil rule under the military governor. Harlow, *California Conquered*, pp. 318–33; James Creighton, *et al.*, to Smith, March 10; Smith to Creighton, March 27; Smith to Roger Jones, May 1, 1849, *California and New Mexico*, pp. 732–37.

California, and San Francisco in particular, were in a curious political state of existence. From the time of the treaty of peace with Mexico until the arrival of Generals Smith and Riley, Colonel R. B. Mason, the former military governor of California, had continued in the exercise of his authority, and the country had been governed by the same laws and usages as during the war, when it was actually a territory belonging to Mexico.[6] In contradiction of at least the intention and understanding of the government at Washington, Colonel Mason had appointed collectors, and collected revenue in the ports of California, and in all respects the military government had been continued. Now, when the people of San Francisco, in their sovereign capacity, had established a local government for their own protection, they found themselves interfered with by a military commander.

The Legislative Assembly, however, went on receiving the support of the whole community. A courthouse was established and courts organized.

[6]Colonel Richard B. Mason, a West Point graduate, served as the military governor of California from May 31, 1847 to February 28, 1849. After succeeding General Stephen W. Kearny, he authorized a mixed form of former Mexican and U.S.-style civil government, going so far as to drawing up a code of laws, but he decided against issuing it because he believed that all matters of government for the territory were vested in the United States Congress, which was indeed the fact. *Appeletons' Cyclopaedia of American Biography* (New York, 1888), IV: 243; Hart, *A Companion to California*, p. 308.

Governor Peter H. Burnett

Courtesy California State Library, Sacramento

Judge Norton finding that Mr. Leavenworth still
made no reply to his note, after waiting a reasonable time, issued a writ of replevin, and gave it to
the sheriff, who called upon Mr. Leavenworth at his
office, presented it and demanded the surrender of
the town records. Mr. Leavenworth refused to deliver them, and the sheriff, calling to his assistance a
number of the citizens, seized the records and deposited them in the courthouse. Mr. Leavenworth
started for Monterey the same evening to consult
with General Riley upon future proceedings. In the
meantime the Legislative Assembly issued an address to the people of California, earnestly calling
upon them to assemble in convention and organize
a provisional government for the territory, prior to
an immediate application to Congress for admission
as a state.

This was the first concerted movement coming
from any authorized body to recommend the formation of a state government for California. Mr. Leavenworth soon returned from Monterey, and brought
along two proclamations issued by General Riley,
which were posted in several parts of the town the
morning following Mr. Leavenworth's arrival. The
streets of San Francisco then presented a most exciting scene. Little knots of people were gathered in
the streets engaged in loud discussion, and crowds
were collected in the vicinity of the proclamations.
The first was a long one, and commenced by stating
that as Congress had failed to extend a government

over California, it became the duty of the residents to organize as such; that he, (General Riley) "in accordance with instructions from *the Secretary of War*," had assumed the civil government of the territory, and that he conceived it his duty to organize the old Mexican system, and put it in active operation until such time as a constitution and laws should be created. The document was both inconsistent and contradictory. It assumed that the territory of California was a conquered territory and should continue to be under the laws and usages of Mexico until Congress should extend over it those of the United States. At the same time, it called upon the people to assemble and organize a government for themselves. The whole broad ground which had been taken by the Legislative Assembly of San Francisco, which was that in the absence of a government extended over us by Congress, gave us the inherent right to establish one for ourselves. Although denied by General Riley in the first part of his proclamation, it was essentially admitted and urged in the latter portion.

The second proclamation was addressed merely to the citizens of San Francisco and related to the seizure of the town records by order of Judge Norton. It called upon all good citizens to assist in restoring them to the "proper authorities."

Various were the feelings expressed, and the opinions offered regarding these proclamations, but a large majority of the people of San Francisco were fully decided in the idea that General Riley had assumed an authority which, even if it was "in accordance with the instructions of the Secretary of War," was one which he had no right to assume and was in fact nothing more nor less than an unjust usurpation of power.

Trouble was again anticipated, and it was understood that, backed by General Riley's proclamation, the former *alcalde*, Mr. Leavenworth, would once again attempt to seize the town records. A few days after the publication of this document, a writ was served upon the town Register, calling for their delivery. He refused to give them up, and when an attempt was made to seize them, a force of about fifty of the most respectable citizens gathered at the courthouse, determined, if necessary, to resist *vi et armis*. The *alcalde's* sheriff presented his writ, and was replied to by William M. Stewart, presiding judge, that the records could not be removed, and seeing that a strong party was arrayed against him, the sheriff left without making any forcible attempt to take them. General Riley refused to lend the *alcalde* the assistance of any military force and matters were soon progressing again as before.

On the 12th of June, a large meeting was held in Portsmouth Square for the purpose of taking steps towards the establishment of a state government for California. The call for this meeting had been signed by a large number of respectable citizens and was issued before General Riley's proclamations

were published. This meeting was addressed by
Honourable T. Butler King, Honourable William M.
Gwin, William A. Buffum, Esq., and other speakers,
all of whom urged the immediate formation of a
state government for California.[7]

In reply to the proclamations of General Riley, a
response was issued by the Legislative Assembly of
San Francisco, written by Peter H. Burnett, set-

---

[7]Thomas Butler King entered Georgia politics and held
elective office in both houses of Congress. During his last
term, King was appointed by President Zachary Taylor
as his representative to California. King arrived in San
Francisco on June 4, 1849, just in time to join the growing
public protest against military rule. The following year he
resigned his seat in Congress to accept appointment by President Millard Fillmore as Collector of the Port of San Francisco, a post he held until he resigned, March 1, 1852.

William M. Gwin was born near Gallatin, Tennessee, and
earned a medical degree. After a stint as U.S. Marshal, he
was elected to the House of Representatives. Like King, he
immediately joined in the festering political scene in San
Francisco, a man fired with the ambition to become one of
the first U.S. Senators from California. *Biographical Directory of the American Congress 1774–1961* (2 vols., Washington,
D.C., 1961), pp. 984; Soulé, *et al., Annals of San Francisco*, pp. 334, 790; Lately Thomas, *Between Two Em-
pires: The Life Story of California's First Senator, William
McKendree Gwin* (Boston, 1969), p. 28.

William A. Buffum, Esq., the latter indicating he was a lawyer, was Edward Gould Buffum's older brother. As to his
arrival date, nothing is known. He was elected, along with
his brother Edward, to the San Francisco City Council
on May 11, 1849, when it was enlarged to include ten more
members, both men taking their seats on May 14. San Francisco *Alta California*, June 16, 1849, p. 2, cl. 1; Bancroft,
California, VI: 210 *note*.

ting forth in a clear and succinct manner the right of the people, in the absence of a government established by Congress, to legislate for themselves and justifying the course which had been pursued by the Legislative Assembly.

In order to arrive, by the shortest and most practicable mode, at the "consummation devoutly to be wished," the establishment of a state government for California, the Assembly united with other citizens of California, and on the first day of August an election was held at which were chosen the various local officers and members of convention, to meet at Monterey on the first of September for the purpose of forming a constitution.

The convention met and a more sensible and dignified body of men never assembled in any portion of the world. After six weeks of severe labour, a constitution was prepared and laid before the people of California for their ratification or rejection. It was a constitution featuring a most radically democratic character, and most admirably adapted to the wishes and wants of the people over whom it was to be extended.[9]

On the 13th of November an election was held at

[9]The document, largely based on the recent constitution which had been adopted in New York, claimed a number of innovative elements, chief among them the concept of a "plural executive," which made the top administrative offices in the state government subject to popular election rather than by executive appointment. See Ellison, *A Self-Governing Dominion*, pp. 22–46.

which the state constitution received almost unanimous ratification. At the same time, a governor and the necessary state officers, members of the state legislature, and two members of Congress were chosen. The choice for governor fell upon Peter H. Burnett, Esq., one of the early emigrants to Oregon, and who there received the appointment as Judge of the Supreme Court, an enterprising citizen of California, and one of the first to declare the rights of her people.

In tracing the causes which have created California a state, it will be seen that a small body of men, the Legislative Assembly of San Francisco, were the first to set the ball in motion, and I cannot refrain from giving them the credit which is their due. The proclamation of General Riley would probably not have been issued to this day, had not the body of which I have spoken taken the preliminary steps, and although General Riley deserves gratitude from the people for what he did, and as a man, is one of "nature's noblemen," I shall forever look upon his assumption of power as Civil Governor of California as unwarranted and unjust.

X

Burgeoning San Francisco

WITHIN THE past six months, the growth of San Francisco has been enormous. During that time at least a thousand houses of all sizes and forms have been erected. The hills around the town are now covered with buildings and every spot of ground near the centre is occupied. When it is taken into consideration that during this time lumber has never been lower than two hundred and fifty, and often as high as four hundred dollars per thousand feet, and carpenters' wages have been at from twelve to twenty dollars a day, it must be conceded that the Californians are, at least, an enterprising people. During this time the price of real estate has risen in direct proportion to the growth of the town; property now being fifty percent higher than it was six months since. A lot on Portsmouth Square, which was purchased some three years ago for fifteen dollars, and sold last May for six thousand, was purchased a few days since for forty thousand dollars! The mere ground-rent of a little piece of land of sufficient size to erect a house upon, in any of the public streets, varies from one hundred to five hundred dollars per month. Rents of houses are, of course, in proportion to the price of real estate. A common-sized lodging room, anywhere near the centre of the town, rents for one hundred dollars per month; an office on a lower floor, from two hundred to five hundred. The Parker House, a hotel upon the Square, is leased for two hundred thousand dollars per annum, and under-leased in small portions, at a profit of fifty thousand more. In the El Dorado, a large building next to the Parker House, a single room on the lower floor is rented for gambling purposes for one hundred and eighty dollars a day, or five thousand four hundred dollars a month—nearly sixty-five thousand dollars per annum. Most of the large rooms in the hotels are rented to gamblers, each table where a game is played paying thirty dollars a day. A man who builds a house in San Francisco usually intends that the rent should cover all expenses of the building in three or four months, and in this he generally succeeds. Mechanics command enormous wages. Carpenters are now getting from twelve to twenty dollars a day, and tinsmiths, bricklayers, paperhangers, and others employed in the construction of buildings, the same; while common day labourers engaged in discharging vessels, digging cellars, and the like, command eight dollars a day for their services. Meals vary from sixteen to forty-two dollars per week and washing costs eight dollars per dozen. A bewildered stranger in search of a night's lodging may procure one by sleeping upon a narrow shelf, called a "bunk," at the moderate charge of two dollars, and

El Dorado

Parker House

Early San Francisco Landmarks
Courtesy California State Library, Sacramento

337

get his breakfast at an eating house in the morning for a dollar and a half. Many of the usual articles of trade, such as clothing, can be obtained here at almost New York prices.

San Francisco possesses one of the most capacious and magnificent harbours in the entire world; one in which the navies of all the maritime powers could ride at anchor in perfect safety. From its entrance to its head is a distance of about twenty miles, and branching from it are two other sizeable bays—San Pablo, and Suisun. The entrance to the harbour is guarded by lofty hills, nearly five thousand feet apart, and could be protected with the greatest ease. But the town of San Francisco itself is not fitted by nature to be a pleasant residence. During the spring, summer, and autumn, cold northwest winds are continually blowing, sometimes with such severity as to destroy buildings, and always filling the streets with a dense cloud of dust. From December to March, during the continuance of the rainy season, the streets, which have been filled with dust in the summer, become perfect pools of mud and mire, so that in some of them it is almost impossible to travel. The climate is one of the most peculiar in the world. During the summer the weather is so cold that a fire is always needed, and the surrounding hills are dry and burned up; while in the winter, in the intermissions between the rains, the weather is delightfully warm and May-like, and the hillsides become clothed with a lovely verdure. Among the improvements in town are several wharves, which have been completed within a short time past. The principal one of these, the central wharf, built by a joint-stock company, extends into the harbour a distance of two hundred and ninety-two feet, and will, when completed, be twenty-one hundred feet in length, enabling vessels to tie-up abreast, and discharge their cargoes directly upon it. Several churches have also been erected; and there are now in the town seven, of the following denominations, viz.: Catholic, 1; Episcopalian, 2; Baptist, 1; Presbyterian, 2; Methodist, 1. There are also two public schools in operation. Some ten or twelve steamboats are plying the Sacramento and San Joaquin Rivers and the Bay of San Francisco. Travelling has ceased to be as disagreeable as it was when I went up the Sacramento in a little open boat. These steamboats run to Benicia, Sacramento City, Stockton, and San Jose; while several smaller ones ply up and down the Sacramento River, to and from the various little towns upon it. The passage from San Francisco to Sacramento City, a distance of less than one hundred miles, is performed in nine hours; the price of passage being twenty-five dollars.

XI

Gold Rush Winners

THAT IMMENSE fortunes have been made in California is beyond a doubt; many of them, assuredly, have been by gold digging and trading, the latter occupation, in some cases, proving even more profitable than the former. The man who has been most fortunate in the mines is, probably Charles M. Weber, a German of whom I have previously referred, who left his rancho on the first discovery of gold. He organized a large group of Indians and placed them to work at various mining points. He purchased their gold from them with blankets at a hundred dollars apiece, and every other article of trade at correspondingly enormous prices. The untutored Indian, who had spent his life roaming over his native hills, subsisting upon acorns and wild game and using the skins of the deer and the wolf for clothing, found himself able to live sumptuously upon flour and some of the little luxuries of life, and clothe his swarthy limbs in an elegant Mexican *serape* or Yankee blanket, by simply parting with his gold, the value of which he had no idea. I have seen Indians at Coloma, who, as recent as three months ago had been naked as newborn babes, and had lived on roots and acorns were now clothed in the most gaudy dresses, and feasting on raisins and almonds that were bought at fifteen dollars a pound.

It is said that Weber, before he gave up the digging of gold, had, by the labour and trade of the Indians, made between four and five hundred thousand dollars. He then purchased the ground on which the flourishing town of Stockton now stands, laid it out in building lots, and is now probably worth over half-a-million dollars, and his sale of lots will double this amount in one year.

John Sullivan, an Irishman, who was driving an ox team when I first arrived at San Francisco, discovered a rich *canon* near the Stanislaus River some time in the summer of 1848. Before the winter was over he had taken from it twenty-six thousand dollars worth of gold dust. With this he established a trading post, purchased property in San Francisco, and is now on the highroad to a large fortune. The *canon* he discovered has ever since been called Sullivan's Diggings, and has been celebrated for the "big lumps" which have been taken from it.[1]

---

[1] John Sullivan came overland to California in 1844. He was first employed by Sutter, then lived on the Yuba River before moving to San Francisco in 1846 where he worked as a teamster, trader, and dabbled in real estate. After his famous strike, he operated a store on Sullivan Creek in Tuolumne. Later by shrewd investment in San Francisco lots, he became rich and founded the Hiberian Savings and Loan Society (Bank). He left an estate of almost a million dollars to his eleven children. Bancroft, *California*, V: 737; Thomas F. Prendergast, *Forgotten Pioneers: Irish Leaders in Early California* (San Francisco, 1942), pp. 88–92.

A man named Stockton, who came to California on the same ship with me and who was a private in our regiment, settled upon the Stanislaus River in the early part of September, 1848. He was a keen, trading genius, and, striking off of the beaten track, bought a mule and started, with a minimal quantity of trinkets and other articles of luxury, into the mountain Indian region. Here his sharpness for driving bargains was brought into full play, and it is said that he sold several boxes of raisins to the Indians for their weight in gold![2]

A young man named Hudson, from New York, I think, discovered a deep *canon* between the town of Coloma and the Middle Fork. This is a place which, in my travel to the Middle Fork and back, I have crossed four times without ever thinking of disturbing it. But in the summer of 1849, Hudson struck into it, and by digging some four feet reached the granite bed of the *canon* on which lay immense masses of gold. In the course of six weeks he had dug some twenty thousand dollars. The gold in this *canon* is in large pieces and of the purest quality, being entirely exempt from the mixture of quartz. The largest piece discovered here, which I had the pleasure of seeing, weighed a little over fourteen pounds clear gold, and was worth nearly two thousand eight hundred dollars. The success of every

[2]This would be William B. Stockton of Company F, 1st Regiment, New York Volunteers. Giffen, *California Expedition*, p. 95. Bancroft, *California*, IV: 499; V: 735.

one who has laboured in this *canon* has probably been more uniform than in any other place in the whole mining region.[3]

A boy, nineteen years of age, named John C. Davenport from New Bedford, took out one day last fall seventy-seven ounces and the next day nearly ninety ounces of pure gold. The *canon* referred to is now called Georgetown,[4] and has become a thriving little community, of about two thousand people who have built themselves comfortable log houses and have settled down quietly to labour and enjoy the fruits of their toil.

A young man, named Samuel Riper from Waterloo, New York, with three companions, went to the Yuba River in June, 1849. Later in company with a Dr. Bullard,[5] dammed off a site about fifty miles above the river's mouth. By severe labour, occupying the party of four for nearly a fortnight,

[3] Hudson's Gulch, named for its discoverer, is located in Oregon Canyon, near Georgetown. By 1862 it produced 1.5 million dollars. California, Division of Mines, *Report of the State Mineralogist*, II (1881): Pt 1, p. 150; Gudde, *California Gold Camps*, p. 162.

[4] Gudde, *California Gold Camps*, p. 129, reports that Georgetown's first deposits were discovered by a young man named Hudson (referred to in *note 3* above), while in his *California Place Names*, p. 119, states that the town itself was established by George Ehrenhaft in 1849.

[5] Dr. Bullard had been shipwrecked on the California coast while en route from Brooklyn, New York, to the Sandwich (Hawaiian) Islands. He made his way to the gold fields and profited handsomely. Gudde, *California Gold Camps*, p. 52; Kyle, *Historic Spots in California*, p. 544.

they succeeded in perfectly drying this part of the river's bed, and commenced washing the earth they found in it, consisting of a reddish gravel, solidly packed into the crevices of the rock. The earth turned out about three hundred dollars per day, and in less than two months the party of four divided among themselves the sum of fifteen thousand dollars! Immediately above this, two of the same party dammed a much smaller place, and in only two weeks took out three thousand dollars worth of gold.

About seventy miles from the mouth of the Yuba River is a curious formation of rock called "The Slate Range"; which extends along the bank of the river. Above it are lofty and precipitous hills, exceedingly difficult and dangerous of descent, but the richness of the slate rock beneath has well compensated all who have endured the toil of descending. The slate lies about four feet below the earth's surface, and between the thin strata the gold is found adhering to the rock. Over sixty thousand dollars worth of gold has been taken from this range during the past summer.

But one of the most curious circumstances in connection with the gold mines occurred at the old Dry Diggings, to which I have previously referred. These were entirely deserted last spring, having been used as a mere wintering place, and abandoned when the weather allowed travelling. As emigration rushed in, however, people again began to settle at the old working places and the Dry Diggings were soon again filled up. The houses were placed in a long valley with a running stream, and as the diggings thus far had all been found in the ravines which ran up into the hills, no one ever thought of trying the valley itself, which was in fact nothing more than a ravine of a larger kind. But within the past summer this whole valley has been completely dug up, and immense quantities of gold have been taken from it. Even the ground on which the houses stood has been uprooted, and one man named Wilson took from under his own doorstep about two thousand dollars worth of gold. In another case, three Frenchmen removed the stump of an old tree which lay across the pathway on the road from the Dry Diggings to Coloma, and in one week dug nearly five thousand dollars. I could well go on multiplying instances of extraordinary success in gold digging, but so many stories of this nature are already in circulation that I will merely add one more.

Dr. H. Van Dyke, with a company of about thirty men, went on to the North Fork and constructed a dam on that river just above its junction with the American Fork. Within the first three days after the drainage was completed, the company had taken out fifteen thousand dollars and afterwards, for nearly a month, made from five to twelve ounces a day per man.

The largest piece of gold which has yet been

found was picked up in a dry ravine near the Stanislaus River, in September, 1848. It contained a large mixture of quartz and weighed a little over twenty-five pounds, being worth five thousand dollars. A piece weighing twenty-seven and a half ounces was found by a young man named Taylor at Kelsey's Dry Diggings on the South Fork, about eight miles from Coloma. I saw this piece at the mill last spring, and it is now in the possession of the Honourable Edward Gilbert, one of our representatives in Congress from California. It is a beautiful specimen, about six inches in length, the gold being inlaid in a reddish stone. This piece was found by pure good luck, having been probably thrown up from the ravine in some loose dirt, where it was picked up by Taylor, lying directly on the surface.

XII

Advice to Newcomers

IT IS PROPER before closing this work, that I should
make a sort of recapitulation and give some advice in regard to prospects and plans of proceeding
in the gold mines of California. To advise is always
a difficult task, and in this instance it is peculiarly
so, but I will endeavour to give a fair statement of
facts and the best advice I can. The number of persons at present labouring in the various portions of
the mining region is about one hundred thousand.
Of these, at least one-third are Mexicans, Chilenos,
Pacific Islanders, and Chinese, and the remainder
Americans, English, French, and Germans. I should
divide their locations as follows: on the North, Middle, and South Forks, about twenty thousand; on
the Stanislaus, Mokelumne, Tuolumne, Merced,
Mariposa, and other tributaries of the San Joaquin,
forty thousand; on Yuba and Feather Rivers, twenty
thousand; and, scattered over the various dry diggings, twenty thousand more. During the past summer and autumn I should estimate the average
quantity of gold dug daily at eight dollars to a man.
Although it is by no means uncommon for an individual to "strike a lucky place" and some days take
out from a hundred to a thousand dollars, others

spend whole days in search and labour without finding more than two or three dollars. From my own experience in the mines I am, however, satisfied that during six months in the year a stout man with health, energy, and perseverance can average sixteen dollars a day in almost any portion of the placers. Still, I would advise all who are in good positions at home to remain there. The labour and hardships consequent upon the life of a gold digger are of a most severe and arduous nature. Prying and breaking up huge rocks, shovelling dirt, washing it with wet feet all day, and sleeping on the damp ground at night, with nothing above but a thin covering of canvass or a leaky log roof are not by any means agreeable to one who has been accustomed to the civilized life of cities. Richelieu says that "the pen is mightier than the sword."[1] Many a fine, young clerk travelling to California with golden dreams of wealth before him has proved, to his sorrow, that the crowbar is heavier than the pen. I hesitate not to say, that the labour of gold digging is

[1]The quotation actually reads: "Beneath the rule of men entirely great, the pen is mightier than the sword." This appears in Edward Bulwer Lytton's play, *Richelieu*, published in 1839, Act II, Scene 2. The play deals with the life of the French aristocrat-prelate, Armand Jean Duplessis, Cardinal, Duc de Richelieu (1585–1642), who served Louis XIII as his minister of state. So the quotation is Lytton's not Richelieu's. *Familiar Quotations* by John Barlett, ed. by Christopher Morley (Boston, 1951), p. 425, cl. 1; *Chamber's Biographical Dictionary*, ed. by J. O. Thorne (New York, 1962), pp. 1081–82.

unequalled by any other in the world in severity. It combines within itself the various arts of canal digging, ditching, laying stone walls, ploughing, and hoeing potatoes, and adding to this a life in the wilds of the mountains, living upon poor provisions, continually exposed either to the burning rays of the sun or the heavy dews of night, and the occupation becomes anything but a pleasant one. However, to a man endowed with a constitution to endure hardship, with hands that have been accustomed to labour and with a heart which suffers not itself to be sorrowed with disappointment, there was never a better opportunity in the world to make a fortune than there is at present in California. To mechanics, especially, there are great inducements; for if they do not choose to labour in the mines, with the wages which I have previously stated as being paid to them in San Francisco and the other towns of Northern California, they may, in one year, save more money than in five in any other portion of the United States.

To those who do come, I would give a few words of advice which may be of service. Bring with you a minimum amount of clothing, as that will only prove a burden. Articles can be purchased in San Francisco almost at New York prices. Never come without money, as gold is not to be found in the streets of San Francisco. You may be delayed several days before going to the mines, and board at from sixteen to fifty dollars a week will soon make a large hole in a small sum of money. Upon arrival at San Francisco be aware of the vices prevalent there. Drinking and gaming are the principal, and, in fact, many a poor fellow, landing there with high hopes, has been fleeced and turned adrift upon society with a broken heart. Purchase no provisions in San Francisco. The expenses of transportation are so great, (freight up the river being from two to four cents per pound, and by teams to the various mining points from fifteen to fifty) that your provisions will cost more in money and time than they would if purchased in the mining area. Flour is now selling in the gold regions at about fifty cents per pound. This seems like a great price, but you will find it cheaper than to carry it with you, and you will also find that it is much easier to pay fifty cents for a pound of flour when you are making sixteen dollars a day than it is to pay three cents when you are making but one. For the same reason, carry but little clothing. A simple change is sufficient, and clothes can always be purchased at reasonable rates in all parts of the mines.

The best season for proceeding to the mines is about the end of August. The waters, which have been swollen by the melting of the snows in the summer, have subsided, and the heat of the summer months has given way to the cooling breezes of autumn. From that time till the middle of December the weather is most delightful, and the opportunities for profitable labour are far better than at any other time. About the middle of December, the rainy season commences; the rivers immediately begin to rise, and one's labour is halted both by this and the inclemency of the weather. The life of the miner during the winter months is exceedingly unpleasant, and I would advise no one to proceed to the gold region after the month of November. The rainy season usually ends about the middle of February, but the roads are exceedingly muddy until the first of March, and from that time till July, labour can be performed to advantage in the various dry diggings, and upon some of the rivers. By this time the hot and sickly season commences, and the waters upon the rivers are at their greatest height. The thermometer ranges from 90° to 120° in the shade at noonday, and the heavy dews of night fall upon the labourer, who has been all day at work beneath a broiling sun. This, of course, produces disease; and in that wild region, where the comforts and attendance that should ever surround a sick man's bed are unknown, disease is usually followed by death. The most prevalent diseases during this time are fever and ague, and bilious fevers of the most virulent nature. But I am satisfied that a large portion of the sickness of the summer months is caused by the exposure consequent upon the present mode of life endured by the miner. When better comforts are available, when good houses are built, and wholesome provisions can be procured, the several mining regions of California will compare favourably with Illinois, Indiana, or any of the new states in point of healthiness.

It has been frequently asked, "In what kind of soil is gold found?" The answer is, that it is found in no one particular kind of soil, but in every variety from the common loose black earth to the hardest clay. I have uncovered, among the dry diggings of Weber's Creek, bits of gold, several weighing nearly a quarter of an ounce, lying in the upper black soil within two inches of the surface. It is sometimes found embedded in a hard white clay, at other times in a red or blue clay. As a general thing, I have found that where the gold is coarse, it usually descends until it reaches one of the above mentioned clays, while the finer particles rest upon the gravelly stratum nearer the surface, thus fine gold is frequently found mingled with red gravel.

In regard to bringing machines to California for the purpose of washing gold, I must caution the miner to be careful and judicious in their selection. Some of the more recent inventions are valuable, especially the Quicksilver Gold Separator, which is constructed to operate with quicksilver in such manner as to save the fine particles of gold which in the ordinary cradles or rockers are lost. The only object of a machine of any kind is to break up and keep in motion a larger quantity of earth than a pan would hold, and at the same time prevent the gold from being lost. I saw, last spring, hundreds of huge, bulky machines, which had been brought round Cape Horn, and which would require a large ox team to convey them to the mining region, lying piled upon the beach of San Francisco, destined never to fulfill the object for which they were intended. There are, however, some small hand machines manufactured in New York, which are really of great use to the gold digger.

A great mistake has been made by people who have emigrated to California, or who have desired to emigrate, in considering it merely as a temporary home. It is for this reason that the life of the miner is at present tenfold more arduous than it otherwise would be, and never was there a more egregious error in regard to the character of the country. Gold is not the only product of the soil in California. Her fertile valleys and rich prairies are capable of producing an untold store of agricultural wealth. Her lofty pines and spreading oak trees afford an abundant supply of material for the erection of comfortable dwellings. Her thousands of streams, pouring down the hillsides, and winding through her plains, furnish an inexhaustible supply of waterpower. Her forests, mountains, and lakes abound with game of every description. In the immense valleys of the Sacramento and San Joaquin Rivers are millions—yes, millions—of acres of land entirely unreclaimed, upon which any man may settle and make a fortune in a few years by the cultivation of the soil. Some hundred and fifty miles above Sacramento City, on the Sacramento River, are large tracts of valuable, well-watered land, much of which is unreclaimed, other portions being for sale at nominal prices. On one of these tracts, at Lassen's[2] Rancho, wheat was raised at an average of forty-five bushels to the acre, and is now selling delivered on the rancho at six dollars a bushel! Cattle bring from forty to a hundred dollars a head, potatoes twenty-five cents per pound, milk two dollars per gallon, butter from one to two dollars per pound, and every product of a farm is at corresponding prices. With the continued growth of California, the demand for all these articles, most of which are now brought from the Sandwich Islands, Chili, and Oregon, must necessarily increase, and I am satisfied that the cultivation of the soil will yet be a more profitable labour than extracting the gold from it.

California is a habitable country, and should be looked upon no longer as a mere temporary residence. A state government has been organized, the sheltering hand of law stretched over its borders,

[2] Peter Lassen went overland to Oregon in 1839 and reached California on the *Lausanne*, landing at Bodega Bay, July 16, 1840. He headed for Sutter's Fort, then pushed on to San Jose where he applied his trade of blacksmithing. In 1841 he built a sawmill at Santa Cruz, but sold out two years later. He relocated to the Consumnes River, became a naturalized Mexican citizen, and acquired the Rancho Bosquejo. He sold half of his ranch lands and stock in 1850 to take a flyer on a steamboat speculation on the Sacramento River only to go bust. He was killed under debatable circumstances in the region north of Pyramid Lake in 1859. Bancroft, *California*, IV: 708; Cowan, *California Ranchos*, p. 20, Entry No. 54.

and life there can be made as comfortable as life in any other portion of the world. Let then the gold digger come, and from the never-failing hills gather a rich supply of treasure. Let the farmer come, and from the abundant soil produce the necessaries of life, and enrich himself from them. Let the mechanics and labourers come, and build up the towns of this great new country, and let the ladies of our land come, and with their smiles bring peace and happiness into the wilderness.

The world was sad!—the garden was a wild!—
And man, the hermit sighed, till woman smiled!

Editor's Epilogue

AFTER LEAVING the mines Gould Buffum divided his time between California politics and a variety of journalistic endeavors. As he began to write the book you have just completed, he was offered the job of city reporter for the San Francisco *Alta California* of which two of the three founders had served with him in the New York Volunteers. He also accepted an offer to be a correspondent for the New York *Herald*.

Interestingly, Buffum arrived in San Francisco on about May 1, 1849 and on May 11 was elected to the enlarged San Francisco Legislative Assembly, a rump municipal council established by citizen demand. Also elected at the same time was William A. Buffum, Gould's older brother who had arrived only recently.

Like the proprietors of the *Alta*, Gould entered the political fray with both his pen and person. It was obvious that his association with the newspaper was the reason for his name to appear on the ballot, but how he and his brother, who had been residents of San Francisco for such a short time, could be elected to public office is not too hard to understand when placed in the context of events in 1849.

Bayard Taylor, another journalist, published an account of his gold rush experiences entitled *Eldorado*. Taylor's book supplies a telling anecdote that amply describes early gold rush politics:

> The choosing of candidates from lists, nearly all of whom were entirely unknown, was very amusing. Names in many instances were made to stand for principles; accordingly, a Mr. Fair got many votes. One of the candidates, who had been on the river a few days previous wearing a high-crowned silk hat with narrow brim, lost about twenty votes on that account. Some went no further than to vote for those whom they actually knew. One who took the opposite extreme, justified himself in this wise: "When I left home, I was determined *to go it blind*. I went it blind in coming to California, and I'm not going to stop now. I voted for the constitution and I've never seen the constitution. I voted for all the candidates, and I don't know a damned one of them."[1]

Buffum, like the *Alta*, played an active role in the struggle against military rule in California. Shortly after its founding, the paper " ... entered earnestly into the work of forming a Provincial Government, and as zealously into the reform of municipal matters in San Francisco. The stand taken by the paper against the high-handed acts of military authorities and town officers appointed and sustained [by them] ... was warmly seconded by the people, and it would be difficult to conceive of closer knit sympathies between the public and a newspaper than

[1] Bayard Taylor, *Eldorado or Adventures in the Path of Empire* (New York, 1949), p. 189.

those enjoyed by the *Alta California* in 1849. It was emphatically the people's organ ... "[2]

Following the successful effort to have self-rule realized through the ratification of the state constitution on November 11, 1849, Gould pulled away from active politics, but continued on the *Alta* staff.

It was at this time that he hurriedly completed the manuscript of his gold rush experiences. On January 1, 1850, it was rushed to his Philadelphia publisher. The book was critically acclaimed by no less a person than Hubert H. Bancroft, California's first and greatest historian. He was unsparing in his praise, remarking:

> It was published while the author remained in California and constitutes one of the most important printed contributions to the history of the state, no less by reason of the scarcity of material concerning the period it covers, 1841–49, than on account of the ability of the author. He was an educated man, remarkably free from prejudice, a close observer, and possessing sound judgment. He is careful in his statements, conscientious, not given to exaggeration, and his words and ways are such as to inspire confidence ... The style is pleasant—simple, terse, strong, yet graceful, and with no egotism or affectations.[3]

With the arrival of the fall of 1852, the *Alta's* owner/editor took a year's leave and Buffum served

[2] Edward C. Kemble, *A History of California Newspapers 1846–1858*, ed. by Helen H. Bretnor (Los Gatos, CA, 1962), pp. 88–90.

[3] Bancroft, *California*, VI: 642; *California Blue Book* (Sacramento, 1907), p. 273.

as editor for a short time, sharing that appointment with three others.[4] Then, almost immediately after the owner's return, Gould decided to return to the East, perhaps to visit his family.

By early 1854, he returned to San Francisco and that fall ran for election to the state legislature on the American or "Know-Nothing Party" ticket.

The American Party enjoyed a meteoric career. It was founded in New York in 1849 as a secret, quasi-fraternal, patriotic organization, the original name being the Order of the Star Spangled Banner. By 1854, it had become national in scope. Its members were sworn to secrecy at their initiation. When questioned about it, members replied, "I know nothing about it"—thus the popular name, "Know-Nothing Party." Each member had to swear to uphold the party's three objectives: to cast their ballots for only native-born candidates for any elective office; to work for a twenty-one year probationary period before any foreign-born could be naturalized, and to combat the Roman Catholic Church. It is amazing when one realizes how popular the American Party became, but it found its Waterloo over the issue of slavery which by 1856 brought about the Party's swift demise.[5]

The Party had special appeal in California be-

[4] Kemble, *History of California Newspapers*, ed. by Bretnor, p. 96.

[5] Wayne Andrews, ed., *Concise Dictionary of American History* (New York, 1967), p. 37.

cause of the anti-foreignism that dated back to the gold rush. Thus, in the 1854 election, a number of Party members were elected to office, among them Gould Buffum who took his seat in the Sixth Legislature when it convened in 1855.

During his single-year legislative term, Buffum, joined by William B. Farwell as co-editor, established the San Francisco *Daily Citizen* as an organ of the Party. The paper commenced publication on May 25 and continued to appear until October 10, 1855, when it was transferred to Sacramento.[6]

To celebrate his election to the state assembly, The San Francisco Press Club sponsored a testimonial affair in Gould's honor. It turned out to be "elegant entertainment" for some twenty guests who "set down to an excellent dinner, not the least satisfactory feature of which was the magnificent style in which it was served up." A reporter rhapsodized in his account of the affair:

> *Alas! I must leave undescribed the gibier,*
> *The salmi, the consomme, the puree,*
> *And fruits, and ice, and all that art refines*
> *From nature for the service of the gout.*
> *The glasses jingled, and the palates tingled;*
> *The diners of celebrity dined well.*

Numerous toasts and speeches were offered. The first speech was given by the honored guest. "His

[6]Kemble, *History of California Newspapers*, ed. by Bretnor, p. 210.

remarks were made in a very feeling and emphatic style, and listened to with profound attention, and at their conclusion were received with a deafening round of applause." The final toast was directed to "Our Gould: A human specimen alloyed with the silver of honesty and the iron of resolution; a conglomerate of rare character in *Alta California*, and not easily manufactured into those links which fetters freedom by even the most cunning workers in political inquiry."

There was, indeed, some prophecy to be found in one of the toasts offered at his testimonial dinner: "To our Guest, the Honorable E. Gould Buffum— his precedents from his connection with the Press are indicative of his future usefulness and fame."[7] This utterance came true following his legislative stint when in April 1856, Buffum was named to be editor of the *Alta*. He served in that capacity until early November 1857 when his former editorial colleague, William B. Farwell, succeeded him.[8] The *Alta's* ownership had changed a number of times and the paper faced increasing competition from rivals that were proliferating yearly. Perhaps for these reasons, Buffum resigned and decided once again to return to the East. The *Alta* reported that on the morning of November 5, 1857, he embarked on the *Golden Gate* "to make a visit to the Atlantic States.

[7] *Alta California*, January 1, 1855, p. 2, cl. 1.
[8] Kemble, *History of California Newspapers*, ed. by Bretnor, p. 97.

He leaves a host of friends and carries with him our best wishes for his success." [9]

It is at this point his remaining years become somewhat muddled. It can be hypothesized that on reaching New York City he approached the *Herald* for a job. That appears certain for he was sent to Paris, France as an overseas correspondent for the paper in early 1858.

On assuming his duties in Paris, he regularly sent copy to the *Herald* and occasionally to the *Alta California*. In the ensuing years, in addition to his dispatches, Buffum authored a number of mostly descriptive articles and wrote two books, based on his European travels: *A Pocket Guide for Americans Going to Europe* (1859) and *Sights and Sensations in France, Germany and Switzerland* (1869), which was published posthumously.

On Christmas Eve, December 24, 1867, death claimed him in Paris. The New York *Herald* reported in a brief notice: "Mr. E. Gould Buffum, an old American journalist, died very suddenly here after taking an anodyne . . . at the time of his death [he] served as the Paris correspondent of the New York *Herald*." [10]

[9] *Alta California*, November 5, 1857, p. 2, cl. 1.

[10] New York *Herald*, December 27, 1867, p. 5, cl. 1. An anodyne is a medicine or drug which alleviates pain. Apparently Buffum suffered from a severe ailment and probably took an overdose, whether intentionally or unintentionally remains unknown. The New York *Times*, December 27, 1867, p. 1, cl. 2, also recorded his death.

The San Francisco *Golden Era* recorded his passing in a poignant but short obituary:

> Gould Buffum, many years connected with the California press, ex-lieutenant of Stevenson's pioneer regiment, good fellow and thriftless, committed suicide in Paris a week ago last Thursday. He has been a resident abroad some ten years, corresponding meanwhile with local and Eastern newspapers. A sea of trouble swamps a worthy craft.[11]

Similar memorial tributes appeared in the two leading San Francisco papers, the *Alta California* and the *Bulletin*. That notice closed with these words: "He was a fluent and graceful writer, a genial companion, and a man of extensive and varied information. His age was about 45 years, and when he left San Francisco was unmarried."[12] The latter was true at his death.

Unlike James Wilson Marshall, Edward Gould Buffum's only monument is his book, *Six Months in the Gold Mines.* But like Marshall's statue at Coloma, it, too, endures as an important part of the historical legacy of the California gold rush.

[11]San Francisco *Golden Era*, January 5, 1868, p. 4, cl. 2. The date of death suggested in this notice would be December 26, which is in error.
[12]*Alta California*, December 29, 1867, p. 2, cl. 1; *Bulletin*, December 30, 1867, p. 2, cl. 5, which reproduces verbatim the *Alta* obituary.

Index

INDEX

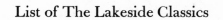
List of The Lakeside Classics

The Lakeside Classics